Signaling without Saying

OXFORD STUDIES IN SEMANTICS AND PRAGMATICS

General Editors

Chris Barker, *New York University*, and Chris Kennedy, *University of Chicago*

RECENTLY PUBLISHED IN THE SERIES

9
The Semantics of Evidentials
Sarah E. Murray

10
Graded Modality
Qualitative and Quantitative Perspectives
Daniel Lassiter

11
The Semantics and Pragmatics of Honorification
Register and Social Meaning
Elin McCready

12
The Meaning of *More*
Alexis Wellwood

13
Enriched Meanings
Natural Language Semantics with Category Theory
Ash Asudeh and Gianluca Giorgolo

14
Parenthetical Meaning
Todor Koev

15
Actuality Inferences
Causality, Aspect, and Modality
Prerna Nadathur

16
From Perception to Communication
A Theory of Types for Action and Meaning
Robin Cooper

17
Signaling without Saying
The Semantics and Pragmatics of Dogwhistles
Robert Henderson and Elin McCready

For a full list of titles published and in preparation for the series see pp. 154–155

Signaling without Saying

The Semantics and Pragmatics of Dogwhistles

ROBERT HENDERSON
ELIN McCREADY

Great Clarendon Street, Oxford, OX2 6DP,
United Kingdom

Oxford University Press is a department of the University of Oxford.
It furthers the University's objective of excellence in research, scholarship,
and education by publishing worldwide. Oxford is a registered trade mark of
Oxford University Press in the UK and in certain other countries

© Robert Henderson and Elin McCready 2024

The moral rights of the authors have been asserted

All rights reserved. No part of this publication may be reproduced, stored in
a retrieval system, or transmitted, in any form or by any means, without the
prior permission in writing of Oxford University Press, or as expressly permitted
by law, by licence or under terms agreed with the appropriate reprographics
rights organization. Enquiries concerning reproduction outside the scope of the
above should be sent to the Rights Department, Oxford University Press, at the
address above

You must not circulate this work in any other form
and you must impose this same condition on any acquirer

Published in the United States of America by Oxford University Press
198 Madison Avenue, New York, NY 10016, United States of America

British Library Cataloguing in Publication Data

Data available

Library of Congress Control Number: 2024907741

ISBN 9780198886341

DOI: 10.1093/9780191994319.001.0001

Printed and bound by
CPI Group (UK) Ltd, Croydon, CR0 4YY

Links to third party websites are provided by Oxford in good faith and
for information only. Oxford disclaims any responsibility for the materials
contained in any third party website referenced in this work.

Contents

General preface	vii
Acknowledgments	ix
1. Introduction	1
1.1 Dogwhistles in social science	2
1.2 Dogwhistles in philosophy of language	6
1.3 An outline of the main proposals	10
2. Dogwhistles as a semantic/pragmatic phenomenon	15
2.1 Previous accounts of dogwhistles	15
2.1.1 The conventional implicature view	16
2.1.2 The inferentialist view	18
2.1.3 The (manner) implicature view	20
2.1.4 The speech act view	23
2.1.5 Mixed views	24
2.2 The social meaning view	26
2.3 Varieties of dogwhistles	28
2.3.1 Saul's 4-way typology	29
2.3.2 Multivocalism	30
2.3.3 'Identifying' vs. 'enriching' dogwhistles	31
2.4 Summary	33
3. A probabilitic pragmatics for dogwhistles	35
3.1 Bayesian Rational Speech Act theory	36
3.1.1 The literal listener L_0	37
3.1.2 The pragmatic speaker S_1	39
3.1.3 The pragmatic listener	40
3.1.4 Implicature calculation in RSA	41
3.2 Social Meaning Games	44
3.2.1 The 'Third Wave'	44
3.2.2 Adding indexical fields to the RSA framework	46
3.2.3 Sociolinguistic speakers and listeners	48
3.2.4 Burnett on Barack Obama	50
4. Identifying dogwhistles	55
4.1 Social meaning games for dogwhistles	56
4.2 A case study of identifying dogwhistles	59
4.3 Exploring the numerical parameters	65
4.4 The grammar of identifying dogwhistles	69
4.5 Non-linguistic identifying dogwhistles	73
4.6 Conclusions	74

5. Enriching dogwhistles ... 75
   5.1 Personas and perspectives ... 76
   5.2 Proposal: Personas induce enrichment ... 85
   5.3 Application and comparison with other views ... 85
   5.4 Other evidence: Experiments on bias ... 87
   5.5 Conclusions ... 88

6. Vigilance and hypervigilance ... 91
   6.1 Vigilance ... 92
      6.1.1 Implicatures in RSA ... 93
      6.1.2 Social meaning implicatures in RSA ... 94
      6.1.3 Vigilance and intention ... 99
      6.1.4 Side-stepping intent ... 104
      6.1.5 Summary ... 105
   6.2 Hypervigilance ... 106
      6.2.1 Modeling hypervigilance ... 107
      6.2.2 Hypervigilance and discourse breakdown ... 111
   6.3 Conclusions ... 113

7. Dogwhistles and trust ... 115
   7.1 Evaluating information sources ... 116
   7.2 Ideology and trust ... 119
   7.3 Social hedges: Fake news and fig leaves ... 123
   7.4 Conclusions ... 127

8. Beyond dogwhistles ... 131
   8.1 Summary ... 131
   8.2 Mask-off moments and discursive health ... 133
   8.3 Lessons on social meaning ... 136
   8.4 Standpoints ... 142
   8.5 Differential communication: The scope of the theory ... 147

References ... 149
Index ... 153

General preface

Oxford Studies in Semantics and Pragmatics provides a platform for original research on meaning in natural language within contemporary semantics and pragmatics. Authors are encouraged to present their work in the context of past and present lines of inquiry and in a manner accessible to semanticists and pragmatists in linguistics, philosophy, and cognitive science, as well as to professional linguists in related subfields such as syntax and lexicology. They are also asked to ground argument in numerous examples from English and, where possible, from a variety of other languages.

This is a companion series to *Oxford Surveys in Semantics and Pragmatics*, which provides critical overviews of the major approaches to research topics of current interest, a discussion of their relative value, and an assessment of what degree of consensus exists about any one of them. The *Studies* series equally seeks to put empirical puzzle and theoretical debate into comprehensible perspective, but its authors generally develop and defend the approach and line of argument which they find most convincing and productive. The series offers researchers in linguistics and related areas—including syntax, cognitive science, computer science, and philosophy—a means of disseminating their findings to potential readers throughout the world.

Dogwhistles mean something different to an ingroup than to the audience at large. For instance, in certain political discourses, 'inner-city neighborhoods' may be taken by some to mean specifically 'Black neighborhoods,' with significant social and communicative consequences. This volume develops and explores a robust new theory of dogwhistles using Rational Speech Act theory (RSA), a Bayesian model of communication. Developing and extending Burnett's RSA analysis of persona signaling, the proposal covers in detail identificational dogwhistles, truth-condition enriching dogwhistles, accidental dogwhistles, and more. The insightful discussion does not presuppose any previous technical expertise; in particular, the RSA theory is clearly and simply explained through a series of examples worked out in detail. The net result is a thorough, compelling case study that takes a pragmatic theory originally designed to explain truth-conditional at-issue meaning and applies it to non-truth-conditional social meaning, building a system on which listeners update their beliefs about a speaker's persona in a way that is parallel to but deeply different than Gricean pragmatic implicature. In addition to constituting a state-of-the-art account of dogwhistles, this study is a paradigm example of how to bring formal pragmatic theory to bear on important sociolinguistic issues.

Acknowledgments

This book has been a multi-year project, extended even further by the COVID-19 pandemic. One effect is that we have had many years to present aspects of this work to colleagues, both publicly and privately. This has most certainly been a boon because the book is better for it, but it has also created certain problems. In particular, in between starting this project (in 2017, long before we even had a book under contract), and finishing this work at the end of 2022, multiple papers have appeared which build off of or critique versions of the present manuscript. We would first like to thank these colleagues who have engaged with our work in their own publications—David Beaver, Ellen Breitholtz, Heather Burnett, Ramiro Caso, Robin Cooper, Quentin Dénigot, Nicolás Lo Guercio, Anne Quaranto, Asad Sayeed, and Jason Stanley (we apologize for anyone we might have missed, as time continues to run on and more work continues to be done). We have learned much from them. As a consequence, we have tried to update our work to contend with their advances, while at the same time maintaining the integrity of the space–time continuum—i.e., we have tried not to substantively change our account so that critiques of our approach, as previously presented, no longer have a target. For the same reason, we have chosen not to engage extensively with work in linguistics and (non-ideal) philosophy of language that has appeared close to publication time which, like this book, aims to clarify relations between meaning, manipulation, and trust. Instead, we proudly defend the position we have defended for the past few years, and look forward to discussions with our cherished colleagues into the future about how to best think about dogwhistles.

We have had the pleasure of presenting versions of this work at a large number of conference venues, including: the 14th and 16th editions of Logic and Engineering of Natural Language Semantics (LENLS), the 22nd Amsterdam Colloquium, a Deutsche Gesellschaft für Sprachwissenschaft (DGfS) Workshop on Secondary Meaning, Expressing Evidence, the Conference on Probability and Meaning (PAM 2020), the 2nd Workshop on Integrating Approaches to Social Meaning at ESSLLI 2019, Semantics and Linguistic Theory (SALT) 31 and 32, and the 18th Szklarska Poreba Workshop. We thank these audiences, as well as colloquium audiences at the Buenos Aires Linguistics and Philosophy of Language Group, City University of Hong Kong, University of Cologne, University of Edinburgh, Gothenburg University, Hokusei Gakuin University, Nagoya Gakuin University, the Ohio State University, the Oppressive Speech, Societies and Norms Workshop at ZAS, the New York Philosophy of Language Workshop, PENN Integrated Language Sciences and Technology Seminar, Queen Mary University London, Ryukoku University, Stanford University Cognition & Language Workshop, Stuttgart University, Tübingen University, and the ZAS Semantics Circle. We would like to thank everyone at those talks and very many other people over the years for valuable discussion and comments, among other kinds of support. We appreciate your interest and attention more than we have words for.

Robert thanks Daniel Gutzmann, Heidi Harley, Gerhard Jäger, Ryan Walter Smith, and Jessica Rett for discussions about this work. Michael Franke, Tatjana Scheffler, and Todd Snider deserve special thanks for sending detailed comments on drafts and talks shared with them. Finally, Robert must thank Betsy Burr, Johanna Skibsrud, John Melillo, Adam Geary, Steve Johnstone, and Scott Pryor for their love and friendship, especially through the years of the pandemic, as well as for many fine discussions about dogwhistles. It was helpful to have the perspective of scholars who have not had their minds altered by too much linguistics and philosophy of language.

Elin thanks everyone who has supported this work and its authors over the years, and especially her family, most of all and first of all Midori Morita and Elis Ottosson. (To briefly break the fourth wall: I love you all so much.) She also thanks her coauthor on this project for being the absolute best.

1
Introduction

On a 2014 radio program, Representative Paul Ryan said the following.

(1) We have got this tailspin of culture, in our inner cities in particular, of men not working and just generations of men not even thinking about working or learning the value and the culture of work.

He was criticized shortly after by fellow Representative Barbara Lee for making a "thinly veiled racial attack." This is because the phrase *inner-city* is code or euphemism for Black neighborhoods (especially stereotypically racialized views of such neighborhoods). Many people heard Paul Ryan say:

(2) We have got this tailspin of culture, in our Black neighborhoods in particular, of men not working and just generations of men not even thinking about working or learning the value and the culture of work.

This example illustrates the notion of a *dogwhistle*—that is, language that sends one message to an out-group while at the same time sending a second (often taboo, controversial, or inflammatory) message to an in-group. While the broader social science literature on dogwhistles is developed, if not mature, the linguistic literature is thin. This is a major lacuna because, as this book will show, dogwhistles are a key phenomenon for understanding deep, underexplored connections between semantics, pragmatics, and sociolinguistics. Even an cursory look at an example like (1) raises questions like the following, which point at these connections:

- Utterances containing dogwhistles send a primary message to the audience and a second message to a subaudience. There is a large semantics literature on secondary content covering presuppositions and implicatures, as well as more 'exotic' phenomena like slurs and honorification. *How does dogwhistle meaning fit into this typology of secondary content?*
- The fact that Representative Lee calls out Representative Ryan for his dogwhistle shows that non-in-group members can be aware of dogwhistles. *How do dogwhistles evolve in a population and spread beyond their original in-group, and what happens to a dogwhistle when a sufficiently large part of the population becomes aware of it?*
- Standard pragmatic theory rests on an assumption of speaker–hearer cooperativity. Dogwhistles complicate this picture because they require a kind of semi-cooperativity where some listeners are intended to be unable to extract an

enriched meaning. *Can Gricean reasoning scale up to a setting in which speakers are reasoning about audiences in an adversarial way?*

- Example (1) contains a classic dogwhistle like *inner-city*, which when used as a dogwhistle clearly has a different referent—namely, Black neighborhoods—than when not used as such. We will show, though, that there are other kinds of dogwhistles, which instead of enriching the semantic content, merely flag the speaker's membership in a particular group. *Given that dogwhistles can be used to convey a speaker's social persona, how can we combine sociolinguistic theories of identity construction with a formal semantic and pragmatic account of dogwhistles?*

- As noted above, dogwhistles can both convey a speaker's persona, as well as enrich the semantic meaning of specific expressions. *Are these distinct phenomena involving different aspects of the semantics and pragmatics of dogwhistles together with sociolinguistic reasoning, or can they be folded into a unified account?*

- *If there are (as we suspect) a multiplicity of types of dogwhistles (we will argue for at least two types), are there particular linguistic devices that are optimal for carrying some kinds of dogwhistled meaning versus others?*

This book will answer these questions, and more, in a novel semantic/pragmatic theory of dogwhistles. The main proposal is that dogwhistles flow out of conversational agents' reasoning about social meanings, and in particular from conventional associations between linguistic expressions and social personas. Before laying out this theory, though, and how it relates to the questions raised above, we first we want to survey the role dogwhistles have played outside of the linguistics literature. Linguists are late to the game in analyzing dogwhistles, as most previous work on the topic has been carried out within political science and philosophy of language. Understanding the place of dogwhistles in these literatures will help contextualize the core proposals this book makes, which are summarized at the end of this chapter.

1.1 Dogwhistles in social science

Most of the work on dogwhistles in the social sciences has taken place in political science, and the primary result from that literature is that dogwhistles work. Across topical domains, and across populations, politicians are able to use coded language to send a taboo, deniable message to one audience, while at the same time sending a second, innocuous message to another audience who would object to the message the first audience received. We started the chapter with an example of the dogwhistle *inner-city* because its efficacy in shaping the opinions of white voters has been confirmed across multiple studies (e.g., Hurwitz and Peffley 2005; Mendelberg 2001; White 2007). For example, White 2007 presented white and Black voters with the prompt in (3), filling the blank with the phrases *Blacks, inner-city Americans, poor Americans*, and *working Americans*.

(3) House Democrats stirred debate today on a proposal that would lead to a major restructuring of the nation's welfare system, with claims that the Republican plan would disproportionately hurt [——] families.

He found that only the dogwhistle *inner-city Americans* significantly altered white voters' willingness to increase spending on food stamps, specifically by driving it downward. The mechanism of the change was out-group resentment. Participants were more likely to assign negative stereotypes to Black people after hearing the dogwhistle than in a control condition, and there was no such effect for the other phrases. In contrast, support for an increase in food stamp funding for Black participants was unchanged in the *inner-city* condition, and there was no change in out-group resentment or in-group identification after hearing the dogwhistle. While there is a long chain of effects we must untangle to get from the meaning of a dogwhistle to the recorded behavioral outcome through out-group resentment, the immediate and concrete lesson of this study for semantics and pragmatics is that a racial dogwhistle like *inner-city* can be used to send a taboo message to a targeted group to shape political opinions, while leaving other groups unaffected.

One question White 2007 does not answer is whether participant behavior is dependent on whether they "hear" the dogwhistle in the sense of decoding it. That is, is the aggregate behavior of Black participants in the experiment due to some respondents not picking up on the coded racial message of *inner-city*, or is it due to recognizing the message and merely reacting to it differently?[1] Albertson 2015 answers this question for a different domain, namely that of coded religious appeals. Religious dogwhistles have also been well-studied, both in American political rhetoric (Calfano and Djupe 2008; Albertson 2015), but also across the world, for instance in Salafist writings (Thurston 2017), or in the Hindutva tweets of Narendra Modi (Pal et al. 2018). As with the work on racial dogwhistles, this literature has confirmed the effectiveness of dogwhistling, though with a deeper focus on the covertness of the relevant language.

Albertson 2015, for instance, asks whether carefully crafted language can increase the appeal of a candidate to religious listeners, while having no obvious religious content to the non-religious. The inspiration for the study comes from an example from George Bush's 2003 State of the Union address, which contains the following line.

(4) Yet there's power—wonder-working power—in the goodness and idealism and faith of the American people.

To most people this sounds like, at worst, a civil-religious banality, but to a certain segment of the population the phrase *wonder-working power* is intimately connected to their conception and worship of Jesus. When someone says (4), they hear a person who must share their religious beliefs. To test this, Albertson 2015 recruited a sample of Pentecostal Christian believers and a general population sample, and presented

---

[1] The question of what happens when dogwhistles become widely known, and thus less coded, is taken up in Chapter 6 in our discussion of what we call *vigilance implicatures*.

them with speeches that ended with either the sentence in (4), or minimally modified versions that contained either an overt religious appeal or a completely secular control. Respondents were then asked a variety of questions to determine their reactions to the speeches, including their likelihood to support the candidate. In a post-test, Albertson (2015) found that 84% of the Pentecostals had heard of the phrase *wonder-working* power, while only 24% of the general population claimed to have heard the phrase before, which already shows that this phrase at least has the potential to act as a dogwhistle.

The results of the study showed that this possibility was made manifest. The phrase *wonder-working power* proved to function as a successful dogwhistle. First, Albertson (2015) found that the covert religious appeal increased the candidate's positive impression scores in the Pentecostal population relative to the non-religious control group. This shows that the dogwhistle does, in fact, reach those that can hear it. In contrast, the dogwhistle had no effect in the general population on either their initial impressions or on their intention to vote for such a candidate. This was true even in the subset of that population that professed a dislike of religious language in politics. This was in stark contrast to the overt religious appeal. In that same subset that disliked religious language, the overt religious appeal caused a significant decrease in likability, as well as decrease in intention to vote for the candidate making the speech.

As in the study by White (2007), Albertson (2015) was able to probe what mediated the link between the content of the dogwhistle and the policy preference measure. In the case of White (2007), the dogwhistle activated stereotypes about Blacks in one population. In the case of the covert religious appeal, the dogwhistle did not seem to work by conveying content about a policy domain or a group of people, but by merely flagging the in-group membership of the speaker. In particular, Albertson (2015) found that in the Pentecostal sample, measures of religiosity did not magnify the dogwhistle effect, but Republican self-identification did. This matches what was found in Calfano and Djupe (2008), namely that the use of religious dogwhistles made Protestant respondents label a candidate more Republican. This suggests that these covert religious appeals do not work by sending covert religious content, but by merely flagging the speaker's partisan identity. We will have more to say in coming chapters about the differences between the kinds of content sent by dogwhistles like *inner-city* and those like *wonder-working power*, but, once again, what we see in these studies is that dogwhistles are effective tools for targeted political communication. One can successfully send a message to an in-group that wants to hear it, while obfuscating that communication to an out-group that would object to the message if they did hear it.

Outside of the political science literature, dogwhistles have also appeared in the literature on advertising. This should not be surprising given that, just like politicians, corporations might naturally want to target multiple demographics simultaneously in an advertising campaign, but keep those communications siloed. For example, Kanner 2000 discusses a Subaru ad campaign from the late twentieth century peppered with references that were meant to send targeted messages to the LGBTQ community, while slipping past straight people who might be uncomfortable about buying a car marketed to gay people. Paul Poux, one of the campaign's developers, said that "it's apparent to gay people that we're talking about being gay, but straight people don't know what's going on" (Palmer 2000). Subaru took this marketing strategy to be a clear success, showing once again in a new domain that dogwhistles are an important tool in sending public messages to large and varied audiences.

Beyond showing that dogwhistles work, the advertising literature has gone beyond other social sciences and identified subtle effects of message targeting, which help explain why dogwhistles are effective as a public messaging strategy of the kind developed by Subaru. In particular, there is clear evidence people have meta-awareness about the kind of message targeting dogwhistles involve. Listeners know that public messages can be targeted, and will change their perceptions of communications based on how they believe they are targeted. For instance, experiments in Aaker et al. (2000) show that if a participant can determine the target market for an advertisement, they will like that advertisement more if they belong to that group and less if they do not. Moreover, the positive effect is exaggerated if the listener belongs to a numerically rare or distinct group. This strand of research has interesting implications for dogwhistles as targeted communications. Even if no other message is sent, listeners will be positively disposed to a speaker if they merely determine they are being dogwhistled to, and this effect is magnified if they see themselves as part of some distinctive group.

This effect clearly accords with what Calfano and Djupe (2008) and Albertson (2015) posit for one mechanism for how religious dogwhistles work. As discussed above, Republican Party self-identification increased the dogwhistle effect already seen in the religious audience, and caused respondents to identify the speaker as Republican. This effect, which goes over and above the religious message, could plausibly be attributed to the effect discovered in Aaker et al. (2000), namely Republicans recognizing a message targeted to them as Republicans, a distinct group they self-identify as belonging to.

What we see across the social science literature is that dogwhistles not only have effects that can be detected under a variety of experimental conditions, but that these effects likely have different genealogies. Some dogwhistles work by making salient negative out-group stereotypes, perhaps making them more linguistically akin to slurs (an idea that we will explore thoroughly in subsequent chapters). Other dogwhistles seem to work by flagging the in-group identity of the speaker for the benefit of in-group members. Finally, the social science literature suggests that there are meta-effects to dogwhistles. That is, beyond whatever information is extracted from the dogwhistle, there is information in the fact that a dogwhistle is being sent. When a listener can detect a targeted communication in an otherwise public message, listeners are more likely to approve of the message. As we develop a linguistic theory of dogwhistles over the course of this book, we will keep these effects in mind. It is a subtle and difficult question to determine how the content and use of a linguistic expression can have behavioral effects through channels like in-group identification or out-group threat, but we take these question as critical for any successful linguistic account of dogwhistles, even if they range beyond the usual kinds of questions asked in formal semantics and pragmatics.

We have focused so far on empirical results showing the efficacy of dogwhistles. We should also consider what this experimental literature takes dogwhistles to be as a linguistic phenomenon. Here the primary theoretical proposal is that dogwhistle language comes in two forms: coded communication and multivocal appeals. Albertson (2015) presents the difference in terms of the deniability of the message. A coded communication sends a taboo message that can be denied, even to the community that receives the message, while a multivocal appeal sends a plurality of messages to a plurality of communities, each of which is undeniable in its target community. We are a bit skeptical of this distinction because our intuition is that all examples of dogwhistles discussed in this literature would be, in principle, deniable, though perhaps there is a distinction between whether the speaker has deniability as a goal. That said, this question of how deniability plays into the semantics and pragmatics of dogwhistles is critical for determining whether and how the message sent by dogwhistles is conventionalized. The next chapter considers this question in detail, and as we construct a typology of dogwhistles, we will also return to the distinction between coded communication and multivocal appeals.

A second major theoretical contribution by social scientists to our understanding of the linguistic aspects of dogwhistles is due to Mendelberg (2001), which has also inspired some of the philosophical approaches discussed in the next section. Mendelberg (2001) insight is to link the effectiveness of racial dogwhistles to wider American conversational norms about race, and to show that subverting these norms requires that the targets of such messages be unaware of their norm-subverting designs. In particular, the theory is that racial dogwhistles exist because there are conversational norms of equality in the context of US politics, and so while people still harbor racist beliefs, overt racist speech is punished, even by those that hold those beliefs. Mendelberg (2001) goes even further and shows through experimental and ecological data that dogwhistles must work, at least in part, in an unconscious way. In particular, people that are receptive to racial dogwhistles become unreceptive once it is explained that the dogwhistle was sent in order to get around the norm of equality. The important theoretical insight is that in order for certain kinds of dogwhistle communication to function, the intent of the message must be concealed from the listener (if not aspects of the message itself). The realization that some dogwhistles must be covert, not just to the excluded audience but to the target audience as well is a critical insight that any theory of dogwhistles will have to reckon with.

1.2 Dogwhistles in philosophy of language

In recent years philosophers of language have expanded their field of study from historically core questions about meaning and reference, especially in the truth conditional domain, and taken up in earnest social and political aspects of language use.

Dogwhistles have appeared in this literature, especially in work that tries to understand how language can be used for social coordination through ideology, propaganda, etc. We are interested in these broader questions this literature takes up (see Chapters 5 and 8, for instance); most of the second half of the book considers questions of this general kind. But first we want to provide a satisfying semantic and pragmatic account of how dogwhistles can be treated as a linguistic phenomenon, and how they relate to current questions in linguistic theory. To this end, we return to the following exploration of previous philosophical accounts in more detail in the following chapter.

Stanley (2015), in his work on propaganda, is the first philosopher of language to tackle dogwhistle speech using tools from semantics and pragmatics. His view is that dogwhistles are expressions that introduce conventional implicatures. In this way, they become analogous to slurs or honorifics, which, in addition to their at-issue content, carry a conventional non-at-issue component as well. To make the analogy concrete, note that a slur like *kraut* would have, at least on the kind of view Stanley is using for his analogy, the at-issue component "German" and the not-at-issue component "I hate Germans." Similarly, a dogwhistle like *inner-city* would have, according to Stanley (2015), the at-issue component "the SNAP program"[2] and the not-at-issue component "the speaker dislikes poor Black people." Dogwhistles, then, under an analysis like this, would fall under the umbrella of *mixed content bearers* in the sense of McCready (2010).

Another proposal on the market is the inferentialist view in Khoo (2017), which diverges from Stanley (2015) in rejecting the idea that dogwhistles, like slurs, involve a conventionalized component. Khoo's idea is that dogwhistles induce certain kinds of inferences, namely those which the existing beliefs of interpreters coupled with the information provided by the dogwhistle combine to yield. Schematically, if the speaker claims that x is C and the interpreter believes that Cs are Rs, then the interpreter will conclude that x is R. It's this kind of inference that Khoo (2017) thinks dogwhistles license. To illustrate this schema, we can analyze the example in (1) using the inferentialist framework as follows. Suppose that the interpreter believes that *inner-city* neighborhoods are Black neighborhoods. Then the speaker saying that people who live in inner-city neighborhoods lack a culture of work licenses the inference that people who live in Black neighborhoods lack a culture of work. This is a kind of invited inference account which relies on the (at-issue) content of the dogwhistle itself and the background beliefs interpreters have, which license a constellation of inferences about things related to that content.

In comparing the proposals in Stanley (2015) and Khoo (2017), we already begin to see the outlines of some of the core debates. For instance, here we see a disagreement about the degree of conventionalization of dogwhistles. In fact, we could introduce a third position, thus connecting the political science and philosophy of language literatures, by recasting the difference Albertson (2015) makes between coded

---

[2] 'SNAP' is the name of a social assistance program in the US, namely the Supplemental Nutrition Assistance Program.

communication and multivocal appeals as one between conventionalized dogwhistles (as they are not deniable) and those that are not conventionalized, and so able to be denied.

This debate about the content of dogwhistles crosscuts a second debate about how dogwhistles interact with the conversational context (however modeled). That is, instead of focusing on the meaning of dogwhistles to explain their communicative effect, some authors instead take their effect on the context to be primary. We can think of this literature as asking the question of what dogwhistles do to a conversational context that makes them distinct from simple assertions.

Recall the Stalnaker (1974, 1978) notion of assertion, which takes the assertion of a sentence denoting the proposition p to be a proposal to all conversational participants to remove from the context set all possible worlds that are inconsistent with p. If no one objects, the default effect of assertion is to remove those worlds with the effect that all conversational participants explicitly take p for granted. Emphasizing acceptance is crucial because it creates space between mutual beliefs and those propositions on conversational record as mutual beliefs.

Camp (2018) exploits this space to provide a new method of interacting with common ground on par with assertion, called *insinuation*, which provides an account of dogwhistles, among other phenomena. The idea is that a speaker S insinuates p by getting the listener to take 'S believes p' as one of their mutual beliefs, but because p was never explicitly proposed or accepted as part of the conversational record, p is deniable. Dogwhistles can then be treated as expressions that, whatever the contribution to the assertions in which they appear, they also insinuate some proposition p. This proposal is nice because it shows clearly how taking a broad view of semantics, pragmatics, and the conversational context broadens the solution space. It allows us to give simple answers in one domain while accounting for linguistic complexity in another. For instance, in this case, dogwhistles are completely mundane in terms of semantic content—they denote simple propositions. They come to have their interesting status in virtue of how they interact with an enriched notion of the common ground.

There is another set of proposals that also make use of a Stanakerian notion of conversational context, but which give dogwhistles an even more oblique effect than the insinuation-based account does. While not strictly about dogwhistles, McGowan (2004, 2012) and Langton (2012), aim to understand hate speech and covert exercitives more broadly. These categories clearly include at least some dogwhistles. On the Stalnakerian account, conversational moves are always made relative to the common ground, which constrains their appropriateness. This is clearest in the case of expressions that bear presuppositions, which cannot be felicitously used unless those presuppositions are met in the common ground.

McGowan (2004, 2012) and Langton (2012) want to extend this notion of permissible conversational move from the area of facts, where classical presuppositions reside, to all manner of norm-governed conversational behavior. For instance, there is a norm against displaying anger or aggression in a conversation, which prevents such conversational moves out of the blue. One function of certain expressions, like expletives, could be to update the conversational state so that participants know that anger is now permissible. The use of an expletive would, in the emotional sphere, remove the presupposition blocking angry conversational displays. This notion of permissibility could extend to some cases of dogwhistles, which could be analyzed as conversational norm shifting devices. Because dogwhistles often involve taboo subjects, their purpose would be to signal that the conversational background should be such that the taboo subject is not, in fact, taboo for the speaker. They would invite participants that recognize the dogwhistle to, in future conversations with the speaker, make conversational moves that would otherwise not be permitted.

Both the insinuation-based and norm-based accounts of dogwhistles treat them as making speech acts that are different than vanilla assertions. While these speech act theories are couched in a Stalnakarian framework, there are others that hearken back to Austin's (1962) original speech act framework. Saul (2018) argues that we must understand at least certain dogwhistles as perlocutionary speech acts—that is, we must view them through their consequences for the listener. In particular, recall that in the experimental literature, certain dogwhistles like *inner-city* appear to work by triggering a willingness to assign racial stereotypes within a subset of listeners. Saul (2018) argues that these kind of facts suggests that instead of focusing on what dogwhistle mean, or how they are deployed by speakers in contexts, we should focus on their perlocutionary effects on those who hear them.

Finally, there is an important set of questions philosophers have asked concerning the place of conscious awareness and intention in dogwhistles. Saul (2018) presents the clearest cognitive typology of dogwhistles. She argues that there are four kinds of dogwhistles based on a pair of two-way splits—the first between intentional and non-intentional dogwhistles, and the second between covert and overt dogwhistles, where the effect of covert dogwhistles on a listener is dependent on their conscious awareness of the dogwhistle.

The covert/overt split is perhaps the more interesting, in linguistic terms, because it bears directly on the question of how dogwhistles transmit information. Saul (2018) takes overt dogwhistles to involve a kind of standard Gricean conversational implicature, but in a coded way. That is, the speaker uses an expression that is perfectly tailored (given the context) so that only a subset of the audience is able to do the requisite implicature calculation to alight on the hidden message. Overt dogwhistles are thus most likely what we immediately think of when asked to consider dogwhistles. More intriguing are covert dogwhistles. Recall from the experimental literature that expressions like *inner-city* can alter a respondent's policy preferences and willingness to assign racial stereotypes, while an overt racial appeal fails to do so. Saul (2018), based on similar conclusions in Mendelberg (2001), argues that these dogwhistles require unconscious uptake by the listener to be effective. In this sense they are doubly covert, being completely hidden from one audience, and unconsciously received by another.

The intentional/non-intentional split is exactly as the name would have it; the distinction involves whether the speaker intends to dogwhistle or not. Of course, speakers can intentionally send coded messages, but Saul (2018) believes that a speaker can also non-intentionally dogwhistle. This is a crucial political fact because it allows dogwhistles to act as conversational contagion. Otherwise well-meaning actors can send harmful covert messages when the dogwhistle itself becomes part of the conversation—e.g., in media discussions about a controversial political ad. This is especially pernicious in the case of covert dogwhistles which, as we have seen, depend on unconscious processes in the listener. In the case of unintentional covert dogwhistles, then, a conversation can be full of harmful messages that all participants are sending and reacting to, but that no one is actually aware of.

The goal of this brief summary of the philosophy of language literature (and of the social science work in the previous section as well), is to begin to situate this work in the conversation about dogwhistles in previous research, and to provide a high-level overview of some of the debates that this work will engage in. We will be returning to the works mentioned here throughout the following chapters, but already we can see some of the core questions that need to be answered.

First, we need a linguistically grounded typology of dogwhistles. Previous authors have considered the same examples of dogwhistles that have repeatedly appeared in the literature, but produced different categorizations. The next chapter considers the place of dogwhistles in pragmatic theory, and in doing so will develop a typology of dogwhistles that situates them relative to related linguistic phenomena based on standard linguistic tests. A second core question that emerges from the previous literature, which is also considered in the next chapter, is where the analysis of dogwhistles should be located in semantic and pragmatic theory. That is, should dogwhistles involve traditional semantic content, or are they best handled through a speech act theory of contextual manipulation, or are they purely a result of standard Gricean reasoning? Perhaps we need some kind of mixed account, or even different accounts for different kinds of dogwhistles. There is very little agreement in the previous literature on these issues. A core goal of this work is to bring some clarity to the issue of how to best provide a unified account of dogwhistles, taking into account the subtypes we will show to exist in the following chapters. Finally, the previous literature, both in the social sciences and in the philosophy of language, shows a preoccupation with how dogwhistles produce their effect. Do dogwhistles work by mere information transfer, and if so, how can that be tied to out-group threat or in-group identification? Finding a way to model these notions in formal semantic/pragmatic theory is a primary result of this work and also provides a through line to the previous literature on dogwhistles.

1.3 An outline of the main proposals

We can now lay out the main proposals of this work in a way that situates them relative to the previous literature on dogwhistles and the questions we posed at the beginning of this chapter. We take our primary contribution to the literature to be that dogwhistle communication primarily concerns social meaning, as understood by the field of quantitative, variationist sociolinguistics first pioneered by Labov (1963).

While the field of sociolinguistics, and the understanding of the nature of social meaning has changed over the past 60 years, at its core is the idea that variation in language allows for meaning to accrue to that variation, with the meaning at issue standing outside the bounds of the kind of truth-conditional meaning that's so well-studied in semantics. For instance, even sub-phonetic differences in the pronunciation of a particular vowel could signal, for example, that the speaker is from a certain place, belongs to a particular ethnic group, has a certain sexual orientation, or is a member of the punk scene. In this way social meaning concerns how our ways of speaking situate us in the social landscape of interlocutors. Our contention is that all of the phenomena we see with dogwhistles, including those described in this introduction, are best understood as flowing from speakers attempting to situate themselves in this way in the social landscape (perhaps in different ways and to different subaudiences, and sometimes deceptively so).

Chapter 2 is focused on laying out the argument for the social meaning account, presenting its virtues, and comparing it to its competitors. We can already see, though, how it finds its own place in ongoing debates about the nature of dogwhistles. In particular, we mentioned the tension between accounts that take dogwhistles to involve conventionalized meaning, and those that take them to involve pragmatic inference. Our approach resolves this tension. Social meaning is conventionalized, but in virtue of being non-propositional, we expect it to behave differently than conventionalized truth-conditional meaning.

Further, additional analytical avenues open up by moving to the domain of social meaning. It is these that we explore throughout the rest of the book. If dogwhistles work in virtue of the kinds of social meanings they bear, we can ask how speakers and listeners react to social meaning in discourse. That is, we can think about the pragmatics of social meaning. In many ways *the pragmatics of social meaning* could have been the subtitle for this work. In Chapters 3 and 4 we introduce Bayesian Rational Speech Act theory, which is a game-theoretic model of the pragmatics of communicating agents. We show how such models can be extended to the domain of social meaning, and further show how they provide a perfect setting to provide an account of dogwhistles.

The fact that such models are inherently interactional will allow us to make good on the fact, well-known from the sociolinguistics literature, that the social meaning of a speaker's utterances is constructed in concert with their listeners. This means that dogwhistles will come into their own in conversations with many participants, where the speaker is trying to manage their social persona across different groups of listeners. In addition, the fact that these models are inherently statistical will allow us to capture important contours of dogwhistled meaning. In particular, we can make sense of the fact that though dogwhistles involve conventionalized meaning, they are still deniable because listeners will detect dogwhistled meaning only probabilistically, yielding in general a likelihood of a particular meaning rather than a certainty of it.

After laying out our core theory in these chapters we begin to extend it. Chapter 5 considers a class of dogwhistles which we call *enriching* dogwhistles. We draw a distinction between those dogwhistles that purely convey social meaning and those that additionally convey some kind of propositional content. For instance, in the example in (1), Ryan uses the classic dogwhistle *inner-city*. The dogwhistle clearly signals something about Ryan's sociolinguistic persona—only certain kinds of politicians talk like that—but as noted, the dogwhistle conveys enriched truth conditional meaning. On hearing the dogwhistle we take *inner-city* to not merely pick out a geographical location but certain racially coded neighborhoods in that location. How does this truth conditional meaning enter the discourse? It cannot be part of the conventional meaning, a view we reject in earlier chapters. It also cannot arise via one of the classes of standard Gricean implicatures, which we also reject in earlier chapters.

Instead, we propose in Chapter 5 that certain sociolinguistic personas can be linked to ideologies. After discussing our approach to ideology and how to formalize it, we show that ideologies can leak propositional content into the common ground. For instance, if I signal through a dogwhistle that I am a racist, and thus willing to have a conversation on racist ideological grounds, if you assent, then certain propositions become part of the common ground, or at the least it will become common ground that I assent to those propositions. Thus, even me signaling my racist persona will give you a hint about the kinds of propositions I might believe. We show that this is enough to generate the kinds of enriched meanings we see with dogwhistles like *inner-city*. We also show how the ideological view relates to critical research in the social science literature that shows how participants can be inoculated against dogwhistles, so that while they may hear the dogwhistle, they will avoid reacting with the negative stereotypes the dogwhistle would otherwise trigger.

In Chapter 6 we take a sharp turn. The previous chapters mostly focus on the speaker's perspective. That is, we consider under what conditions it is optimal behavior to dogwhistle. The Bayesian RSA framework, though, allows us to take either the speaker or the listener's perspective. We can thus ask—how should a sociolinguistically aware listener react to hearing a possible dogwhistle? We show that taking this perspective allows us to identify a novel class of implicatures in the social meaning domain, which we call *vigilance* implicatures. We show that these implicatures are the exact analogue of another class of implicatures called reference implicatures, which have been studied in the truth-conditional domain.

After describing vigilance implicatures, we consider a type of listener that takes to the extreme the idea that a sociolinguistically aware listener should be on the lookout for dogwhistles, especially when dogwhistling would be utility-maximizing for the speaker in the current conversation. These listeners we call hypervigilant, and they stand out by aggressively labeling messages as dogwhistles. We consider cases of hypervigilance, especially in social media, and provide an analysis in a slightly modified version of the social meaning games we begin with. The idea is that instead of using empirically grounded estimates of the frequency at which certain kinds of speakers use certain kinds of messages, such listeners use ideological distance as a metric. We show

how such a shift produces hypervigilance and relates to certain results in the *cheap talk* games discussed by Farrell (1993).

Chapter 6 can be viewed as exploring some consequences of the core analysis we present. The final two chapters move further beyond this core analysis of dogwhistles and how they are deployed by speakers and interpreted by listeners. The first extension we make is in Chapter 7, where we consider the role dogwhistles and social meaning more generally could play in questions of trust. In particular, theories of testimonial evidence, and when it should be trusted, often place a premium on truth-tracking. Agents with a track record of truthful statements should be a better bet for trust, and so such theories usually take them as trustworthy, and, conversely, those whose speech doesn't track truth should not be trustworthy. This leads to a possible paradox involving interlocutors who are known to frequently make assertions that are not truth-tracking, but which inspire fanatical followings of trustful listeners. We show in this chapter that social meanings have the ability to explain this paradox. The core idea is that listeners may choose to track the truth of a speaker's utterances in order to establish trust, but may also choose to track faithful reporting of social meaning, especially when the reported persona links up well with their own ideologies. It is this latter option that will allow us to explain interlocutor trust in untruthful speakers.

The final chapter, Chapter 8, ranges broadly. We aim to consider approaches to phenomena that open up once we have a theory of dogwhistles. We start by considering questions of discursive health, and the provocative idea that speakers resorting to using dogwhistles might suggest that the discourse is otherwise healthy, at least comparatively speaking. The alternative is for the speaker to go *mask-off* and use messages that unambiguously signal their sociolinguistic persona—perhaps taboo. We explore some situations in which going mask-off might be the right move, and show how they track political polarization. We then turn to a grab-bag of questions which arise when considering social meaning and its place in the theoretical landscape of meaning in semantics and pragmatics. What is the structure of the domain of social meanings? What can we say about interactions of social meaning and more standard truth-conditional meaning? How might implicatures arise from the projection of social meanings and the use of dogwhistles? It turns out that our proposals about dogwhistles earlier in the book have more general consequences in some cases, and open up avenues for examination in others.

Finally, we conclude the book at the end of Chapter 8 by moving beyond dogwhistles in particular to consider coded communication more generally, whether involving social meaning or truth-conditional meaning. The theory we develop in this book is a theory of dogwhistles, but there's nothing stopping it from being applied to communication which is accessible to some listeners and not others, an extremely wide domain, perhaps the domain of all language use. We close with a few examples and suggestions for the future.

2
Dogwhistles as a semantic/pragmatic phenomenon

This chapter situates dogwhistles within the prior literature in semantics, and especially pragmatics. We will interrogate the naive, folk-definition of dogwhistles—expressions that send one message to an in-group, while sending a second, often taboo message to an out-group—in order to understand what kinds of messages these are, how a speaker comes to send them, and how they can be received. In doing so, we will also consider previous approaches to dogwhistles, which vary quite substantially in how the meaning of dogwhistles is distributed across semantic and pragmatic components, how and what aspects of dogwhistles are conventionalized, and in the inventory and typology of various kinds of dogwhistles they assume. In working our way through this previous literature in section 2.1, we will stake out our own position on the issues raised in the previously literature. The overarching picture we come to in section 2.2 is that at its heart, dogwhistles involve *social meaning*, a unique, non-propositional category of meaning over which pragmatic inferences can still be made.

The final section of this chapter, namely 2.3, will consider whether dogwhistles are a monolithic category, or whether we need a typology of such expressions. We will see that there are a variety of axes on which one can divide dogwhistles, but that there is only one axis that is directly linguistically relevant. In particular, we will draw a novel distinction between two kinds of dogwhistles, consisting of one class that traffics only in social meaning and a second which involves both social meaning and standard propositional inferences.

2.1 Previous accounts of dogwhistles

In this section we will survey some of the major previous accounts of dogwhistles. While dogwhistles are relatively understudied compared to prima facie related phenomena, like slurs, for instance, there are still a variety of accounts on the market. The parameters along which these accounts differ are perhaps not so surprising. Previous authors differ with respect to the question of whether dogwhistles bear some kind of conventional meaning. If dogwhistles do bear conventional meaning, authors can then differ with respect to the precise content that is conventionalized. Among those authors that are unwilling to imbue dogwhistles with special conventional content, the question of how to generate dogwhistle inferences becomes a pragmatic one. Here, once again, authors differ on whether these inferences should be generated via standard Gricean mechanisms, or perhaps involve a different kind of pragmatic reasoning.

We will take each of these kinds of previous accounts in turn. Critical for us is the question of conventionalization. We will come to argue in section 2.2 that dogwhistles involve conventionalized social meaning. This proposal will allow us to resolve certain tensions between those purely pragmatic accounts and those accounts that take dogwhistles to involve something like a conventional implicature in the truth-conditional domain. First, though, we must introduce those accounts, as well as the problems we believe they fall short of resolving.

2.1.1 The conventional implicature view

Recall that in addition to expressions that bear at-issue content alone (hereafter *AI-content*), there are expressions like slurs, honorifics, etc., which carry a conventional not-at-issue component as well (hereafter *NAI-content*). The NAI-component of such expressions, for historical reasons going back to Grice 1975, have often been called conventional implicatures.[1] For example, a slur like *kraut* would have AI-component "German" and a NAI-component "I hate Germans." In general, terms like *kraut* which carry both AI- and NAI-components can be referred to as *mixed content bearers* (McCready 2010). Stanley (2015) argues that dogwhistle language should be analyzed as mixed content bearers. In particular, he says that a dogwhistle like *welfare* would have the AI-component "the SNAP program" and the NAI-component "Black people are lazy." There are a series of reasons to believe that this is not the case.

Our first argument, which we call the *knowledge argument*, is based on what it takes to plausibly say a speakers knows the meaning of a word. We argue that the requirements for knowing the meaning of dogwhistles seem quite different from those for widely accepted cases of mixed content. Take the case of pejoratives. Can a speaker know what *kraut* means without knowing it is derogatory? It seems not. Conversely, can a speaker know what *welfare* means without knowing this association with Cadillacs, etc. (Stanley 2015, pp. 158–159)? We think the answer is: Yes. The whole idea of a dogwhistle is that the (so-called) NAI-component is not accessible to some speakers. Thus, the NAI part must not be part of the conventionalized truth-conditional meaning.

An immediate objection to the knowledge argument would be that we are just dealing with different dialects. If so, it's not unexpected that what's needed to know the meaning of the expression varies across speakers to the extent that their dialects differ on the meaning of dogwhistles. This argument seems to beg the substantive question concerning the knowledge argument, but there are other reasons to think it incorrect.

While this view might explain the effect of dogwhistles in mixed company, it fails to explain the use of dogwhistles with an in-group. Lo Guercio and Caso (2022) caution

---

[1] They are also sometimes thought of as expressive content, which often receives something of a similar treatment in terms of compositional behavior in popular theories of these phenomena within linguistics.

that we have to be careful in these scenarios to distinguish the dogwhistle expression from the 'act of dogwhistling' using said expression. We think the critique holds up even when restricting ourselves to considering just the dogwhistle expression and its semantic import. The point is that under the conventional NAI account a dogwhistle is indistinguishable from expressions like slurs, at least in terms of how they commit their users to contents. We think this wrongly predicts how dogwhistle expressions function, even among speakers who share a dialect. Imagine choosing between a racial dogwhistle and a racial slur. We could imagine speakers choosing the former to appear less strident (or even to stake out or try to stake out a small space of deniability), even in in-group scenarios surrounded by fellow racists. A NAI account collapses these distinctions, which we think has bad consequences. It seems to us that dogwhistles can in fact be subtly used or not used strategically, even in in-group communicative contexts, which wouldn't make sense if the subtext of dogwhistle were part of its conventional meaning for the in-group.

Ultimately what we'll propose in section 2.2 and subsequent chapters is that we do, in fact, have distinct groups of speakers, as the dialect account would propose. Critically, though, the way groups of speakers are distinct is not in virtue of the conventional truth-conditional meaning of their expressions—i.e., how we would think of genuine lexical-semantic dialectal variation—but rather because of variation in background knowledge about language *use patterns* across the groups. We think this way of thinking about things preserves important distinctions between dogwhistles and NAI-content-bearing expressions, while allowing us to capture the subtleties of dogwhistle use across both in-groups and out-groups.

The final argument against a mixed content account of dogwhistles, what we call the *deniability argument*, gets at the heart of what it means for content to be conventional. The use of dogwhistles is prompted by a desire to veil a bit of content, but to still convey it in some manner. Deniability is essential. If a bit of content is conventional, it's not deniable any longer. This can be seen with pejoratives, which clearly carry conventional NAI content.

(1) A: Angela Merkel is a kraut.
    B: What do you have against Germans?
    A: #I don't have anything against Germans. Why do you think I might?

Such dialogues are fine with dogwhistles; in the following, there seems to be no entailment that A has the relevant attitude.

(2) A: Elin is on welfare.
    B: What do you have against poor people?
    A: I don't have anything against poor people. Why do you think I might?

Generalizing, we can identify a dialogue-based test for conventional content. In a dialogue in which participant A says 'X,' where $[\![X]\!]$ is a mixed content bearer with AI content Y and NAI content Z. If participant B responds with 'It's not cool to say Z,' then it is incoherent for A to respond 'I didn't say that Z" (if Z is stable using conventional truth-conditional content).[2] By this test, dogwhistles of all types can be concluded to not be conventional in this sense, and thus a fortiori, not mixed content bearers.

We take the knowledge and deniability arguments to present a strong challenge to the mixed content bearer view of dogwhistle language.

2.1.2 The inferentialist view

The polar opposite of the conventional implicature view is the inferentialist view of Khoo (2017). While the conventional implicature view treats dogwhistles as expressions that bear lexically specified NAI-content, the inferentialist view lays down the deflationist gauntlet. The claim is that there is essentially no special linguistic phenomenon at work in dogwhistles. Instead, Khoo's idea is that dogwhistles do nothing more than induce certain kinds of inferences, namely those which the existing beliefs of interpreters coupled with the information provided by the dogwhistle combine to yield.

Schematically, if the speaker claims that x is C and the interpreter believes that Cs are Rs, then the interpreter will conclude that x is R. It's this kind of inference that Khoo thinks that dogwhistles license. In the example we have focused on, if the interpreter believes that inner-city neighborhoods are Black neighborhoods, then a speaker saying that people who live in inner-city neighborhoods lack a culture of work licenses the inference that people who live in Black neighborhoods lack a culture of work. This is a kind of invited inference account which relies on the (at-issue) content of the dogwhistle itself and the background beliefs interpreters have, which license a constellation of inferences about things related to that content.

This kind of account gets around the problems of treating dogwhistles as conventional implicatures. Most importantly, the dogwhistle effect is not conventionalized and is entirely listener-based, which preserves the speaker's deniability. This is the critical fact that conventional implicature accounts miss. At the same time, an account that is based entirely on the extensional content of the dogwhistle and the listener's background beliefs is too weak. As Khoo himself notes, the account predicts that any two coextensive terms should induce the same dogwhistles, but they don't. We thus seem to require a theory in which the dogwhistle inferences are tied to specific linguistic expressions, but are not a part of their conventionalized semantic meaning, as with a conventional implicature. This is a tricky middle way to find.

Khoo's solution is to appeal to work of Elga and Rayo (2016) on belief fragmentation. The idea is that thinking of Xs in one way may not deliver the same inferences as

---

[2] The condition about statability is important because it's been argued that (for example) expressive content can't be paraphrased using exclusively truth-conditional content-bearing expressions (e.g., Potts 2007). The result of this is that the expression 'that Z' doesn't really make sense for expressives already. For the present case, this isn't an issue, because the proposal around dogwhistles in the literature is that they carry conventional implicatures, not expressives, and conventional implicatures pretty clearly are paraphrasable by truth-conditional means in the same way that presuppositions are usually taken to be (McCready 2014).

thinking of them in a different way, so even coextensive terms may not give the same inferences. Indeed, Khoo indicates (in his fn. 19), that a metalinguistic theory of these words is probably needed, conceding "beliefs about the code words themselves may be relevant." We agree with this suggestion, though he doesn't provide any details of how he thinks it should be realized. We think it's precisely the use of the dogwhistle that has to be taken into account when trying to compute what meaning is transmitted and what the likely intentions of the speaker are.

This point undermines an inferentialist account, though. The need to look more closely at the linguistic expressions themselves invalidates the inferentialist theory, which has its focus on *content*. We must move to a view which induces the inferences arising from dogwhistles on the basis of the forms of the messages themselves, as in the picture we develop in subsequent chapters.[3] This matches the conclusion from Lo Guercio and Caso (2022), who show in recent work that dogwhistles pass Lewis (1975) tests for conventionalization in language. We simply must respect the fact that dogwhistles are, in some sense, lexicalized, even if not lexicalized in the way that conventional implicatures are, much less the way in which standard truth-conditional content is. What we will see is that what is conventionalized in dogwhistles is an aspect of their social meaning rather than their truth-conditional content.

This last point about lexicalization is critical. The reason is that we read Khoo as, beyond the particulars of his proposal, staking out a general deflationary position with respect to dogwhistles. That is, dogwhistles are not, as a phenomenon, distinct from any kind of normal inferences about content listeners make in the process of interpreting language. The result is a very thin theory of dogwhistles. The fact that dogwhistles are lexicalized, in some sense, and also arbitrary in the structuralist sense,[4] is enough for the linguist to conclude that there is a linguistic phenomenon here. We are not merely dealing with inferences about (propositional) content. Rather, we can (and must) point to particular expressions and ask 'what do these expressions mean (and not other similar expressions) which yields the observed dogwhistle effects (e.g., deniability, multivocality, etc.)?'

While we believe we clearly have a linguistic phenomenon at hand, we can now replicate Khoo's challenge on the assumption that there is in fact a linguistic phenomenon at issue: (i) are dogwhistles actually distinct from other kinds of linguistic phenomena, and (ii) do we really need a new theory to account for them? The view we come to is that (i) dogwhistles are ultimately not so different from other phenomena involving social meaning. We see in section 2.2 and then in Chapters 3–5

---

[3] This is not the only way to address the problem of intersubstitutability. Breitholtz and Cooper (2021) instead develop a hyperintensional treatment which takes extensionally equivalent expressions to potentially denote type-theoretically distinct objects, which can still play similar roles in inference while possibly triggering distinct inferences. However, the way in which enrichment is handled in their theory involves hearer access to topoi—roughly, certain kinds of reasoning patterns—and speaker beliefs about their access, which then informs a game-theoretic calculation. While similar to our approach, that fact that the theory doesn't make reference to social meaning means that it doesn't have access to the principled explanation for observed patterns of dogwhistle recognition that do quite clearly involve social facts. We view this as a fatal weakness of the account.

[4] Consider, for a completely clear example of this arbitrariness, the case of Gritty in Chapter 4, whose meaning is entirely opaque.

that dogwhistles can be placed solidly alongside other sociolinguistic phenomena where speakers signal their social personas through their choice of language variants. Dogwhistles stand out, though, because they arise in scenarios where there are large audiences, risky messages, and a certain amount of uncertainty about the social meaning of particular messages, as we will show. Thus, dogwhistles, while not distinct in kind, emerge only in very particular kinds of discourses. Studying social meaning in these extreme cases, we hope, allows us to get a better picture of how it works in more usual (and usually simpler) cases.

From this study, what we will see is that (returning to the second question posed above) dogwhistles actually require a fairly thick theory, contra Khoo. Even if we are semi-deflationist in the sense that we propose a unified account of dogwhistles and a variety of sociolinguistic and pragmatic phenomena, we believe dogwhistles are a complex phenomenon, one that reveals the need for a theory that allows for interactions between truth-conditional meaning and social meaning, as well as a theory of pragmatics that can combine information from these multiple sources. The rest of this work, as we construct and motivate this theory, can be seen as an argument against the deflationism of a Khoo-style inferentialist account, where dogwhistles can be accounted for by agents making bog-standard logical inferences from their beliefs (a set of propositions) and the proposition expressed by what the speaker said.

2.1.3 The (manner) implicature view

In jointly considering the conventional implicature and default inference views, we have what looks like a paradox. We do not want to let dogwhistles have conventionalized content (for reasons of deniability), but we have to recognize that certain expressions are, by convention, dogwhistles. One way out that immediately comes to mind is to try to treat dogwhistles via Gricean implicature. Here is it important to lay out the scope of our claims. There are a variety of semantic theories that could be considered Gricean. In fact, even the game-theoretic treatment we develop in the following chapter can be taken to be in harmony with Grice (e.g., Franke and Jäger 2016), only operating at a different level of description. We do not mean to challenge here the deep connections between traditional Gricean and probabilistic approaches to meaning. Instead, we take Gricean pragmatics to have given us a typology of implicatures defined by how they arise via the interaction of maxims. The question we raise here is whether we can simply slot dogwhistles into one of the standard cells in the typology. We think the answer is a clear no.

If we were to try to slot dogwhistles into a Gricean typology of implicature, the most natural would be a Manner implicature. As an implicature, the enriched content would be deniable, but we could attribute the fact that particular expressions can be identified as dogwhistles to the fact that Manner implicatures involve 'non-standard' ways to say things. That is, just as the phrase *caused to stop* generates implicatures because it is a non-standard way to say *stopped*, a dogwhistle like *inner-city* might not be lexicalized as such, but merely recognized as a non-standard way to say *Black neighborhoods*. Upon such recognition by listener's who are aware of the dogwhistle, its use would trigger a Manner implicature, which would be deniable, just as we want. This is an attractive story, and while implicature accounts have been floated for certain examples of dogwhistles (e.g., Saul 2018), it is surprisingly hard to make these approaches work.[5]

Manner implicatures are bit mysterious, but broadly they work in virtue of the fact that listeners will assume that speaker will describe normal events with normal language. For instance, if a speaker says that *George made the car stop*, the listener ask why the speaker didn't say *George stopped the car*, which is equivalent as far as the truth conditions are concerned, but is more complex and also a non-normal way of speaking. This makes it a worse thing to say with respect to Manner. The Manner-based conclusion is that there must have been some reason that it would be inappropriate to say that *George stopped the car*. This would be true, for instance, if what is relevant is not that he stopped the car, but that it happened in a non-standard way, which is the implicature actually generated by *George caused the car to stop*.

A Manner implicature account of dogwhistles, then, should go something like this:

The speaker said *inner-city*. Assuming she is cooperative and following Manner, she would have said *Black neighborhoods*......

We must already stop because we have a problem. Classic Manner implicatures involve non-standard ways of saying the same thing. This assumes that *Black neighborhoods* and *inner-city* mean the same thing (e.g., *stop the car* vs. *made the car stop*), but we have already seen that dogwhistles must not have this conventionalized content given that they are deniable. This was the core argument grounding our rejection of the conventional implicature view of Stanley (2015).

Suppose we grant this equivalence, though. The Manner implicature is still difficult to derive. The problem concerns what is implicated by the use of *inner-city*. If we step back, we usually think of implicatures as involving some asserted S with meaning P that is enriched through the implicature calculation process to arrive at the content $P + E$ for some enrichment E. For instance, in the case of a standard manner implicature, like that arising from saying $S = $ *made the car stop*, the utterance of S meaning P competes with $S' = $ *stopped the car* also meaning P, to give us $P + E = $ *stopped the car in a weird way*. We are being pedantic about this point because it reveals that the

---

[5] Instead of manner, Saul 2018 proposes a Relevance implicature account of some dogwhistles, but this does not work either, which is surprising given how powerful the Relevance maxim is taken to be (e.g., Sperber and Wilson 1986). She considers the case of George Bush mentioning the Dred Scott decision as a pro-life dogwhistle that emerges via Relevance due to the fact that mentioning this case in the context of a question about abortion is not relevant unless you are familiar with pro-life discourse. But there are immediate problems here. A pro-life person familiar with this discourse would not detect a dogwhistle because it *would* be relevant for them given their background assumptions. It is the out-group members who would have a relevance implicature triggered, but these are precisely the people who shouldn't detect the dogwhistle. A Relevance implicature view could never get off the ground because of this informational asymmetry. Savvy listeners, the ones who detect the dogwhistle, are by definition more knowledgeable about the conversation, the speaker, their goals, etc. They will, thus, always generate fewer Relevance implicatures than the naive listener.

proposed Manner implicature doesn't match the standard schematic. We have been thinking about *inner-city* competing with *Black neighborhoods*, i.e., our S and S′, but the latter is also the enriched meaning we aim to get to through the implicature computation process. That is, in virtue of S and S′ competing, we want to reach S + E = *inner-city Black neighborhoods*. This is radically different than the standard case, which if truly parallel would involve saying *made the car stop* in order to implicate that you *stopped the car*. This is obviously ridiculous.

The reprise of the 'what is said' argument along with this new 'what is implicated' argument deeply undermine a standard Manner implicature account. Even if we grant a meaning equivalence between *inner-city* and *Black neighborhoods*, which we know can't actually be right, the relationship between alternative utterances and enriched meanings is completely wrong. If we try to fix these problems, we run into others. Ultimately, to make a standard Manner implicature account work, we must find some X with the same extension as *inner-city* whose avoidance licenses the inference that *inner-city* must refer to *Black neighborhoods* in the city. There are just no plausible candidates for X.

While we think that there is no way to generate the dogwhistle inference via a standard Manner implicature, there are interesting implicatures that could be generated through the competition between expressions like *inner-city* and *Black neighborhoods*. While we do not ultimately propose a Gricean account, it is worth considering these inferences because we believe they exist and because we will eventually be able to generate them in our own account, though through a different non-Gricean route. Once again, let's return to our script.

> The speaker said *inner-city*. Assuming she is cooperative and following Manner, she would have said *Black neighborhoods*. She didn't. It must be because she cannot say *Black neighborhoods* without violating one of the other maxims.

But which one? And what is the resulting implicature supposed to be? We have no good choice among the standard Gricean maxims, but it seems like what the listener concludes of the speaker is something like: "It's not polite / safe / socially sanctioned for the speaker to say *Black neighborhoods*." Thus, the listener infers that the speaker believes that "We have got this tailspin of culture, in our Black neighborhoods in particular, of men not working...." But, because saying this would violate our new 'maxim' *Safety*). The listener also derives a variety of meta-conversational inferences. In particular, (i) the speaker believes there is at least one listener who would disapprove of their saying *Black neighborhoods*, (ii) the speaker believes *inner-city* is veiled enough that at least part of the audience that disapproves of *Black neighborhoods* will not disapprove of *inner-city*, (iii) the speaker is being semi-cooperative by being under-informative to a subset of the audience.

While these inference seem to be correct ones to draw when noticing a speaker using a dogwhistle, they are clearly not 'normal' Gricean implicatures. The implicatures are not about enriching the content of an utterance, but all involve a meta-conclusions about the conversation, its participants, their attitudes, etc. All of these inferences will be recoverable in the analysis of dogwhistles we provide using social meaning. In addition, we will be able to account for the core dogwhistle enrichment that happens with dogwhistles that affect truth conditions, that is, the additional content a listener who detects a the dogwhistle is able to recover. As we have seen, a Gricean account making use of one of the standard classes of implicatures, and in particular, a Manner implicature account, is not up to the task.

2.1.4 The speech act view

The Austinian (1975) motto is that we must not just know what our utterances mean, but also what they do. With all the discussion of subaudiences, (dis)approval, covert moves, and so forth, dogwhistles would seem to be the ideal candidates for an account in terms of Speech Act Theory. We know of no such previous work, but there is influential research in a broadly Austinian framework on perhaps adjacent phenomena like slurs and hate speech (McGowan 2012; Tirrell 2012; Popa-Wyatt 2016) and pornography (Langton 2012).

What unifies this research is the idea that these varieties of speech all have an exercitive force (especially conversational exercitive force, following McGowan 2004). The speech in question serves to grant permission to the listener to hold particular views or engage in particular acts. For instance, using a slur to refer to a person or group of people instead of a non-slurring expression, would at least narrowly, give the listener permission to also use slurs. It would signal that they are in a conversation where such speech is acceptable. Taken to its extreme, slurs could give the listener permission to hate the target of the slur or even commit genocidal violence (Tirrell 2012).

We do not want to spend too much time tearing down a counter-analysis that does not exist, but we think that a unified analysis of dogwhistles through speech acts, whether exercitives or not, will run into problems. The trouble is that we do not think that dogwhistles have a general unified illocutionary or perlocutionary effect. There are clearly dogwhistles that can have similar permission-granting effects to hate speech, in particular the racial dogwhistles in political speech that we have touched on repeatedly (e.g., Mendelberg 2001; Hurwitz and Peffley 2005). We could treat these as covert exercitives giving a subaudience that is alert to the dogwhistle permission to indulge in racist attitudes that they may be predisposed to.

The problem is that it is hard to find a similar exercitive effect in other attested examples of dogwhistles. Take Bush's dogwhistle to evangelical voters in his State of the Union address. At best, the perlocutionary effect is something like affecting solidarity or eliciting a common spirit. There is no clear sense in which Bush is giving the audience permission to otherwise speak or act in a particular way, or expecting them to do so. The takeaway is that while certain dogwhistles or uses of dogwhistles could absolutely behave as exercitives (a view which we would in fact endorse), it is not the case that we can identify dogwhistles as such in general.

Of course, if there is no unified account of dogwhistles in terms of previously identified speech acts, we could try to make an argument that dogwhistling itself is the Speech Act in question. That is, alongside commanding and promising, we would have dogwhistling. We are quite amenable to this view, much more so than trying to reduce dogwhistles to other kinds of speech acts. Just as you might want a formal account of how the content and mood of an expression interacts with the context to have the force of a promise or a command, the analysis we develop in subsequent chapters explains which expressions can act as dogwhistles and how they come to have that effect in particular contexts. While we do not, in this book, do the work of integrating dogwhistles into Speech Act Theory, we think it would be possible and profitable. This work could then be seen as a formal account of dogwhistle speech acts.

2.1.5 Mixed views

The previous accounts we have considered have tried to analogize dogwhistles to various kinds of meaning that have been previously well studied. There are more recent accounts that involve novel, or even mixed types of meaning. Lo Guercio and Caso (2022) provide one such account. For them, dogwhistling involves a two-step process. The dogwhistle encodes a conversational perspective, which is treated as a not-at-issue conventional implicature. On receiving the at-issue content along with the perspective, the listener is able to generate what they call a *positioning* message. A new term is needed because the positioning message can come about via a implicature, perlocutionary inference, or even as an entailment—i.e., a conventional inference downstream from the conversational perspective.

It should now be clear why we label this account a 'mixed view.' It involves complex linking between multiple kinds of meaning categories already discussed. For this reason, many of the arguments against the other accounts discussed up to this point carry over to this kind of 'mixed view.' For instance, Lo Guercio and Caso (2022) take an anti-abortion dogwhistle like *Dred Scott Decision* to carry a conventional implicature that the speaker occupies an anti-abortion perspective, where c_w and c_t are the time and world of the context of utterance.

(3) {c : the speaker of c occupies an anti-abortion perspective at c_w at c_t}

As part of the conventional meaning, though not-at-issue, we would expect this proposed dogwhistled content to be undeniable, as with a slur. Thus, this kind of account is subject to the same objection to the pure conventional implicature view, namely that dogwhistles are, in fact, canonically deniable.[6]

The second step to their account follows the detection of the dogwhistle—here the conventional implicature that the speaker occupies a certain conversational perspective. The listener can use facts about the speaker's perspective to generate other kinds of inferences, whether by implicature, entailment, perlocutionary inference, or other means. This is an interesting idea, and in principle we have no objection to

---

[6] Lo Guercio and Caso (2022) propose that there is a dialectal difference involved in dogwhistles, as opposed to slurs, which accounts for their deniability. We have addressed the shortcomings of account based on truth-conditional dialectal variation above where we consider the pure conventional implicature view. Those arguments carry over to this case.

it. Of course, we could object to particular analyses of particular dogwhistles. For instance, Lo Guercio and Caso (2022) argue that listeners on hearing the phrase *Dred Scott decision* and detecting the speaker's conversational perspective generate a relevance implicature that the speaker will not appoint pro-choice judges. We do not think a relevance implicature account goes through (for our reasons, see footnote 5 in this chapter), but that does not mean that we would object to the general idea of implicatures following from the detection of a conversational perspective.

Looking ahead to Chapter 5, we will argue that detecting a dogwhistle will allow listeners to, in certain cases, assign speakers an ideology. These ideologies have some commonalities with Lo Guercio and Caso's conversational perspectives. We think that it is quite reasonable that knowing the speaker's ideology could facilitate all manner of inferences about what was said, and so Lo Guercio and Caso's insights about the second step in a dogwhistle inference could be imported into our account. This does not mean our proposals are equivalent, though. In addition to the fact that we do not treat dogwhistles as introducing conventional implicatures, we do not take ideologies to be genuinely part of the dogwhistled meaning. Here we differ from the analysis in Lo Guercio and Caso (2022), where the analogues of our ideologies are in fact part of the meaning of the dogwhistle itself.

This aspect of Lo Guercio and Caso (2022) actually causes problems, which our account avoids, because we could imagine the same expression triggering various kinds of conversational perspectives. For instance, an evangelical dogwhistle spoken by a pastor might signal that the speaker bears a kind of purely theological conversational perspective, but the same expression used by a right-wing politician could reveal them to be taking a Christian nationalist perspective. We would have to assume that the same expression is massively truth-conditionally ambiguous across many dialects. While in principle possible, this is not something that is familiar from other kinds of not-at-issue expressions.[7]

Rather than attempting to place dogwhistle content into the lexical semantics, as we will discuss in the following section in more detail, we take dogwhistles to involve social meaning. Social meaning is known to be multi-way underspecified or even ambiguous. For instance, apical pronunciations in English gerunds (g-dropping) is known to be associated with a variety of social personas, from lazy, to relaxed, to ignorant, or just unpretentious (e.g., Campbell-Kibler 2007a, 2007b). In our account, we can naturally say that a dogwhistle is consistent with a variety of kinds of personas and it is those personas that are related to ideologies, or conversational perspectives, in the parlance of Lo Guercio and Caso (2022). It is precisely this account that we will develop over Chapters 3–5. First, though, let us dig into the social meaning view more deeply now that we can contrast it to these other approaches to dogwhistled meaning from the previous literature.

---

[7] Note that this is another argument we can add to those against the conventional implicature view in section 2.1.2, which must include dialectal variation in the truth-conditional content of the dogwhistles.

2.2 The social meaning view

Having explored previous account of dogwhistles, as well as possible accounts using the standard semantics / pragmatics toolbox, we come to our own positive proposal, which is that dogwhistles involve particular kinds of inferences over the *social meaning* of expressions. Chapter 3 will begin to develop formal models of social meaning. Our goal for this section is much narrower. We aim to introduce the general idea of social meaning and show how it solves the conceptual problems of treating dogwhistles in the ways we have discussed so far—conventional implicatures, Gricean implicatures, etc.

Modern work on social meaning goes back to the foundational work of quantitative, variationist sociolinguistics. Labov (1963) study of Martha's Vineyard English famously documented how the pronunciation of a diphthong had become a proxy war in a larger ideological battle. The unique pronunciation of [ai] on the island had, over time, been drifting toward how it was pronounced on the mainland. As mainland controlled tourist businesses began to push out local fisherman as the core of the economy, fisherman and their supporters began to revive the older diphthong. The particular pronunciation of the diphthong became, then, a core marker of how the speaker was positioned in this fight for economic control of the island.

In Labov's study, the pronunciation of [ai] had clearly become imbued with meaning, but it is equally clearly not the standard denotational meaning dealt with in formal semantics / pragmatics, not the least because it involves sub-morphological and even sub-phonemic distinctions, a situation which is intractable on the assumptions of standard denotational semantics. Yet, it is clearly a kind of meaning. It is this kind of *social meaning* that has been at the heart of sociolinguistics for 60 years. While the contours of how we think of social meaning have changed over time along with our understanding of identity, at its core, the social meaning of an expression is the information it carries about how the speaker fits into the social landscape (Bucholtz and Hall 2005; Eckert 2012). Because the social landscape is large, we expect to find expressions associated with broad social categories like *masculine* or *feminine*, but also fairly boutique social categories like *supporter of traditional lifeways on Martha's Vineyard*. In the next chapter we dig more deeply into how these social meanings are connected to bits of language, and how those social meanings sum together to characterize an interlocutor's *persona* (i.e., their fully specified place in the social landscape). For now, though, we already have enough to lay out the essential picture of a social meaning approach to dogwhistles which can make sense of the puzzles we have seen thus far which stymie other approaches.

Our core proposal is that a dogwhistle like *wonder-working power* in the Bush example we started with (see (4)) has three key features: (i) it bears social meaning, i.e., signals a persona, (ii) some members of the audience would disapprove of the speaker bearing the social persona the expression signals, and (iii) there is some uncertainty in the disapproving audience (up to complete obliviousness) as to whether the expression bears the social meaning in question. When these features hold, a speaker like Bush is able use *wonder-working power* to signal to evangelicals that he is an evangelical as well—that is his position in the social landscape—while listeners who might disapprove of having an overtly evangelical president would have no idea that the speaker is situating himself in this way.

What does this approach buy us? First, it solves the tension we noted between the conventional implicature account of Stanley (2015) and Khoo (2017) inferentialist account. The problem, recall, is that we do not want to associate dogwhistles with a conventional, possibly truth-conditional, secondary component because they are deniable, unlike slurs. At the same time, we have to say that certain expressions are, by convention, dogwhistle expressions in virtue of the fact that we can have seemingly synonymous expressions where only one is a dogwhistle. With an extra meaning dimension at our disposal, we sidestep this problem. Synonymous expressions can differ in their status as dogwhistles because while bearing the same truth-conditional content, they can differ in terms of their social meanings. In fact, we expect them to. Sociolinguistics is built on the notion of a variant. When there are multiple ways to say the same thing (truth-conditionally), these difference are easily recruited to signal other things, like the speaker's position in the social landscape.

Deniability also quickly follows once we move to this new domain of meaning. Social meanings, as the literature attests, are more mutable than truth-conditional meaning. Consider the literature on the apical versus velar pronunciation of *-ing* (e.g., Campbell-Kibler 2007a, 2007b). The apical variant [in] does not just have a simple, fixed social meaning, but is related to a field of personas the speaker could bear ranging from uneducated to relaxed and unpretentious. The actual social meaning conveyed by its use depends on many other contextual factors. Thus, it makes sense to treat social meaning as involving probabilistic associations between forms and their social meanings. Once we see this, we immediately arrive at a pair of nice consequences.

First, we understand how dogwhistles are deniable. With only a probabilistic link between social meaning and expressions, there just is room for the speaker to say that the listener erred in assigning them a social category, even if it was a good guess. In this way, social meanings emerge in a deniable way that is closer to conversational implicatures than conventionalized truth-conditional content (whether at-issue or not). Importantly, as we show in subsequent chapters, this social meaning view is tractable, unlike a Gricean, conversational implicature approach.

Second, the probabilistic turn helps us understand a core feature of dogwhistles, namely (iii) above, which is that some listeners can fail to 'hear' the dogwhistle. If social meanings are probabilistically associated with expressions, then it is a simple step to allow that probability to vary across members of a speech community. That is, some speakers can be unaware that a phrase like *wonder-working power* is commonly used in the evangelical community, and thus that it is good evidence for the speaker's social persona. Here we can hearken back to the question of whether dogwhistles are reducible to dialect differences. The answer is both a yes and a no. Under the social meaning view, yes, expressions that behave as dogwhistles can emerge out of dialect differences in a certain sense. At the same time, no, the dogwhistle effect is not due to expressions being lexicalized as such in a particular dialect—according to the strict definition social meaning, all dialects will link personas and pieces of language in the same way. Instead, it emerges due to the variation in what knowledge members of a speech community have about how other members of the speech community use language to situate themselves in social space, and in particular about the frequency in use of particular expressions. This is entirely expected from a sociolinguistic standpoint. Members that belong to a community will have more knowledge about the style or ways of speaking of members of that community than outsiders will. This fundamental fact could explain how dogwhistles come into existence, though we will not pursue this line of inquiry much in this book.

We think that a social meaning view of dogwhistles is both intuitive and plausible. It also avoids the stumbling blocks that we have identified for approaches that take dogwhistles to involve standard, truth-conditional content, whether that content is lexicalized as a conventional implicature, derived through Gricean enrichment, or the result of a default inference from the propositional content of what was said. While the social meaning approach to dogwhistles suppresses the role of truth-conditional / propositional content, there are ways to allow for the social meanings of expressions to trigger propositional inferences. We clearly want this to be a possibility given the findings of the previous literature, where dogwhistles appear to alter the behavior of respondents on surveys about policy preferences and racial attitudes (e.g., Mendelberg 2001; Hurwitz and Peffley 2005). We need a way for inferences about the social meaning of what was said to affect the propositions a listener is willing to endorse (or at least consider).

Building just such a system is the goal of Chapter 5. In the meantime, it is enough to point out that this is also a property of social meaning more broadly. For instance, hearing a Vineyarder use the non-standard [ai] would be a good signal that they would agree to certain propositions, which would then shape the common ground. For instance, we could imagine that certain presuppositions would either not fail or be accommodated by such a speaker in virtue of hearing this vowel alone. There is thus a clear connection to the kinds of denotational meanings in context that are standardly studied in semantics / pragmatics. We see here another connection between dogwhistles and standard kinds of social meaning. The fact that we see propositional effects for dogwhistles does not preclude treating them, at their core, as a social meaning phenomenon.

2.3 Varieties of dogwhistles

The previous section presented the major proposals to date on the semantics and pragmatics of dogwhistles. We ended the section with our own positive proposal, namely that dogwhistles involve social meaning. Of course, determining that dogwhistles involve social meaning does not answer the question of whether dogwhistles are a unified phenomenon. In this section we will consider various typologies for dogwhistles that have been proposed in the previous literature. We end this section with our own typology, which posits two kinds of dogwhistles. Both can be given an account in terms of social meanings, which we will do in Chapters 4–5, but as we will see, the second type recruits propositional meaning in a way that that the first type does not.

2.3.1 Saul's 4-way typology

Saul (2018) presents a 4-way typology of dogwhistles based on two cross-classifying features. The first concerns whether the speaker means to dogwhistle, that is, a split between intentional and non-intentional dogwhistles. This distinction is required because it has been shown that dogwhistles can still have a dogwhistle effect in listeners when 'mentioned,' not just 'used' (Mendelberg 2001). The result that, for instance, a newscast replaying a controversial, dogwhistle-bearing advertisement in order to discuss the controversy can still generate a dogwhistle effect, even if the newscaster didn't intend to dogwhistle. This is an interesting distinction, and one that is actually quite difficult to model in our system. The reason is that, for us, dogwhistles come into play through speakers and listeners negotiating the personas they bear. In the case of a newscast where the newscaster only mentions a dogwhistle, it should be clear that its mention should not factor into the persona the newscaster bears. We will consider this puzzle in more depth after we present our initial analysis.

The second split that Saul identifies is more directly linguistically relevant in virtue of shaping how the messages conveyed by an utterance are integrated into the common ground. For this reason it also shapes our analysis of dogwhistles, especially as it pertains to so-called *enriching* dogwhistles, as discussed below and in Chapter 5. What Saul points out is that dogwhistles can be both explicitly and implicitly received by an audience. The former she calls *overt* and the latter *covert*.

Overt dogwhistles correspond, roughly, to the way we have been discussing dogwhistles so far. In particular, there is a savvy subaudience who knows about the dogwhistle in a declarative way. When the speaker uses it, the savvy audience is able to extract information from the message that an unsavvy audience cannot. For instance, when Albertson (2015) explored religious dogwhistles, she found that Pentecostals explicitly recognized the phrase *wonder-working power* and in virtue of this, could identify a religious appeal in political speech using that phrase.

The covert case, in contrast, involves dogwhistles that seem to require a particular kind of target audience ignorance in order have an effect. That is, declarative knowledge of the dogwhistle, unlike with *wonder-working power*, dissolves the dogwhistle effect. Saul (2018) appeals to the research on racial dogwhistles in Mendelberg (2001). In this work, Mendelberg shows that an advertisement with a racial dogwhistle can shift the voting intentions of white voters who score high on a racial resentment inventory. But, if the racial dogwhistle is explained to these voters to be a dogwhistle, this has an inoculating effect and their voting intentions change on seeing the ad to be more like those of non-racially-resentful voters. Mendelberg explains this fact as follows.

When certain voters are not explicitly conscious of the dogwhistle, observing it can trigger implicit racial bias. When the dogwhistle is made consciously explicit, though, the racial attitudes it conveys will compete with (and possibly lose to) other attitudes that are consciously accepted—i.e., norms of racial equality. Saul (2018) perceptively sees that these dogwhistles are phenomonologically different than overt dogwhistles.

We will take up the case of covert dogwhistles in Chapter 5, but we point out here the critical features of covert dogwhistles that will help us assimilate them to other cases of dogwhistles. First, whether or not the listener has been inoculated against a covert dogwhistle, the expression seems to carry the same information. Listener knowledge of the dogwhistles does not change the dogwhistled content, only how the listener reacts to that content. Second, covert dogwhistles do not just depend on linguistic knowledge—i.e., awareness of the dogwhistle—they also depend on sociologically relevant features of the listener. Mendelberg (2001) shows that for the covert dogwhistles she considers, the listener must not be aware of the dogwhistle, and in addition must be white and score high on a racial resentment inventory.

Both of these features allow for a promising account of the covert / overt distinction within our social-meaning-based theory of dogwhistles. The fact that the conventionalized meaning of a dogwhistle does not change across covert and overt uses will allow us to keep our theory of dogwhistle expressions uniform, and thus exactly like our theory of the more commonly recognized overt dogwhistles. All the action governing the distinction takes places at the level of the listener, and so what we need is a theory about the uptake of dogwhistles that can draw a distinction between conscious and unconscious uptake of the dogwhistled content, and how that interacts with the common ground, the plausible home of Mendelberg's "norm of equality." Crucially, this uptake can be mediated by sociolinguistically relevant features of the listener, like whiteness. This fact will allow an account of covert dogwhistles to slot perfectly into the broader theory we develop. In particular, if dogwhistles traffic in social meanings, it is a small extension to make their effects depend on the space of possible social personas available to the listener.

We pursue just such an account in Chapter 5, the result being a complete subsumption of Saul (2018) 4-way typology into our social meaning account. The four kinds of dogwhistles will emerge, not as different kinds of dogwhistles *per se*, but as an effect of how a uniform class of dogwhistles interacts with different kinds of participants in discourse.

2.3.2 Multivocalism

Instead of dogwhistles, much of the political science and marketing literature talks about *multivocalism*. The reason is that this literature makes a distinction between covert messages the speaker would deny—which are sent by dogwhistles—and those that a speaker would not deny—which are sent by multivocal expressions. It is important to note, though, that this distinction is orthogonal to the question of whether the message is risky. For instance, in the case of (4) from George Bush's State of the Union address, the message sent by the phrase *wonder-working power* is risky. If the wrong audience, an audience that disapproves of explicit religious appeals in political speech, detects that Bush is signaling that he is an evangelical, there will a penalty. That is, as Albertson (2015) shows, they will be less likely to vote for him. That said, if you confronted Bush with this message and asked him whether he was an evangelical, and whether he believed there was wonder-working power in the blood of the lamb, he would undoubtedly assent. That is his sincerely held religious belief.

In contrast, the Paul Ryan example in (1) provides a case of a bona fide dogwhistle as classified by the multivocalism literature. When Paul Ryan was called out for his statement about "inner-cities" and the "culture of work" his office issued, not a retraction, but a denial.

> It is clear that I was inarticulate about the point I was trying to make. I was not implicating the culture of one community—but of society as a whole. We have allowed our society to isolate or quarantine the poor rather than integrate people into our communities. The predictable result has been multi-generational poverty and little opportunity. I also believe the government's response has inadvertently created a poverty trap that builds barriers to work.

When pressured further, he explicitly denied there being a racial component to his message.

> This isn't a race based comment it's a breakdown of families, it's rural poverty in rural areas, and talking about where poverty exists—there are no jobs and we have a breakdown of the family. This has nothing to do with race,...

For the multivocalist view, then, this would not be a multivocal message because Ryan denies voicing one of the potential messages. Instead, it would be a dogwhistle.

While this is an interesting distinction, we will not be making it. First, as we will show in Chapter 4, our account can handle, in a unified framework, cases where the speaker would agree to the covert message, as well as cases where the speaker would deny it. This means that we can model the distinction that the proponents of multivocalism make. The reason we don't draw a hard distinction between dogwhistles and multivocal expressions is that there is no linguistic distinction to be made. That is, there are no expressions that can only be dogwhistles or only be used in multivocal appeals. Thus, even if this is a genuine categorical distinction, it is not one that is reflected in language. We think it is better simply to call all of these expressions dogwhistles, and then model in our system how speakers can use dogwhistles to make claims they would deny, as well as (possibly risky) claims they would not deny.

2.3.3 'Identifying' vs. 'enriching' dogwhistles

We come now to our own typology. We want to emphasize that we do not think that previous typologies are not correct, just that they are not narrowly linguistically relevant. For instance, Saul (2018) makes a distinction between dogwhistles that are consciously used and those that are unconsciously used by the speaker. This is an interesting distinction, but it is not one that we would need to linguistically model in order to understand the semantics and pragmatics of the language of dogwhistles. Instead, we want to focus on distinctions that hew closely to the kinds of messages sent by dogwhistles. Along these lines, we draw a primary, and novel, distinction between two kinds of dogwhistles. The first we call *identifying dogwhistles*; the second we call *enriching dogwhistles*.

In identifying dogwhistles, the content sends one message to all audience members, while the dogwhistle transmits information about the speaker's true identity to a sub-audience. The George Bush case considered in (4) probably best fits in this category. Bush's *wonder-working power* doesn't seem to convey some secondary message about the power at hand. All speakers hear *wonder-working power* and interpret it as power that works wonders. The message sent to a subaudience, the audience that hears the dogwhistle, is about Bush himself. In particular, it flags him as an evangelical because only evangelicals talk like that.[8] We call these *identifying* dogwhistles because the covert content concerns the speaker's identity.

Identifying dogwhistles contrast with enriching dogwhistles. The canonical case would be Ryan's use of *inner-city* in (1). With enriching dogwhistles, the content sends one message to all audience members, while the whistle sends and places an addendum on that message for a sub-audience. For instance, Ryan's use of *inner-city* conveys to all audiences a geographical location inside cities, but then to a sub-audience, it specifically picks out Black neighborhoods in those cities. Of course, on detection, the fact that Ryan used a dogwhistle will allow a listener to infer things about Ryan's identity, just as with identifying dogwhistles. That said, we can draw a distinction between identifying and enriching dogwhistles because the enriching dogwhistle clearly involves a covert message, or *enrichment* of the content of what is said, which is missing from identifying dogwhistles.

These cases are likely extremes. We don't mean to draw a hard boundary between the two kinds of dogwhistles. Instead, what this distinction does is make clear the two kinds of covert messages a dogwhistle can send—i.e., messages about the speaker's persona and enrichments of the at-issue content. In fact, when we come to our analysis in Chapters 4 and 5, what we will see is that all dogwhistles send information about the speaker's identity, or persona. Whether the dogwhistle will also exhibit enrichment is dependent on the personas at issue, background assumptions related to those personas, and the at-issue content of the utterance. Some uses of dogwhistles will lead to strong enrichments, like the *inner-city* example (1), while others will lead to weak or absent enrichments, as with *wonder-working power* in (4). These are our canonical

---

[8] One might wonder what the difference is between sending a message with the content *I'm an evangelical* and, in our sense, flagging oneself as an evangelical. The difference here is comparable to the difference between explicitly claiming an identity for oneself and indicating (constructing) one's identity via the use of sociolinguistic identity markers. This distinction is brought out by our use of sociolinguistic signaling games in the formal analysis.

cases, but we expect dogwhistles to mostly fall on a cline between these two poles. Our Chapter 5 analysis of enriching dogwhistles, in particular, will make this expectation a formal part of the analysis.

2.4 Summary

This chapter has presented the previous literature on dogwhistles (and dogwhistle-adjacent phenomena, like exercitives), in an effort to situate dogwhistles within the larger realm of semantic and pragmatic phenomena. We were able to rule out accounts of dogwhistles using standard theoretical tools, most notably conventional and Gricean implicatures. We instead advanced our own proposal, which is that dogwhistles involve social meaning and inferences that flow from social meaning. We additionally presented a typology for dogwhistles, that unlike other proposals, focuses on the kind of messages dogwhistles convey. In particular, we see dogwhistles conveying two kinds of messages: (i) information about the speaker's persona, and (ii) enrichments to the truth-conditional content of the dogwhistle. In subsequent chapters we will come to see that even the truth-conditional enrichments are dependent on the listener retrieving the social meaning conveyed by the dogwhistle. The result is a unified, social-meaning-based approach to dogwhistles.

A consequence of treating dogwhistles as bearing social meaning is that once we move to this new meaning domain, we expect listeners to draw inferences about why a speaker would use an expression bearing the social meaning it does, and that speakers would pick the expressions they use knowing listeners will be doing so. That is, we must recapitulate pragmatic theory in the domain of social meaning. To do so, we will move away from a Gricean analytic framework, whose maxims have no clear analogue in the social meaning domain. Instead, the next chapter will introduce a pragmatic theory for social meaning in the Bayesian Rational Speech Act (RSA) framework (Franke and Degen 2016; Franke and Jäger 2016; Goodman and Frank 2016, among others). Subsequent chapters will then extend this framework to build a comprehensive account of dogwhistles, the meanings they convey, and how they behave and evolve in discourse.

3
A probabilitic pragmatics for dogwhistles

The previous chapter situated dogwhistles within the wider field of pragmatics. In particular, we argued that dogwhistles involve pragmatic inferences over certain social conventions of language use. In this way, dogwhistles are not expressions that bear conventionalized meanings, but expressions that are commonly used in particular ways by particular speech communities. This allows in-group members to draw pragmatic inferences from a dogwhistle that out-group members cannot, while allowing a speaker to maintain deniability about what was said by a dogwhistle through deniability about group membership. While we propose that dogwhistles involve a kind of meaning mostly novel to formal semantics, namely social meaning, in an ideal situation the pragmatic mechanisms that operate over these meanings will be those same mechanisms involved in reasoning about standard truth-conditional content. The goal of this chapter is to lay the foundation for just this kind of unified account of the pragmatics of truth-conditional and social meanings.

We lay that foundation in this chapter by introducing the Bayesian Rational Speech Act (RSA) framework (Franke and Degen 2016; Franke and Jäger 2016; Goodman and Frank 2016, among others), which is a pragmatic theory that can be used to model the behavior of agents in signaling games. After reviewing the recent pragmatics literature making use of RSA, we then introduce the reader to so-called *Social Meaning Games* (SMGs), which are a variety of RSA signaling games introduced by Burnett (2017, 2019) to unify variationalist sociolinguistics and modern game-theoretic pragmatic theory. This game-theoretic approach to sociolinguistic interaction will provide firm ground for building an account of dogwhistles. We will have to extend the account in the next chapter to handle the simplest kind of dogwhistles, and then extend it again in Chapter 4 for modeling more complex cases. This chapter, then, lays out the formal ideas that will reoccur through the rest of this work. In building off a theory of sociolinguistic variation that itself builds off a theory of pragmatics, we come to a satisfying result—dogwhistles can in fact be analyzed in a unified pragmatic theory and thus belong to a class of empirical phenomena that includes sociolinguistic inferences as well as classical Gricean implicatures.

Before introducing the RSA framework, though, we want to take a step back to consider this choice of analyzing dogwhistles in a Bayesian setting. First, as we argued in Chapter 2, we do not believe that dogwhistles can be analyzed as Manner implicatures. This precludes a simple Gricean analysis of dogwhistles. Moreover, this observation immediately causes problems for this goal of a unified analysis of pragmatic phenomena involving truth-conditional meaning and those involving social meaning.

Going beyond the question of whether a classical Gricean account of dogwhistles is possible, we can also ask whether it is even appropriate. While not all, some varieties

Signaling without Saying. Robert Henderson and Elin McCready, Oxford University Press. © Robert Henderson and Elin McCready (2024). DOI: 10.1093/9780191994319.003.0003

of Gricean pragmatic analysis have a strongly intentional flavor. Conversational agents make rational, conscious decisions about what to say and how to interpret what is said against a background of shared knowledge and a norm of cooperativity. There are reasons to be skeptical of such approaches to dogwhistles, most notably due to the evidence that some dogwhistles require unconscious uptake (Mendelberg 2001). Moreover, there are even plausible cases where neither the speaker nor hearer are consciously aware of the dogwhistle (Saul 2018). The pragmatics of dogwhistles under a Bayesian RSA account can sidestep these issues. As is usual in game-theoretic applications, the process of selecting a strategy involves convergence toward the maximization of a utility function, which admits both intentional and non-intentional interpretations (as for example in game-theoretic formalizations in evolutionary biology).

While we will be leaving Gricean pragmatics behind for the core analysis of dogwhistles, the proposal we develop and the way we interpret it is close in spirit to how Gricean pragmatic models are treated throughout the literature in formal semantics and pragmatics. For Grice, pragmatic phenomena are explained as a consequence of the fact that conversation is a rational, optimizing, goal-directed activity. From these assumptions flow the conversational maxims, which, whether interpreted normatively or not, are a second level of analysis expressing certain regularities in pragmatic behavior. They are less explanatory tools than epistemic tools used to categorize pragmatic phenomena and to clarify how complex implicatures can arise by naming the various pragmatic pressures that interact to produce them.

This is precisely how we want to interpret the analysis of dogwhistles developed in this work. While we take model construction seriously, the aim in this work is not to construct a comprehensive explanatory model of dogwhistling agents, but rather to use various game-theoretic models as an epistemic tool to tease out the core theoretical issues that undergird dogwhistles as a semantic and pragmatic phenomenon. In the Bayesian RSA framework, instead of specifying various maxims and exploring their interactions, this amounts to specifying the conversational participants' prior beliefs about language meaning and use, and providing utility functions for speakers and hearers. With these in place, pragmatic phenomena emerge, just as in a Gricean account, as the result of rational, optimizing, goal-directed activity—namely, that speakers and hearers take conversational actions that maximize their utility in a probabilistically optimal way given the structure of the game.

3.1 Bayesian Rational Speech Act theory

The traditional way of dividing semantics and pragmatics is that semantics concerns the conventional meaning of expressions, while pragmatics concerns the meanings conveyed by uttering those expressions in a context, which is computed based on the conventional meanings in light of the mutual knowledge, conversational goals, etc. of the conversational participants. The RSA framework captures this traditional divide and the enrichment of semantic meaning in context through a process of speakers and listeners recursively reasoning about each other's conversational moves.

The base case is that of the **literal listener** L_0, who does no pragmatic reasoning and takes the meaning of an utterance to merely be the conventional meaning of the sentence uttered. In this way, L_0 acts as a proxy for the semantics proper, the ground on which pragmatic enrichment takes place. At the next level, the **pragmatic speaker** S_1 observes the state of the world w and picks her utterance u to maximize the likelihood that the literal listener L_0 will infer that the state of the world is w. Going up one more level, we have the **pragmatic listener** L_1, who reasons about the state of the world given that the pragmatic speaker S_1 chose to utter u for the literal listener L_0. This process could continue with an even more pragmatically sophisticated speaker S_2 picking an utterance u to maximize the likelihood that L_1 would take u to mean w (by reasoning about S_1 uttering u to maximize the likelihood that L_0 would take u to mean w), though as we go higher up this chain of meta-reasoning, there are diminishing returns for optimizing information transfer. Already at three layers, with a pragmatic listener interpreting an utterance of u by a pragmatic speaker for the literal listener, we can model a variety of interesting pragmatic phenomena.

We will consider some examples of how RSA can model classic cases of conversational implicature below, but first we need to formally flesh out how this recursive reasoning process takes place. In particular, we need to know what it means for the literal listener L_0 to infer the state of world w based on the conventional meaning of an utterance u. We also need to understand how speakers can compute the likelihood that utterances will be interpreted in particular ways and how these probabilities percolate up and affect the way that higher order speakers and listeners choose utterances and interpretations.

3.1.1 The literal listener L_0

Let's start with the literal listener L_0, who tries to extract as much information as possible from an utterance based solely on its conventional meaning. In order to keep things as simple as possible, we can begin by treating these conventional meanings themselves exactly as they are treated throughout formal semantics, namely as propositions. An utterance u (or more precisely, a declarative sentence borne by u) denotes a function from worlds to truth values, namely

$$[\![u]\!] : \mathbb{W} \to \{0, 1\}$$

When the literal listener hears an utterance, she wants to take the information sent by u and update her beliefs about the probability that any particular world is the actual world. This is just vanilla Bayesian inference which we can define as follows—for each possible world w,

$$P_{L_0}(w|u) \propto [\![u]\!](w) \times P(w)$$

gives the probability of w given u, which is 0 if u is false at w and otherwise is weighted by the prior probably the literal listener assigns to w.[1] Note P_{L_0} is defined as a proportion, which means that the literal listener can always determine the relative likelihood of any two worlds given an utterance. Even better, as long as Bayesian inference takes place over exhaustive and mutually exclusive domain, like worlds, we can directly compute these conditional probabilities because they must sum to 1.

Consider, for instance, a toy example with just two mutually inconsistent propositions p and q, which would induce an equivalence class over worlds, namely w_p, w_q, and $w_\emptyset$ where both are false. If L_0 were completely uniformed about p and q, then her prior over these worlds would be uniform

$$P(w_p) = P(w_q) = P(w_\emptyset) = \frac{1}{3}$$

On hearing an utterance of p ∨ q, L_0 would compute a new probability distribution over the space of worlds satisfying the following constraints given by P_{L_0} for each world:

$$P_{L_0}(w_p|u_{p\vee q}) \propto 1 \times \frac{1}{3}$$

$$P_{L_0}(w_q|u_{p\vee q}) \propto 1 \times \frac{1}{3}$$

$$P_{L_0}(w_\emptyset|u_{p\vee q}) \propto 0 \times \frac{1}{3}$$

Intuitively, we can see the result of this calculation. If L_0's prior beliefs are uniform, then it is incredibly informative to learn that a world—here $w_\emptyset$—is inconsistent with the utterance. It means that it should be given zero probability and that we can take that world's prior probability mass and equally distribute it over the remaining worlds. That is, L_0's posterior probability over worlds on hearing p ∨ q would be

$$P(w_p) = P(w_q) = \frac{1}{2}$$

While this makes sense intuitively, we can directly compute it by solving for the proportionality constant of the conditional probabilities above. Letting c be the proportionality constant, we have

$$P_{L_0}(w_p|u_{p\vee q}) = c \times \frac{1}{3} \text{ and } P_{L_0}(w_q|u_{p\vee q}) = c \times \frac{1}{3}$$

Because $P_{L_0}(w_p|u_{p\vee q})$ and $P_{L_0}(w_q|u_{p\vee q})$ sum to 1, we can add these formulas

$$1 = c \times \frac{2}{3}$$

---

[1] The reader may have been expecting a more standard form of Bayesian inference, namely $P(w|u) \propto P(u|w) \times P(w)$, but we assume that the literal listener hews as closely to the conventional semantics as possible and takes the probability of messages $P(u|w)$ to be directly given by their truth conditions. The probability of the message p in a world that satisfies p is 1, and the probability of the message p in a world where it is false is 0. We raise this point because we will weaken this coupling below when we move to dogwhistles, where agents are reasoning about personas and not possible worlds.

and solve for c. With c we deduce that

$$P_{L_0}(w_p|u_{p \vee q}) = 1\frac{1}{2} \times \frac{1}{3} \text{ or } \frac{1}{2}$$

which is the same as the probability of w_q given the utterance of $p \vee q$.

What this toy example shows is that through Bayesian inference, a literal listener can probabilistically update her beliefs about the state of the world based on the conventionalized propositional content of an utterance. A pragmatically aware speaker will send messages to such a listener taking into account that she will do just the kind of inference described here.

3.1.2 The pragmatic speaker S_1

Speakers pick utterances, but not just any utterances. A cooperative speaker is an epistemic ally. She observes the state of the world and picks an utterance that will help a listener know the state of the world. A pragmatic speaker tries to do so in an optimizing way. In the RSA framework, this means picking an utterance u in world w that will maximize $P_L(w|u)$ for some listener L.[2] Another way of saying this is that the speaker's utility is a function of how listeners interpret messages. For the pragmatic speaker S_1, the utility calculation is a function of how the literal listener interprets messages and the cost of those messages

$$U_{S_1}(u, w) \propto \ln(P_{L_0}(w|u)) - C(u)$$

The cost is important because the space of possible messages is large, and it is well known that pragmatic reasoning does not take place against all possible alternative utterances, but against a constrained subset that are considered to be roughly equal on some measure. Consider, for instance, Horn scales in the scalar implicature literature (e.g., Horn 1972; Sauerland 2004), which exist solely to constrain the alternative sentences that are considered in pragmatic reasoning. If someone says *Bill ate three cookies*, then to determine what they are trying to communicate, I should consider why they didn't say *Bill ate four cookies*, but the Horn scale for *three* explains why I need not consider why the speaker didn't say *Bill ate three cookies and no more than three cookies*. Even though it is relevant to the topic at hand and involves similar expressions of scalar quantity, it is too complex relative to what was actually said to be an alternative to what was said. The cost function allows us to implement this idea, where Horn scale alternatives would have equal costs, while utterances with scalar expressions off the scale would be highly punished. The bigger takeaway is that speakers want to pick utterances that will maximize the probability that the listener grasps the state of the

---

[2] Note that instead of using the raw probability given by P_L, it is helpful to instead use log-probability. Taking the log of a function will not alter its maximum, while making this maximum easier to compute in some cases. Also, we will sometimes want to further manipulate the speaker's utility in real space, and so it is helpful to already be working with log-probabilities.

world, but they make that choice among alternative utterances that are of roughly equal cost—whether in complexity, novelty, politeness, or in the case of dogwhistles, social costs like the listener's approval.

Having a definition of speaker utility is useful, but it doesn't define what the speaker does, only what is best for the speaker to do. Just as we model listener behavior as probabilistically picking meanings (i.e., worlds) for observed utterances in accordance with $P_L(w|u)$ above, we want to treat speakers in the reverse, namely probabilistically picking utterances for observed worlds. That is, we want to define $P_S(u|w)$, and do so using the speaker's utility function. The simplest way would be to set $P_{S_1}(u|w)$ to be proportional to $U_{S_1}(u, w)$, but this would mean speakers behave perfectly rationally, picking utterances at a frequency that perfectly matches the amount of information about the observed world that the literal listener can extract from the utterance while minimizing its cost. This is not plausible. We want to model speakers as more or less rational, but sometimes selecting costly utterances or failing to perfectly simulate what the literal listener will do with a message. We can introduce this kind of noise by scaling utility by a factor $\alpha > 0$, called the temperature, which acts as a knob to control rationality as follows

$$P_{S_1}(u|w) \propto \exp(\alpha \times U_{S_1}(u, w))$$

As α tends toward ∞ speaker behavior becomes aggressively rational, that is, categorically selecting the message that maximizes utility. Around zero, lower utility messages become comparatively more likely. This allows us to model a slightly less rational speaker that selects an option that does not maximize utility more often then she should. On its own, though, particular values of α are not interpretable. They depend on the range of utilities at issue, which depends on what kinds of costs are associated with messages, among other factors.

We now have two layers of recursive conversational structure, which can model pragmatics in the RSA framework. We have a listener that by rote interprets utterances according to the conventional semantics, and a pragmatic speaker that selects utterances for this listener to interpret. This speaker is called *pragmatic* because she models the decision-making behavior of another agent in making her own decisions. Crucially, these decisions are not purely based on this second agent that she models, otherwise she could be dispensed with. Rather, the pragmatic speaker S_1 considers what L_0 will do with her utterances, but only in a boundedly rational way, and taking into account the costs to herself of the utterances she makes.

3.1.3 The pragmatic listener

We started this section by considering the literal listener L_0, who does Bayesian inference to determine which world is most likely given a message. The pragmatic listener does exactly the same thing, but instead of grounding this inference in the conventional semantics of expressions, the pragmatic listener L_1 is, well, pragmatic. She reasons about the actions speakers take. That is, she infers the likelihood of the world given a message on the basis of the probability that a pragmatic speaker would send the observed message in that world (weighted, of course, by her prior for that world)

$$P_{L_1}(w|u) \propto P_{S_1}(u|w) \times P(w)$$

The pragmatic listener is simply stated, and this elegance is one of the attractive features of the RSA framework, but it masks an equally beautiful, though complex, recursive computation that traces the outline of the kind of reasoning that all pragmatic theories must assume takes place in conversation. Listeners interpret utterances by trying to suss out why a speaker would make that utterance, assuming that the speaker made the utterance reasoning about how the listener would interpret it. This is the structure we see when unraveling the definition of P_{L_1}, which contains an instance of P_{S_1} that can be expanded to

$$P_{L_1}(w|u) \propto \exp(\alpha \times U(u, s)) \times P(w)$$

the speaker's utility function as described above can itself be expanded, yielding

$$P_{L_1}(w|u) \propto \exp(\alpha \times (\ln(P_{L_0}(w|u)) - C(u)) \times P(w)$$

Note that this formula contains the literal listener. We see, then, that the pragmatic listener reasons about how the pragmatic speaker would send messages to a listener that knew the shared conventions of their language. We can now substitute the definition of P_{L_0} in this formula, which ends the recursion, giving

$$P_{L_1}(w|u) \propto \exp(\alpha \times (\ln([\![u]\!](w) \times P(w)) - C(u)) \times P(w)$$

The RSA framework is encapsulated in this formula, which provides a theory of pragmatics from the listener's perspective. On hearing an utterance, the listener does a Bayesian inference to determine which world is most likely given the utterance. This means reasoning about what message a boundedly rational pragmatic speaker would send in that world, which reduces to a question of how a literal listener would interpret that message minus the cost of sending it. While compact, even after working through the recursive process of interpretation, the RSA framework allows for a wide range of pragmatic phenomena to be understood. This is true even if we restrict ourselves to thinking about the pragmatic listener L_1 (recall that we can continue this recursive reasoning process to consider how a listener L_n will reason about a message sent by a speaker S_n by simulating how that speaker would select a message for a listener L_{n-1}). In the next section we will consider a case study to show how the RSA framework can be used to model classic scalar implicatures.

3.1.4 Implicature calculation in RSA

To see how pragmatic enrichment takes place in the Bayesian RSA framework, let's consider the classic case of scalar implicatures. Suppose you know that we bought three croissants at the boulangerie for breakfast, but you've woken up late and want to know if there are any left to eat. You ask, *Have you eaten any of the croissants? I've eaten some,*

I say. You will be consoled, understanding me to say that I haven't eaten them all, even though I never committed to that fact or explicitly stated it. The standard Gricean story explains how you came to this conclusion as follows. You think:

1. S said *I ate some of the croissants*
2. But why didn't S say *I ate all of the croissants*? It's certainly relevant, and it's stronger, and it's not a more complex a thing to say.
3. The only option is that it must be because S does not hold the belief that *I ate all the croissants*.
4. But S is surely informed about what S has eaten and what S hasn't. That is, S must hold the belief that *I ate all the croissants* or S must hold the belief that *I didn't eat all the croissants*.
5. The first of the options in (4) is inconsistent with point (3), so it must be the case that S didn't eat all the croissants.

We can capture this same scalar implicature in the RSA framework, and once again, it boils down to listeners reasoning about speakers, assuming that, all else being equal, pragmatic speakers should make utterances that allow a listener to extract as much information as possible.[3]

For this example, we can assume there are 4 worlds that are currently live options— w_0, w_1, w_2, and w_3—where S ate zero, exactly one, exactly two, and exactly three croissants, respectively. Against this backdrop, we assume the speaker makes a choice between three utterances, which we'll label NONE, SOME, and ALL. Finally, we take L_0 to have a uniform prior over worlds: upon waking, truly, who knows or can even imagine how many croissants have been eaten? We can directly compute the literal listener's reaction to hearing the critical ALL and NONE utterances. Because the prior is uniform, the posterior has an equal probability distributed over all world states consistent with the utterance's conventional content.

L_0 **Posteriors**

Variant	w_0	w_1	w_2	w_3
SOME	0	0.33	0.33	0.33
ALL	0	0	0	1

It is just as easy to calculate P_{S_1}, namely the probability that a pragmatically aware speaker will make particular utterances in particular states. In worlds w_1 and w_2, the speaker must use SOME, while in world w_0, NONE is required. Let's focus, then, on the critical state w_3 because it is the only state where the speaker has options. Assuming

---

[3] Note that the standard Gricean story requires a step where the listener assumes the speaker is informed about the issue at hand (i.e., *S believes p* or *S believes ¬p*. In RSA terms, this means that the listener must not just determine $P(w|u)$, the probability of the world given the utterance, but $P(w|u, s)$, the probability of the world given the utterance and some speaker type s, where s can be informed or not. This richer system where listeners make a joint inference including speaker informativity is explored in Goodman and Stuhlmüller (2013). For the toy example shown here, we will ignore this inference, and take listeners to assume that speakers are fully knowledgeable about the state of the world.

there is no difference in cost between SOME and ALL, a perfectly rational speaker must produce them in proportion to the probability that L₀ will select w_3 on hearing that utterance—that is, ALL should be selected 3/4ths of the time.

$\mathbf{P_{S_1}}$

World	NONE	SOME	ALL
w_0	1	0	0
w_1	0	1	0
w_2	0	1	0
w_3	0	0.25	0.75

We come to the crux of the analysis. The preceding sets the table for how a pragmatic listener should react to hearing an utterance like *I ate some of the croissants*. The intuition is that L_1 makes her decision about what this utterance means by reasoning about what S_1 would do in various scenarios. In particular, note as above that were it the case that the speaker ate all the croissants, that is, were it the case that we were in w_3, it is relatively unlikely that a pragmatic speaker would use *some*. It is this fact that will guide the pragmatic listener into assigning more probability to w_1/w_2.

Recall that L_1 takes the probability of a world given an utterance—i.e., $P_{L_1}(w|u)$—to be proportional to $P_{S_1}(u|w)$ weighted by her prior for that world. We have already computed $P_{S_1}(u|w)$, and we know L_1 has a uniform prior over worlds. Thus,

$$P_{L_1}(w_3|\text{SOME}) = \frac{0.25}{2.25} = .11$$

while

$$P_{L_1}(w_1|\text{SOME}) = P_{L_1}(w_2|\text{SOME}) = \frac{1}{2.25} = .44$$

That is, the speaker is much more likely to be reporting that w_1 or w_2 is actual, even though what was said is consistent with w_3. This is precisely the kind of pragmatic enrichment we aimed to model. While the speaker never said that there were any croissants left over, the listener is safe to assume there are, assuming that the speaker picks utterances to maximize the ability of a literal listener to extract the most information possible from them.

We have provided this example to illustrate how the RSA framework can be used to model implicature calculation—that is, how conventional semantic meanings can become enriched in context. Of course, the space of pragmatic inferences is much wider than classical implicature calculation, and the RSA framework has been used successfully outside this narrow range. There have been, for instance, studies on hyperbole (Goodman and Frank 2016) or politeness (Yoon et al. 2016). When we consider the range of phenomena that have been explored using RSA models, we can see that RSA is truly a framework—that is, a basic conceptual structure for thinking about how agents reason about each other's use of language. On this framework, we can graft various modules onto the basic structure to help us think about the particular phenomenon at hand. As long as the phenomenon grows out of agents reasoning about each other's language use, it is likely amenable to an RSA treatment. In the next section we will see how this modularity of the RSA framework works as we extend it to deal with sociolinguistic phenomena, and eventually, dogwhistles.

3.2 Social Meaning Games

As we have seen, the RSA framework allows us to model implicature calculation through a recursively structured probabilistic signaling game. In these games, the signals are utterances bearing standard truth-conditional content. There is nothing in the RSA framework, though, that would prevent players from reasoning over other kinds of meanings. In recent influential work, Burnett (2017, 2019)extends the standard RSA framework to do precisely this, so that it can be used as a formal foundation for variationist sociolinguistics (Labov 1966, et seq.), while unifying this field with formal pragmatics.

3.2.1 The 'Third Wave'

One of the core ideas of so-called *Third Wave* variationist sociolinguistics (see Eckert 2012 for a review), is that linguistic variation is not the product of pre-existing, static social identifies to which those variants are attached. People do not just pick or get assigned an identity and then speak in accordance. Instead, sociolinguistic practice is deeply creative, with speakers, though their linguistic choices, constantly creating a place for themselves in social space. Under this view, linguistic variation is the ferment from which speakers construct, entrench, and mutate social identities though their stylistic practices.

Eckert (2008) calls this ferment the indexical field, and to give an example, she considers the contrast between apical and velar pronunciations of the final segment in *-ing* participles, i.e., [in] ~ [iŋ]. A naive theory of variation would say that one form is used in the dialect of one group of speakers, while the other is used in some other dialect. Eckert (2008), though, sees a much more complex situation. In experimental work (Campbell-Kibler 2007a, 2007b), participants associate a range of contrasting properties to speakers using one variant versus speakers using the other:

[in] ~ [iŋ]

uneducated ~ educated

relaxed ~ formal

lazy/effortless ~ effortful

inarticulate ~ articulate

unpretentious ~ pretentious

Crucially, while we have pairs of binary oppositions, these oppositions do not necessarily crosscut. A person who is educated can also be relaxed. A person can be formal, but unpretentiously so. These properties thus form an indexical field for the variants. Which properties a hearer will assign to a speaker will depend, not just on the variant, but on speaker's entire style, including all of their other linguistic choices, as well on as the context in which the conversation is taking place. For instance, the speaker might, through dress and word choice, come off as educated, but if the conversation is taking place in a bar, hearing the apical variant would likely be interpreted as relaxed and consonant with the surroundings, not as inarticulate or lazy.

Switching to the speaker's perspective, the Third Wave view of variation and sociolinguistic practice comes into view. Each point of linguistic variation will be associated with a indexical field of currently active social meanings. (We say *currently active* because Eckert 2008 makes the important point that these indexical fields are also constantly in flux depending on how they are being used.) The task of the speaker is to pick among these variants—i.e., to construct a linguistic style—that conveys and is consonant with the particular persona the speaker aims to construct for herself. It's these personas (in the sense of Podesva 2007; Eckert 2008; Zhang 2008), constructed in part through style, that are linked with sociocultural identities as we commonly think of them.

Podesva (2004, 2007), for instance, discusses the case of a gay medical student named Heath, who subtly modulates fine-grained aspects of his phonetic production throughout the day as he moves from a professional context in a clinic to a barbecue with friends. At the barbecue in particular, he greatly exaggerates the aspiration of his stop-release bursts and increases his use of falsetto and creaky voice to construct a *diva* persona. How does the diva persona link up with these acoustic correlates? It does so through the social meanings of those variants and the stereotype of the diva. Canonically, the diva is demanding and requires everything to be just so. This kind of attention to detail and fussiness would be consonant with the use of a variant that had in its indexical field pretentiousness, effortfulness, and articulateness. These are the properties assigned to always and exaggeratedly releasing stop bursts, which often need not be released at all. In fact, we would expect Heath to also prefer the apical participle as discussed above, which would fit with the persona he constructs (though Podesva does not discuss this variable). Similarly, the diva is highly emotive, which would be properties indexed by exaggerated phonation of the type that Health employs. We see, then, that there is a persona, the diva, that a speaker can choose to take on in context (but need not take on in every context) by choosing particular linguistic variants whose social meanings, in accordance with that context, guide the listener to assigning the speaker that persona.

Finally, we can link personas to identities, though once again, this process is not deterministic and is highly context dependent. In the case of Heath, he would identify as a gay man throughout the day, but as Podesva (2004, 2007) discusses, he takes on the diva persona only at the barbecue. Clearly then, the diva persona and gay identity are separable, even in the same person. In fact, they are clearly just different things.

The canonical diva in terms of persona is a female vocalist, especially of the operatic sort. The link between this persona and gay identity involves a long chain of reasoning through linguistic ideologies. For instance, Podesva (2007) indicates one likely route, namely that the diva is emotive in ways that are not heteronormatively appropriate for men. Thus, by employing the diva style, a man can signal that his identity is not in line with heteronormative categories. We can now see the full style of reasoning that distinguishes Third Wave theory from previous approaches to variation. Identities, as usually construed, are related to (but not determined by) personas through broader linguistic and cultural backgrounds and ideologies, and these personas are related to (but not determined by) the linguistic variants chosen by the speaker through the social meanings of those variants.

This process is inherently creative given the fact that the choice between variants in pursuit of a style will be dependent on the conversational context in highly specific ways. There is no simple algorithm to make these choices, especially not one as simple as merely speaking the dialect of some chosen identity group. This process, though, is creative in a second, deeper way. Eckert (2008) notes that while there may be fairly entrenched and stereotyped personas—jock, diva, goth, redneck, soccer mom, etc.— there is ample room to create novel personas to meet current conversational needs. As an illustration, Zhang (2008) discusses the case of Chinese financial managers, who have different speaking styles depending on whether they work for international banks or state-run national banks. The latter use more variants characteristic of Beijing, especially those associated with a persona known as the *Beijing Smooth Operator*. That said, this persona is stereotypically masculine, so female state-run bank managers tend to avoid some of the variants whose indexical fields are dominated by properties deemed most masculine, thus constructing a slightly altered, feminine version of the Smooth Operator. The point is that variants are likely to have broad indexical fields, and speakers are likely to have large variety of variants to choose from. This means that speakers have freedom to creatively construct styles, or subtly modulate well-known styles, as long as the collection of properties indexed by the chosen variants is coherent, allowing listeners to place the speaker in social space through her constructed persona.

3.2.2 Adding indexical fields to the RSA framework

Burnett (2017, 2019) takes the core ideas of Third Wave variationist theory and cleanly translates them into the RSA framework. In vanilla RSA, we consider speakers and listeners as they recursively reason about each other's choices in producing and interpreting expressions that bear truth-conditional meaning. To extend this process to include sociolinguistic interaction, we want speakers and listeners to engage in the same process, but to take into account the fact that expressions bear, not just truth-conditional meanings, but social meaning as well. Recall that, following Eckert (2008), an expression's social meaning can be identified with its indexical field—a set of properties, some of which are in opposition.[4] Given this structure, Burnett (2019) treats the universe from which expressions get their social meanings exactly as one would expect:

A *universe* for social meanings is a pair $\langle \mathbb{P}, < \rangle$ where
- $\mathbb{P} = \{p_1, ..., p_n\}$ is a finite set of properties
- $<$ is an irreflexive relation on $\mathbb{P}$

Now we can say that an utterance, in addition to its standard truth-conditional meaning given by $[\![\cdot]\!]$, also has a social meaning, which is given by $[\cdot]$, and is simply a subset of the universe

$$[u] \subseteq \mathbb{P}$$

This subset, along with the properties related to its members by the opposition relation $<$, has just the structure of Eckert's indexical fields.

There is a large outstanding question here, which is how the social meaning relation is compositionally determined. When considering the RSA framework as a theory of pragmatics, we worked with utterances denoting propositions and compositionally determined in the usual way. Taking Third Wave theory seriously, we have to acknowledge that utterances are complex sociolinguistic performances, with choices between variants taking place everywhere from lexical choice down to low level aspects of phonetic production. The default theory would be that these choices are tracked by simply taking the union of the indexical fields of the variants deployed in the utterance. In practice, we will tend to zoom in on a particular variant of interest, as Eckert (2008) does with the apical/nasal participle contrast, and treat the social meaning of utterance as equivalent to that of the critical feature.

Now that we have a way to assign social meanings to expressions, we can consider how they are related to larger, extralinguistic structures that interact with indexical fields, like personas. Burnett (2017, 2019) treats a personas as a maximally consistent sets of properties, where the second bullet enforces consistency (a persona can't include a property and its opposite), and the third bullet is maximality (a persona can't have a persona inside of it).

π is a *persona* just in case
- $\pi \subseteq \mathbb{P}$
- There are no $p, p' \in \pi$ such that $p < p'$
- There is no π' such that $\pi \subset \pi' \subseteq \mathbb{P}$

---

[4] Sometimes the phrase 'social meaning' is used more broadly to include expressions whose content situates the speaker in social space in some other manner than directly via this kind of indexical field. For example, honorifics situate their users in social hierarchies, indicating what they take to be speech appropriate to the current situation and conversational participants, though honorifics shouldn't necessarily be analyzed as directly involving indexical meanings of the kind discussed here (see McCready 2019 for one way to think of their content).

Because personas and social meanings are made of the same stuff, namely sets of properties, we can model how they are related. A persona is possibly signaled by some variant, if that variant's social meaning overlaps with the persona—that is, if the variant indexes a property that is part of that persona.

We thus have two available perspectives on the social meanings of expressions. On one hand we have the indexical field for that expression, while on the other, we have the set of personas it can be used to convey. Burnett (2017, 2019) calls the latter the Eckert-Montague field, and it will be helpful to have the following way to consider the social meanings of expressions in these terms. The Eckert-Montague field of an utterance denotes the characteristic function of the personas they are consistent with

$$[\mathbf{emf}(u)](\pi) = 1 \text{ iff } \pi \cap [u] \neq \emptyset$$

The relation between an utterance's indexical field and its Eckert-Montague field is very similar to how propositions are related to contexts in a theory like Heim 1982, where a proposition (a set of worlds), projects all future contexts, which are those sets of worlds consistent with it. Similarly, when a speaker chooses a variant, she projects all future personas that she could be assigned, ruling out just those that are inconsistent with the chosen variant. This connection is what sets up the game for our RSA agents to play. Speakers want to pick utterances whose social meanings will allow listeners to identify their desired persona. Listeners want to pick personas for speakers in a rational way given some utterance which they have observed—that is, by extracting as much information as possible from the social meaning of that utterance given their prior beliefs about the speaker's persona.

3.2.3 Sociolinguistic speakers and listeners

Neo-Gricean pragmatics tends to take the listener's perspective. That is, we ask what meaning a pragmatic speaker takes from a message sent by a pragmatic speaker. This was reflected in the previous section, where the pragmatic listener L_1 was the deepest layer considered in the recursive process laid out in the RSA framework. In Third Wave variationist sociolinguistics, though, the focus is on the speaker. Listeners, of course, play a role (and they will play a larger role when we begin to consider dogwhistles, which will involve a mix of sociolinguistic and classical pragmatic inference), but as we saw in the previous section, the focus of current sociolinguistic theory is the speaker who selects among variants in constructing a style. For this reason, Burnett (2017, 2019), in developing her sociolinguistic signaling games, centers the analysis on S_1, the sociolinguistic speaker. Just as in RSA pragmatics, S_1 selects utterances for a literal listener. In this case, though, the literal listener is familiar with the sociolinguistic conventions of the language. That is, she knows the space of possible personas, as well as the indexical fields of particular variants, and so she knows which personas are consistent with which utterances.

More formally, for any utterance u a speaker who knows the sociolinguistic conventions of a language knows which personas are in that expression's Eckert-Montague field—that is, she knows the characteristic function of personas given by **enf**(u). This allows us to define the literal listener L_0 for social meaning games in a way perfectly parallel to the literal listener in the pragmatic games we considered previously.[5] The literal listener, on hearing some utterance u, does Bayesian inference to determine the speaker's persona π using the sociolinguistic conventions of the language, namely

$$L_0(\pi|u) \propto [\mathbf{enf}(u)](\pi) \times P(\pi)$$

Note that here, personas are playing the part of worlds, and instead of checking that a world is consistent with the proposition denoted by the utterance—i.e., $[\![u]\!](w) = 1$—we check whether the persona is consistent with that utterance's social meaning. The inference the literal listener does otherwise proceeds in exactly the same manner. In particular, the result of the inference is that the prior probability mass of those personas inconsistent with the utterance's social meaning will be redistributed over those personas that are consistent with its social meaning. Because personas, just like worlds, are mutually exclusive and exhaustive, we can directly compute the relevant conditional probability, and will do so in the next section when we consider a concrete example.

Moving to the sociolinguistic speaker S_1, we can almost directly import the analysis from vanilla RSA. There is one important difference, though. When we think of standard semantic/pragmatic interaction, we imagine the speaker observing the world and reporting what is observed. This does not exactly transfer cleanly to sociolinguistic interaction. As we have seen, a major result of the Third Wave is that speakers do not speak following some identity they have, but creatively and actively construct a style that is related to a persona they want to convey, and eventually to identities they may have. That is, speakers do not merely observe their place in the social world and report it, but have a say in their place in that social world. More pointedly, we want the speaker's utility to be determined, not just by how informative to a listener some utterance is (weighted by the cost of the utterance), but also by how much that utterance helps the speaker construct her chosen persona. If we let ν be a function from personas to real numbers encoding the speaker's preferences for personas, we can define utility for the sociolinguistic speaker S_1 following Burnett (2019):

$$U_{S_1}(u, \pi) \propto \ln(P_{L_0}(\pi|u)) - C(u) + \nu(\pi)$$

Finally, just as with the pragmatic speaker, we want the sociolinguistic speaker to be boundedly rational in her choice of utterance. That is, the probability that she chooses

---

[5] Note that L_0 is given in a slightly different, though equivalent, form in Burnett (2019). Our deviation here from her presentation is merely to emphasize the similarities between social meaning games and standard pragmatic games in the RSA framework.

some utterance u given a persona π is proportional to its utility, though perturbed by noise:

$$P_{S_1}(u|\pi) \propto \exp(\alpha \times U_{S_1}(u, \pi))$$

In sum, we now have a theory of sociolinguistic interaction in the RSA framework that only minimally deviates from pragmatic theory as developed for truth-conditional content. There are only two core differences. The first is that speakers and listeners now reason about the personas speakers have in virtue of the sociolinguistic properties their utterances index. The second is that speakers do not report on the world, but help construct it—that is, speaker utility for an utterance–persona pair is weighted by how much the speaker wants to assume that persona. Beyond these slight architectural differences, social meaning games are different from standard pragmatic games in terms of perspective. We focus on what the sociolinguistic speaker does, not how listeners react to such speakers. In the next section, we consider how these games play out using an example Burnett (2019) considers, namely Barack Obama choosing between whether to use the apical or the nasal variant of the *-ing* participle.

3.2.4 Burnett on Barack Obama

Recall that whenever using the *-ing* gerund, English speakers have a choice between a velar and an apical variant. The former is associated with an indexical field including properties like pretension, effort, formality, articulateness, competence and so on, while the latter indexes properties like unpretentiousness, relaxness, laziness, lower education, etc. An English speaker must attend to the social situation and the persona she wants to assume in order to select a variant that is concordant with that persona. Social Meaning Games will allow us to model this choice.

As an example, Burnett (2019) considers the case of Barack Obama, whose use of these two variants has actually been studied (Labov 2012). Labov found that in a casual setting, namely a Father's Day BBQ at the White House, Obama used the apical variant 72% of the time, while in taking questions with reporters just after the BBQ, his usage rate plummeted to 33% of the time. Clearly the social situations, as well as the personas Obama wants to project in these two settings, are quite different, and these differences are controlling his use of the variants. Obama's identity didn't change across this short period of time, nor did his role of being president. A BBQ at the White House is clearly a presidential event and he was just as much acting as a president there as when taking questions from reporters. The difference is that in the latter scenario, it would be appropriate for Obama to project the persona of a competent leader, while projecting that same persona at the BBQ would be inappropriate. He would come off as pretentious, a person who can't relax and be with the little people. He would come off as an asshole.

Burnett (2019) models these dynamics by taking the variants to have the following simplified indexical fields

$$[\text{in}] = \{\text{competent, aloof}\}$$
$$[\text{iŋ}] = \{\text{incompetent, friendly }\}$$

If we assume that these are all of the properties available for the construction of personas, and that incompetence is incompatible with competence (and similarly for friendliness and aloofness),

$$\text{competence} > \text{incompetence}$$
$$\text{aloof} > \text{friendly}$$

then we can construct the following personas, which are maximally consistent subsets of $\mathbb{P}$:

$$\{\text{competent, aloof}\} \sim \{\text{competent, friendly}\} \sim \{\text{incompetent, friendly}\}$$

Burnett (2019) calls these personas, respectively,

$$\text{stern leader} \sim \text{cool guy} \sim \text{doofus} \sim \text{asshole} \sim \{\text{incompetent, aloof}\}$$

Obama's task, then, is to choose between velar and apical variants in such a way so that he comes off as the stern leader in the press conference, but plays the cool guy at BBQ. Presumably, he wants to avoid playing the doofus or the asshole in all scenarios.[6]

Speaker preferences for personas are handled via the affective value function v over personas. Burnett (2019) treats Obama's preferences at the BBQ as follows:

$$v$$

Persona	Properties	Values
Cool Guy	{competent, friendly}	1
Stern Leader	{competent, aloof}	0.5
Doofus	{incompetent, friendly}	0
Asshole	{incompetent, aloof}	0

The result is that Obama might be licensed in choosing a more costly variant, even if it only slightly increases the likelihood that the listener assigns him the Cool Guy persona—or, assuming the apical and nasal variants do not alter the cost of the utterance, the result is that speaker will be biased toward choosing variants that better signal the Cool Guy persona, even if those variants are otherwise less informative for the listener. We will be assuming that the apical and nasal variants are equally costly, so to compute Obama's utility, we need only find the probability that the literal listener assigns to personas given utterances, which is to say that we need to compute the first

---

[6] Even here, though, there might be context-based preferences. For instance, it is likely preferable to be a doofus at the party and an asshole in the press conference, while the reverse is the worst of all possible outcomes. We won't model these subpreferences, though, because in this toy example neither will ever be in contention.

term in

$$U_{S_1}(u, \pi) \propto \ln(P_{L_0}(\pi|u)) + v(\pi).$$

Unraveling the literal listener, this means computing

$$U_{S_1}(u, \pi) \propto \ln([\mathbf{enf}(u)](\pi) \times P(\pi)) + v(\pi),$$

where $[\mathbf{enf}(u)](\pi)$ is given by the sociolinguistic conventions of the language and $P(\pi)$ represents the listener's prior beliefs about the speaker's persona.

Starting with the conventional meaning, we know that **enf**(-in) will return 1 for any persona that is not the Stern Leader and **enf**(-iŋ) will return 1 for any persona that is not the Doofus. In other words, on hearing **enf**(-in), the listener will know, by sociolinguistic convention, that the speaker does not have the Stern Leader persona, and will re-weight the probabilities of the other personas accordingly. This is precisely the same procedure familiar from RSA pragmatics; we rule out those possibilities inconsistent with the semantic content of an expression, redistributing their probability mass over those options that remain.

The listener's priors, or, taking the speaker's perspective, what the speaker believes the listener's priors to be, are critical for determining the utility of the available variants. Consider how Obama might be thinking about his audience at the BBQ. Suppose Obama is concerned about coming off as too aloof at the party. He is worried that his normal Stern Leader persona is not appropriate for the party, and even worse, that it might be interpreted as the even less appropriate Asshole persona. That is, he is worried about speakers who have a higher prior belief that he is aloof as opposed to friendly. We can construct the listener that Obama is particularly worried about as follows:

Listener Priors (P)

Persona	Properties	Prior
Cool Guy	{competent, friendly}	0.2
Stern Leader	{competent, aloof}	0.3
Doofus	{incompetent, friendly}	0.2
Asshole	{incompetent, aloof}	0.3

As noted above, because personas are exhaustive and mutually exclusive, given the priors for a listener, we can directly compute $L_0(\pi|u)$ for any persona and message. In this case, the probabilities for each persona on hearing each variant are:

Listener Posteriors

Variant	Cool Guy	Stern Leader	Doofus	Asshole
-iŋ	0.25	0.375	0	0.375
-in	0.286	0	0.286	0.428

Note that Burnett actually uses log-probabilities to calculate speaker utility, but it is helpful to see the raw probabilities here to compare them to the listener's priors. What we see is that on hearing the nasal variant, a speaker who already thinks Obama is aloof will have confirmation of their beliefs. This variant is inconsistent with the Doofus persona, and its probability mass is reapportioned over the remaining three personas, with a 3/4ths majority going to aloof personas. In contrast, using the apical variant completely rules out the Stern Leader persona. Some of that probability mass is moved into the Asshole persona, but, overall, even speakers biased toward assigning Obama an aloof persona now have more evidence that his BBQ persona is not an aloof one.

Obama's utility, and so ultimately what he should do, is rooted in these facts—namely, how a literal listener will react to his utterance. In particular, we compute his utility by taking the log-probabilities describing how the listener will assign personas based on the utterance, and then weight those probabilities by the speaker's preferences for personas.

Obama's Utility (U_S)

Persona	Properties	Prior
Cool Guy	-in	-0.253
Cool Guy	-iŋ	-0.386
Stern Leader	-iŋ	-0.481
Asshole	-in	-0.847
Asshole	-iŋ	-0.981
Doofus	-in	-1.253
Stern Leader	-in	$-\infty$
Doofus	-iŋ	$-\infty$

The top line result is what a perfectly rational Obama should do given his preferences. He should use the apical -in variant in attempt to construct the Cool Guy persona. Sure, sometimes this will backfire and the listener will assign him the Asshole persona, but over the long run, the payoff for being seen as the Cool Guy at a higher rate is worth it.

Note that we have highlighted in gray the second-best scenario(s), which is to use the nasal variant and construct the Stern Leader persona, or luck out and still get tagged as the Cool Guy. These second best strategies do, in fact, emerge when we compute what Obama would do were he not optimally rational—that is, when we compute $P(u|\pi)$ with the temperature α set above 1. Burnett (2019) finds that a temperature of $\alpha = 8$ results in a speaker that picks the apical variant 72% of the time, with the nasal variant being chosen otherwise. This is what was observed for Obama at his BBQ.

This example shows how Burnett's (2017, 2019) Social Meaning Games can be used to model sociolinguistic interactions. The account has a series of important pluses. First, it hews closely to previous work in the RSA framework on implicature calculation. This means that this work promises a unification of formal pragmatics with Third Wave variationist sociolinguistic theory, which would be a huge advance. It is not often we see somewhat distant fields of linguistics begin to blend together in such a way, and when it does happen (e.g., Distributed Morphology allowing morphology to be done as Minimalist syntax), the result can lead to rapid advances.

A second major advance provided by this framework is that it allows us to model social agents, just like we can model pragmatic agents. We can use this to explore the evolutionary trajectory of dogwhistles (or other sociolinguistic phenomena) in a population, or to generate predictions about how human agents should behave in experimental (or real-world scenarios). It is thus a formal model that radically opens up the space of data that we can bring to theories of sociopragmatic interaction.[7]

While we wholeheartedly endorse Burnett's approach, we cannot use her adaptation of the RSA framework without further modification. In the next chapter, we will make the minimal modifications necessary to begin to understand how dogwhistles work. Even this minimal extension, though, will not be sufficient for handling the entire space of dogwhistle phenomena, but it provides a solid starting point with connections to the previous literature, tracing its origins through Social Meaning Games and back into the RSA framework for pragmatics.

---

[7] We have already seen this, for instance, in work like Dénigot (2022) which uses the RSA model for dogwhistles built in the following chapters to inform the construction of artificial agents to detect dogwhistles in text.

4
Identifying dogwhistles

The previous chapter reprised the game-theoretic account of variationist sociolinguistic interaction in Burnett (2017, 2019). When variants exists in a language, social meaning can accrete to these variants, which then allows speakers to choose between the variants to construct a style of speaking that best signals the persona they want to have. Taking the listener's perspective, when confronted with a speaker producing some selection of variants, she must reason about the social meanings of those variants, as well as why they were chosen, in order to situate the speaker in social space.

Thinking back to Albertson's (2015) work on religious dogwhistles discussed in Chapter 1, the connections begin to come into focus. Recall that Albertson considered cases like the following.

(1) Yet there's power—wonder-working power—in the goodness and idealism and faith of the American people.

She found that religious voters were more likely to recognize the phrase *wonder-working power* as a religious reference, and to be more likely to support a candidate who made such religious appeals. Listeners that were opposed to religious appeals in politics who did not recognize the phrase failed to punish the speaker, while those that identified the dogwhistle were less likely to disapprove of the speaker. Moreover, as found in Calfano and Djupe (2008), this process was less about religiosity *per se* and more about partisan identity. Listeners who can detect such religious dogwhistles are more likely to label the speaker as Republican, and this party identification is what mediates voter preferences.

This interaction looks very much like a more complicated version of the story we told in Chapter 3 for standard sociolinguistic interactions. The speaker, here President Bush, wants to convey a conservative Republican persona, but he doesn't want all listeners to assign him that persona, only those that would approve of him as such. He thus picks variants whose social meaning will guide only a subset of the listeners into assigning him the conservative Republican persona, while simultaneously leading listeners who would dislike that persona away from it. This is, in essence, our proposal for dogwhistles of this kind—what we have called *identifying dogwhistles*. Identifying dogwhistles involve the kind of inferences found in standard variationist sociolinguistic contexts, but performed in a strategic way in an adversarial setting.

Our goals for this chapter are to understand what contextual conditions make identifying dogwhistles possible, to understand when it is rational for speakers to use identifying dogwhistles, and to understand what kind of language makes for a good identifying dogwhistle. To reach these goals we must go beyond standard sociolinguistic theory in terms of how to think about variants, and also beyond the formal model of variation developed in Burnett (2017, 2019). Interactions involving identifying dogwhistles do not just seem more complicated, but prove to require richer formals systems to model them. By building such a model, we will begin to see more clearly the shape of the phenomenon.

4.1 Social meaning games for dogwhistles

Recall that at the heart of Burnett's Social Meaning Games is the sociolinguistic speaker S_1 who picks variants to maximize the likelihood that a listener will assign that speaker their desired persona. In these games, S_1 picks variants for a literal listener L_0 who is completely aware of the sociolinguistic conventions of the language. We see this in the definition of L_0

$$L_0(p|m), \propto [\textbf{enf}(m)](p) \times P(p),$$

where $\textbf{enf}(m)$ returns the set of personas the utterance is consistent with. In order to deal with identifying dogwhistles we want to step away from this assumption. To see why, consider again the case of George Bush's use of the phrase *wonder-working power*. The point of using the dogwhistle is that some speakers will recognize the tight connection between the phrase and his conservative evangelical persona, while others will not. That is, we don't want to treat the social meanings as lexical facts, incontrovertibly linked with particular personas. Instead, we want to allow there to be uncertainty about which expressions flag which personas. Otherwise stated, we want listeners to have beliefs about a speaker's persona—the prior $P(p)$—but also beliefs about how personas and messages are connected. Formally implemented, this amounts to letting listeners have priors over the set of personas $\mathbb{P}$, but also beliefs about $P(m|p)$—namely how closely utterances are linked to particular personas.[1] This consideration has us redefine the literal listener as

$$L_0(p|m) \propto P(m|p) \times P(p).$$

Note that we can always recover Burnett's 2019 literal listener by restricting the value $P(m|p)$ can take to 0 or 1, and forcing it to take the same value for every listener. This, in a nutshell, is what it means for some content to be lexicalized. The new definition, then, is a generalization of Burnett's, and makes space for dogwhistles. Literal listeners come from a population that can be more or less certain about how an utterance flags a particular persona. Dogwhistles can emerge from this ferment when one group of

---

[1] The term 'belief' might be a bit too strong, to the degree that one takes the content of belief to be available via introspection. Listeners will have formulated, from their experience, some idea about the particular social messages different kinds of people send and at what frequency. This will obviously differ across listeners, but need not be consciously accessible in the general case.

listeners is aware of the tight connection between bits of language and a persona, while another is unaware.

Allowing utterances to weakly or strongly signal personas for different listeners is necessary for dogwhistles, but it is not sufficient. As a phenomenon, dogwhistles emerge in adversarial contexts. In the case of identifying dogwhistles, speakers exploit variation among listeners' acquaintance with an expression's social meanings in order to get one group of listeners to assign the speaker a persona they approve of, while coaxing listeners who might disapprove of that persona to assign a more innocuous one. Note that in this description we are explicitly taking into account listener preferences for personas. Burnett (2017, 2019) makes the important point, following Third Wave sociolinguistic theory, that speakers do not just observe facts about themselves and then report, given those facts, where they must be situated in social space. Instead, speakers actively try to construct a persona. When we consider dogwhistles, the picture becomes more complicated. Speakers do not just report their personas, nor do they construct them unilaterally. Instead, they construct them in concert with their listeners.

Along these lines, we follow Yoon et al. (2016) and Burnett (2017, 2019) in assuming that the utility calculation takes into account the message's social value, which is given by two functions. First, the speaker has a function v_S that assigns a real number (positive or negative) to each persona representing their preferences.[2] We propose to include a second function for listeners, v_L, that also assigns a real number (positive or negative) to each persona representing their (dis)approval. Less formally, speakers want to present themselves in a certain way, but speakers will also be sensitive to whether listeners will approve of that persona or not.

With these functions we can now calculate the speaker's utility, though we must diverge again from Burnett (2017, 2019). In that work, utilities are computed over persona–message pairs, which allows for reasoning about what persona would be useful to convey. We instead focus on what message should be sent given the particular persona structure and how personas might be received. Thus, we consider a generalized formulation which calculates the utility (in terms of social meaning, which we indicate by the superscript Soc) for the message directed to a particular listener, without considering the particular persona it is intended to convey. Here, the utility is dependent on the affective values of the range of personas consistent with the message and on the likelihood that the particular persona is recovered given the message, as follows:

$$U^{Soc}_{S_1}(m, L_0) = \sum_{p \in [m]} \ln(P_{L_0}(p|m)) + v_{S_1}(p) P_{L_0}(p|m) + v_{L_0}(p) P_{L_0}(p|m).$$

---

[2] Here we slightly diverge from Burnett (2017, 2019) in which the speaker's value function is restricted to non-negative real numbers. We need this extra flexibility because with only non-negative dispositions for personas, listeners could force speakers to dogwhistle 'against their will.'

Note that we continue to assume, following the RSA model, that a sociolinguistically aware speaker S_1 addresses a literal listener L_0. More generally, the utility of a message for a level S_n speaker will be computed relative to a level L_{n-1} listener.

When only one listener is addressed, identifying dogwhistles reduce to ordinary social meaning—modulo our revisions to the literal listener. The speaker should choose a signal which maximizes U_S. Dogwhistles come into their own when speakers address groups of individuals with mixed preferences over personas, different priors for the speaker's persona, and different experiences resulting in the assignment of different likelihoods for personas given a message. The simplest way to assign utilities to the group case is to sum over all listeners.[3] In line with the assumption, we use the following metric (for G a group):

$$U_{S_n}^{Soc}(m, G) = \sum_{L_{n-1} \in G} U_{S_n}^{Soc}(m, L_{n-1})$$

Note, though, that we think the method of simple summation should only be taken as a starting point. There are probably cases in which this way of calculating utilities is overridden—e.g., if one particular powerful person in the audience is known to have a highly negative affective value for a particular persona which she is likely to recover. Generalizing from this case, the observation that one might care differently about the views of particular individuals within the audience means that a simple summation technique can't be right for every case. Also, in the case of a particularly pernicious persona (i.e., one for which v_L yields an extremely low value), the possibility of later penalty may preclude the use of the dogwhistle in the first place despite present advantage. Modeling this requires a move to a repeated game setting (cf. McCready 2015). We will consider some of these kinds of scenarios in Chapter 7, which deals with extensions of the work developed in this book.

Finally, as we have already seen, we can model speakers who more or less rationally deploy dogwhistles by perturbing the utility calculation using a temperature value:

$$P_{S_1}(m|p) \propto exp(\alpha \times U_{S_1}^{Soc}(m, L_0))$$

With this we have a complete, RSA-style model for identifying dogwhistles extending Burnett's (2017, 2019)Social Meaning Games. In the next section we will fully work out an example of how a sociolinguistically aware speaker reasons through the use of an identifying dogwhistle. The goal is to explore the contours of this model, and to show it allows for identifying dogwhistles to be deployed to maximize the speaker's social utility.

---

[3] This is the simplest way, but is of course a simplification: ordinarily speakers won't care to the same degree about the reactions of every member of a group, given various patterns of power dynamics, social influence, and network centrality. There are various methods for addressing these aspects of group structure, but we will not consider them here.

4.2 A case study of identifying dogwhistles

Jill Stein is in a predicament.[4]

It is 2018. She has just been asked about vaccines. She knows her base is basically all anti-corporate, but she also knows her base contains a passionate anti-vaxxer minority that hold a position others in her party don't like. She knows that her anti-corporate bona fides are solid, but the question wouldn't be coming up unless there was some uncertainty about her stance on vaccines. She realizes, though, this is the perfect occasion for a dogwhistle. Her audience has only three types of listeners—the passionate anti-vaxxer, the clueless pro-vaxxer, and the knowledgeable pro-vaxxer—and she can satisfy most everyone while maintaining plausible deniability if her strategy is discovered.

We assume that Stein is choosing between messages whose social meanings always mark her as anti-corporate, but mark her as either pro- or anti-vaccine. That is, she could use the phrase *big pharma*, which is an anti-vaxxer dogwhistle, or a phrase like *corporate scientist*, which has no traction in the anti-vaxxer community, but which, in virtue of emphasizing that these are not public servant scientists, could flag the speaker as anti-corporate. Thus, we have the following expressions and the set of personas they are consistent with.

Expressions and Their Consistent Personas

big pharma	{anti-vaxxer, anti-corporate}
	{anti-vaxxer, pro-corporate}
	{pro-vaxxer, anti-corporate}
corporate scientists	{pro-vaxxer, anti-corporate}
	{anti-vaxxer, anti-corporate}
	{pro-vaxxer, pro-corporate}

We further assume that Stein takes all listeners to have the same priors about her persona.[5] That is, they believe that she is probably anti-corporate, but it is equally probable that she is a pro- or anti-vaxxer (which is why the question is being asked). We represent that with the following priors over personas. The particular numbers do no matter so much as the order. Listeners have a larger and equal degree of belief that she is pro- or anti-vax. They have some smaller degree of belief that she is an

---

[4] We should note that we developed this example before COVID; we might not have chosen attitudes toward vaccination as the personas at issue in our example in 2022, when the kinds of social meanings out there with respect to vaccination have changed a lot, and when this set of questions might be a more fraught experience for the reader.

[5] The selection of these numbers might seem arbitrary. First, we would like to point out that the particular numbers are not so important. More important are the relations between numbers. These relations we pick along lines that can be defended. For instance, the idea that antivaxx listeners will assign higher affective value to speakers they detect as antivaxx than listeners who are not antivaxx. One still might worry how fined-tuned our numerical parameters need to be. In the following section we consider how altering all numerical parameters, including this one, shapes the predictions of the model.

anti-vaxxer, but somehow pro-corporate. Finally, we take listeners to assign a very low, but still non-zero probability that Stein is both pro-corporate and an anti-vaxxer.

Priors for Stein's Persona

{pro-vaxxer, pro-corporate}	.05
{pro-vaxxer, anti-corporate}	.40
{anti-vaxxer, pro-corporate}	.15
{anti-vaxxer, anti-corporate}	.40

She also supposes her audience is polarized on this issue, but that there is structure to this polarization. Often constituencies are composed of highly-motivated, warring subconstituencies with a larger center consisting of people with opinions, but who are somewhat less invested. Along these lines, we assume the anti-vaxxers care a lot about the issue, and the savvy pro-vaxxers, as demonstrated by their knowledge of anti-vaxxer discourse, also care a lot about Stein's stance. If she is detected as liking vaccinations at all, the anti-vaxxers will be angry and savvy pro-vaxxers will love her, and vice versa. We see in the following two figures that anti-vaxxers and savvy pro-vaxxers are mirror images of each other, with both groups slightly punishing the speaker for being pro-corporate, all else being equal.

$v_L(p)$ for Anti-vaxxers

personas	Values
{pro-vaxxer, pro-corporate}	-125
{pro-vaxxer, anti-corporate}	-100
{anti-vaxxer, pro-corporate}	75
{anti-vaxxer, anti-corporate}	100

$v_L(p)$ for Savvy Pro-vaxxers

personas	Values
{pro-vaxxer, pro-corporate}	75
{pro-vaxxer, anti-corporate}	100
{anti-vaxxer, pro-corporate}	-125
{anti-vaxxer, anti-corporate}	-100

An unsavvy pro-vaxxer has a more attenuated belief. We assume that if a person like this discovers Stein to be anti-vaxxer, they will highly object. That said, the vaccine culture war circa 2018 is not something they are highly invested in. If Stein is detected to be a pro-vaxxer, they are happy, but it's considered a kind of default position and so not as big a deal as for the savvy pro-vaxxers. Like the rest of the audience, we assume these listeners slightly disapprove of pro-corporate politicians. The reason is that this is an audience for Stein, and so is presumably at least possibly part of her coalition.

$v_L(p)$ for Unsavvy Pro-vaxxers

personas	Values
{pro-vaxxer, pro-corporate}	50
{pro-vaxxer, anti-corporate}	75
{anti-vaxxer, pro-corporate}	-125
{anti-vaxxer, anti-corporate}	-100

While the audience cares a lot about Stein's persona, encoded in the affective value function v_L, we assume for the purposes of this example that Stein is a completely amoral politician and as such is accommodating to her audience. She has no preferences among personas, and only wants to maximize her audience's reception of her. This amounts to setting $v_S(p)$ to 0 for all personas, as we see below. While this assumption is probably accurate only for a certain kind of craven political discourse in which one tries to be all things to all people, an advantage of the framework we have constructed is that it allows us to explicitly model such extreme strategies, and to identify real-world agents who might employ such a strategy.

$v_S(p)$

personas	Values
{pro-vaxxer, pro-corporate}	0
{pro-vaxxer, anti-corporate}	0
{anti-vaxxer, pro-corporate}	0
{anti-vaxxer, anti-corporate}	0

Finally, Stein believes that listeners might not uniformly take certain messages to go with certain personas. In particular, she assumes that all anti-vaxxers are savvy about the phrase *big pharma* and its place in anti-vaxxer discourses, but pro-vaxxers might know about *big pharma* and might not. Second, all speakers realize that a phrase like *corporate scientists* is pro-vax, by virtue of mentioning scientists, but anti-corporate (in virtue of tying those scientists to corporate interests). Note that we assume anti-vaxxers and savvy pro-vaxxers have the same probability structure below—this actually attenuates the utility of a dogwhistle. The less an out-group is aware of in-group messaging, the more useful it will be to dogwhistle. We break down for each group the prior probabilities of the message *big pharma* given the various personas at issue as follows:

- **Savvy listeners**—While it is possible (consistent with the social meaning of the phrase), that a speaker might use 'big pharma' to signal they are just anti-corporate, these listeners know this is phrasing used by their anti-vaxxer/anti-corporate allies. Also note this phrasing is inconsistent with a pro-vaxxer and pro-corporate persona, which we assume speakers know based on knowing the social meaning of the phrase. This is why the conditional probability is zero.

Likelihood of 'big pharma' for savvy listeners (both Pro- and Anti-vax)

personas	Pr(m|p)
{pro-vaxxer, pro-corporate}	0
{pro-vaxxer, anti-corporate}	.1
{anti-vaxxer, pro-corporate}	.1
{anti-vaxxer, anti-corporate}	.8

- **Unsavvy listeners**—Listeners not aware of anti-vaxxer discourse consider this phrase to be consistent with an anti-vaxxer persona, but take it to be primarily an anti-corporate phrase. That is, these listeners don't see the tight connection between 'big pharma' and anti-vaxxer personas. This is why we call them unsavvy.

Likelihood of "big pharma" for unsavvy listeners

personas	Pr(m|p)
{pro-vaxxer, pro-corporate}	0
{pro-vaxxer, anti-corporate}	.7
{anti-vaxxer, pro-corporate}	.1
{anti-vaxxer, anti-corporate}	.15

- **Population likelihoods for 'corporate scientists'**—We assume the phrase 'corporate scientist' is linked to personas in a uniform way across all listeners. In particular, we take this phrase to all but rule out being anti-vaxxer, but to lean anti-corporate. The reason is that anti-vaxxers already have in-group language to disparage the sector, yet the phrase does not convey positive affect.

personas	Pr(m|p)
{pro-vaxxer, pro-corporate}	.6
{pro-vaxxer, anti-corporate}	.8
{anti-vaxxer, pro-corporate}	.1
{anti-vaxxer, anti-corporate}	.1

We are now in a position to calculate the social utility of various messages for Stein when she addresses listeners of each of these three types—the savvy pro-vaxxer, the savvy anti-vaxxer, and the unsavvy anti-vaxxer. We begin with a savvy pro-vaxxer listener (L_{SPV}), and compute U_{Stein}^{Soc} for the message 'big pharma' once in gory detail for illustration purposes.

$$U_{Stein}(\text{big pharma}, L_{SPV}) =$$

$$\sum_{p \in [\text{big pharma}]} \ln(P_{L_{SPV}}(p|\text{big pharma}))$$

$$+ v_{S_1}(p) P_{L_{SPV}}(p|\text{big pharma})$$

$$+ v_{L_{SPV}}(p) P_{L_{SPV}}(p|\text{big pharma})$$

4.2 A CASE STUDY OF IDENTIFYING DOGWHISTLES

Now substituting each persona consistent with 'big pharma' for p, and recalling that $P_{L_{SPV}}(p|\text{big pharma})$ is the posterior over personas computed via Bayes' law, we get the following three lines to sum. Note that we only have three lines because 'big pharma' is inconsistent with a pro-corporate, pro-vax persona so the listener throws out that possibility and updates their priors once having received the phrase 'big pharma.'

$$= \ln(.11) + (0 \times .11) + (100 \times .11)$$
$$+\ln(.04) + (0 \times .04) + (-125 \times .04)$$
$$+\ln(.85) + (0 \times .85) + (-100 \times .85)$$
$$= -85$$

Thus, Stein's utility for using 'big pharma' with a pro-vaxxer who is savvy about anti-vax discourse is negative. This is the effect of detecting the dogwhistle, namely that the phrase 'big pharma' signals anti-vaxxer personas, which they disapprove of. Stein would be safer using 'corporate scientist' with listeners of this type, as the following chart shows.

$U^{Soc}_{Stein}(m, \textbf{Savvy pro-vaxxer})$

Message	Utility
big pharma	-85
corporate scientists	62

In comparison, the unsavvy pro-vaxxer has a much higher utility for 'big pharma.' This is the dogwhistle effect because the unsavvy pro-vaxxer does not hear the whistle—namely that 'big pharma' highly codes for the anti-vaxxer persona. Note that the residual negative relative to the message 'corporate scientists' is from the fact that it doesn't rule out anti-vaxxer personas like other phrasing. That is, it is more cagey though it doesn't strongly reveal the speaker as an anti-vaxxer to these listeners.

$U^{Soc}_{Stein}(m, \textbf{Unsavvy Pro-vaxxer})$

Message	Utility
big pharma	32
corporate scientists	40

Finally, the anti-vaxxer shows the opposite pattern from the savvy pro-vaxxer. This is because they also hear the dogwhistle, but endorse its message.

$U^{Soc}_{Stein}(m, \textbf{Savvy Anti-vaxxer})$

Message	Utility
big pharma	73
corporate scientists	-84

In comparing these utilities, we already see the identifying dogwhistle effect, namely that a message's utility can be greatly increased when listeners fail to realize how tightly it's correlated with a persona they disapprove of. For us, the effect is due to the fact that a listener's (dis)approval of a persona affects the utility of a message in proportion to the probability they assign that persona given the message. If some listeners are unaware that a message tightly signals a persona, their reaction to that persona can be discounted relative to other listeners that are aware (and may have an opposing reaction).

While we already have an analysis of what makes an identifying dogwhistle a dogwhistle—a message such that the value of $P_{L_0}(m|p)$ across the population is correlated with the affective value of that persona—the model also makes predictions about when it is optimal to deploy such language. In particular, it makes predictions about audience structure. If we sum message utilities over each listener in a audience, the optimal message will depend on the proportion of different types of listeners (the speaker thinks) are in the audience. In general, given n kinds of listeners, it will be optimal to use a dogwhistle over a disavowal if the following equality holds—where x_n is the number of listeners of type L^n.

(2) $(x_1 \times U_S^{Soc}(\text{DOGWHISTLE}, L^1)), ..., (x_n \times U_S^{Soc}(\text{DOGWHISTLE}, L^n)) >$

$(x_1 \times U_S^{Soc}(\text{DISAVOWAL}, L^1)), ..., (x_n \times U_S^{Soc}(\text{DISAVOWAL}, L^n))$

To evaluate this formula, let's consider our intuitions about the scenarios. We have the following core intuitions:

1. If Stein thinks she is talking to any number of pro-vaxxers, whether or not that person is savvy about anti-vaxxer discourse or not, she is best to issue a disavowal.
2. If Stein thinks she is talking to any number of anti-vaxxers, she should obviously not disavow and instead issue the dogwhistle.[6]
3. If Stein is talking in mixed company, things are more complicated, but the ratio of anti-vaxxers to pro-vaxxers (of both types) will determine whether it's best to dogwhistle.
   (a) If there are too few anti-vaxxers in the mix, she can afford to alienate them, issue a disavowal, and reap the utility of signaling her pro-vaxxer stance to a primarily pro-vaxxer audience.
   (b) In this calculation, the savvy pro-vaxxers matter more than the unsavvy. That is, the lower the ratio of savvy pro-vaxxers to anti-vaxxers, the more pro-vaxxers we need in total to make it worth her while to issue a disavowal.

Our model captures this dynamic. First, note that because the utilities for "big pharma" / "corporate scientists" are $-85/62$ and $32/40$ for pro-vaxxers of both types, it is just

---

[6] Actually, she may want to issue a direct appeal, but we have not modeled a third explicitly anti-vaxxer message, though we could. In previous experimental work (e.g., Albertson 2015), listeners who would approve of a direct appeal don't seem to prefer it over the dogwhistle, though this probably depends on their listener model, that is, who they think might else be listening.

always better to avoid the dogwhistle if we have a uniformly pro-vaxxer audience. Second, note that because the utilities for "big pharma" / "corporate scientists" are $73/-84$ for anti-vaxxers, it is always best to use the former in a pure anti-vaxxer crowd. Finally, some calculations using the formula in (2) shows that we capture our third intuition above. To make things concrete, imagine that Stein is speaking to audience of about 5000 people. She believes that 400 are hardcore anti-vaxxers, but only about 100 are pro-vaxxers that follow the anti-vaxxer literature and are familiar with that discourse. This is a scenario where it would be optimal to use a dogwhistle. This would change, though, if the ratio of listeners were to change. For instance, adding a few dozen savvy anti-vaxxers, or a thousand more naive listeners would change the calculation away from the dogwhistle. It would no longer be safe to use.

4.3 Exploring the numerical parameters

Through this case study we have seen how our analysis allows us to model the use of identifying dogwhistles in discourse. In particular, we have seen an instance where it is utility optimizing to use an expression that signals a risky persona in virtue of the fact that the expression will most likely only signal that persona to a section of the audience that would actually approve. The reader will likely have noted, though, this result is due to the setting of a variety of numerical parameters—speaker and listener affective values for personas, listener awareness of how personas and expressions are linked, audience size and composition, etc. One would be right to wonder how brittle the account is, that is, how sensitive the dogwhistle effect is to a fine-tuning of the parameters. What we find is that the utility of dogwhistling emerges under a fairly broad and plausible space of parameter settings. Moreover, the parameters allow us to model some interestingly different kind of social agents, both speakers and hearers, that are likely to exist and behave differently from one another.

First, we consider the question of brittleness. Do we have to fine-tune the numeral parameters to allow dogwhistling to emerge, or can it arise fairly easily across a broad range of (hopefully plausible) parameter settings? We can show that we need not fine-tune the parameters much at all to make dogwhistling a plausible conversational strategy. Even better, there are a variety of extreme scenarios where dogwhistling would be either optimal or not, and those cases correspond to plausible actual conversational scenarios.

First, let us consider the role of the affective value functions for the speakers and listeners, starting with the speaker. The situation we have considered above in the case study is the one where dogwhistles are most likely to be deployed, i.e., one in which the speaker has no preference for the persona they bear. They are instead completely malleable by their audience. For this kind of speaker, it is extremely helpful to have words that differentially signal personas to subsets of the audience which will allow them to extract the most social utility from a communicative act. We think this is a good result. It is probably not an accident that we associate dogwhistles with political speech, or other kinds of mass communication, like advertising. These are precisely the kinds of conversational scenarios where the speaker wants to be all things to all people.

While we tuned this parameter in the example above to facilitate dogwhistles, this is not at all necessary. The speaker's values for various personas, as long as they are not too extreme relative to the range of values audience members assign to those personas, merely alter what the audience composition must be for them to take the use of a dogwhistle to be rational. In particular, if the speaker is relatively willing to have a persona associated with a dogwhistle (relative to other personas), then they will be willing to dogwhistle with relatively fewer ideological co-partisans in the audience—that is, in a situation where it is more socially dangerous to do so. The inverse is also true. If a speaker is relatively unwilling to have a persona associated with the dogwhistle, they will resist using it unless they believe there is a large number of members of the audience who will hear the dogwhistle and approve. We can think of such speakers as being on the edge of some kind of in-group, and can be peer-pressured into using dogwhistles in particular kinds of social situations. Note that here the general deniability of dogwhistles is especially useful for such speakers.

We do not need to fine-tune to speaker's affective values for personas to get the dogwhistle effect. We can, though, rig this parameter to rule out dogwhistling in two scenarios. Both are interesting in their own right. First, if the speaker absolutely does not want to be associated with the persona a dogwhistle carries, then assigning a large negative value to that persona (up to $-\infty$) will ensure that the speaker always gets the most utility from messages whose average $P(p|m)$ across the population for the hated persona is the smallest. This is good. For instance, for a committed anti-racist activist well aware of racist dogwhistles, those messages could rise to the level of taboo words. In the opposite camp, there may be speakers who assign very high positive values to (up to ∞) to certain personas. This speakers will try to pick messages that maximize the average $P(p|m)$ for the persona in question. These will likely not be dogwhistles, though, which are precisely expressions that some members of the average audience will not recognize are tightly linked with the valued persona. Instead, such speakers should, all things being equal, prefer messages that more explicitly identify that they bear the persona in question for all listeners. These speakers are beyond dogwhistles and would extract more social utility from overt appeals. We will explore cases of this kind further in Chapter 8.

Turning to the listeners' affective value functions, the situation is slightly more complex. The effect of a single listener on the speaker's message choice vis-a-vis dogwhistling is negligible. What matters is the structure of the population as a whole, as well as how certain messages are linked with personas in that population. Once again, fine-tuning of listener affective values for personas is not required to make dogwhistling the optimal strategy. We only need a general setup where there are two classes of listeners L and L', and two personas p and p' such that, all else being equal: (i) $v_L(p) < v_L(p')$, but $v_{L'}(p) > v_{L'}(p')$, and (ii) there is some message m, the dogwhistle, that flags the speaker as p' for L with greater probability than it does for

L′, and is at least consistent with p for L′. As long as we have this general relationship between some personas, messages, and listener affective values, there can be conversations where dogwhistling is optimal. Whether a particular conversation will count as such depends on the proportion of L and L′ listeners in the audience, where the correct proportion depends on the precise values at issue, but we can at least see in this minimal example that, all things being equal, as long as the L listeners outnumber the L′ listeners dogwhistling will be optimal. This is, of course, not the only such situation, it is just that the proportion will be affected by how other parameters are set.

While we do need the particular inequalities described above for dogwhistling to be utility-maximizing, the situation described by those inequalities is not only plausible, but likely the norm in most public discourse. What it describes is a scenario where listeners who are familiar with a certain kind of rhetoric used by a kind of speaker, do in fact, like that kind of speaker, while people who may not like that kind of speaker much are not necessarily aware of the rhetoric they use. We take this to be the normal situation for essentially all in-group language. Members of the in-group like other members and know how they talk, while the average disapproving out-group members would not know how group members talk precisely because they don't associate with those people they don't approve of. We find ourselves in a best case scenario in terms of modeling. The general constraint we need is quite plausible and allows the phenomenon we are interested in to emerge under a variety of particular parameter settings as long as they fit the general, and plausible, pattern.

Finally, we want to consider a very special kind of listener that mitigates against the use of a dogwhistles. These are listeners who, like the approving listener, are aware of the link between some message and a persona, but whose affective values assigned to that persona are negative. These listeners have a policing effect on the conversation. If the negative affective values they assign to certain personas are large enough, they can prevent dogwhistling because they would overwhelm the utility speakers would get from in-group members who hear the dogwhistle and reward the persona associated with it. Once again, such listeners are plausible. They correspond to listeners who, rather than merely disapproving of the in-group in question, actively oppose it. We would expect that people who oppose a group would assign large negative affective values to its members along with being familiar with in-group rhetoric in virtue of arguing with / monitoring members of that group. Once again, though, no fine-tuning is necessary. Even with such listeners in the audience, dogwhistling can still be an optimal strategy. We just require there be enough listeners of other types to counterbalance.

The last parameter we must consider is the listener priors over the speaker's personas. As with affective values for listeners, when considering whether to dogwhistle, we care less about the priors of individual listeners and more about the kinds of priors we see across an audience. Dogwhistling will be a viable strategy as long as there is some amount of uncertainty with respect to the speaker's persona across the audience. As in all kinds of Bayesian accounts, strong priors blunt the effect of evidence, in this case the message that the speaker chooses to send. Thus, dogwhistles, which we argue exist to allow a speaker to get two sub-audiences to assign them different personas, require that their persona not be fixed across an audience. That said, cases where the audience as a whole (or sub-audiences) have strong priors generate interesting dynamics, which, once again, we think we see in actual conversation.

First, consider the case where the audience has a strong prior that the speaker does not, or can with only great difficulty, bear the persona the dogwhistle is linked to. An example might be a member of a marginalized group bearing a persona that is linked to ideologies that disparage that group (see Chapter 5 for more this connection between ideologies and personas). While it may be possible in principle for such a speaker to bear such a persona, the audience priors might nearly preclude it. In this case, the speaker could use an expression that is a dogwhistle, in virtue of being differentially linked with personas across the population, but which would not have the dogwhistle effect in terms of coaxing different sub-audiences to assign the speaker different personas. Such speakers could then use what would be dogwhistles in certain contexts, uttered by certain speakers, without a similar effect. We see natural examples of this with the phrase *inner-city*. While in certain contexts the phrase *inner-city* can be used as a racist dogwhistle, a web search for that phrase easily turns up a plethora of art and education NGOs with *inner-city* in their names. It is clearly not the case that these organizations are constantly dogwhistling. Instead, in virtue of the work these organizations do, the audience will have a very low prior that these are racist agents. Thus, the organization can use the phrase *inner-city* without sending a covert signal that they bear a taboo persona.

We see equally interesting effects when the audience has strong priors that the speaker does, in fact, bear a persona linked with the dogwhistle. One might think that this would mean that the speaker should always dogwhistle, but that is not exactly true. It depends on how those priors are distributed across the audience. If all audience members have the same priors, and they are highly certain the speaker bears a persona linked with the dogwhistle, then all other things being equal, dogwhistling will be more optimal than if those priors are lower. (In these situations it might also be better to just use an overt appeal, though we do not model this; again, see Chapter 8.) The reason is that the speaker is likely to incur the negative affective values assigned to that persona by out-group members in virtue of the prior alone, and so it is better to use the dogwhistle, removing all doubt for in-group members, and gain whatever boost they provide in terms of affective value for that controversial persona.

More interesting is the case where only subsets of the audience have strong priors that the speaker bears a controversial persona. In particular, consider the case where in-group members do so, namely agents who assign a high affective value to that persona and are familiar with in-group language, i.e., dogwhistles, associated with that persona. In this situation, dogwhistles actually lose their utility because there in-group signaling effect is baked in. The speaker is then freer to use more neutral terms that are not inconsistent with the dogwhistle persona.

While it is hard to observe agents not using dogwhistles, we have seen something like this effect in the political realm surrounding apologies. For instance, when

Donald Trump refused to immediately disavow the support of participants in the Charlottesville white supremacist rally, only to slowly walk it back a few days later, it had no effect on perceptions of him as an ally to the participants. Keegan Hankes, a senior research analyst at the Southern Poverty Law Center's Intelligence Project, who monitors white supremacist forums, has reported, "When they hear the President say things like, 'I'm not a racist,' they turn around among themselves and say, 'He just has to say that for practical reasons,' 'he just has to say that basically to get himself cover, to do the things that we want him to do'" (Simon and Sidner 2019). That is, the first act increases the priors of the in-group members that Trump supports them. The later apology can then be discounted as what he has to do to increase the affective values assigned by out-group members.

This is exactly the same logic that can mitigate the use of dogwhistles by certain speakers. If in-group members are assured that the speaker bears the persona they approve of, as modeled by their strong priors, then optimal speaker behavior, all things being equal, will tilt toward not using a dogwhistle in order to gain more utility from out-group members who may disapprove of personas expressed by the dogwhistle were they to detect it. In-group members can always ignore this evidence, which is not enough to overwhelm their strong priors, just as white supremacists were able to tell themselves that Trump had to say he's not racist, and that he wasn't really disavowing them or their support.

4.4 The grammar of identifying dogwhistles

We have focused in this chapter on how speakers and listeners pick utterances and assign personas given that identifying dogwhistles exist. To do this we have just assumed that there are bits of language whose association with a persona varies across a population. We now want to ask what kind of language is likely to have this property. What are the linguistic properties of a good identifying dogwhistle? There is unlikely to be an exhaustive list of criteria, but there are clearly tendencies that we can make sense of in the framework developed here.

First, let's consider an instructive example of what would make a bad identifying dogwhistle. At first pass, one might think that dogwhistles are merely in-group slang. This is true, perhaps broadly construed, but canonical cases of slang make poor identifying dogwhistles precisely because they must be used in adversarial contexts. Recall from Chapter 2 that a core pragmatic property of dogwhistles is their deniability, in two senses. First, a dogwhistle allows the speaker to deny the message it conveys. Second, a dogwhistle allows the speaker to deny that a hidden message was even sent. In the case of identifying dogwhistles, this latter kind of deniability requires that $P(u|p)$ be non-zero for at least one persona p across the population (and ideally for an innocuous persona relative to each listener). The danger of using in-group slang is that a listener might not be able to associate it with any persona—formally, that the probability of u given p is 0 for all known personas p.

To give an example, suppose in the canonical case of identifying dogwhistles that George Bush, instead of using the phrase *wonder-working power* had used the phrase *shekhinah power*. These would be roughly synonymous, with the latter using the word *shekhinah* that evangelicals, especially Pentecostals, have borrowed from rabbinic literature for the miracle-working power of the Holy Spirit. Likely those same Pentecostals who recognized the religious source of the phrase *wonder-working power* would also recognize *shekhinah power*. Non-religious voters, and even mainline Protestants, though, would likely be completely unaware of this word. In this situation, $P(u|p)$ would be 0 for all personas, leaving the conversational context, as far as social meaning is concerned, in the absurd state. Every calculation for L_0, S_1, L_1, etc. in this scenario would return 0.

It is nice to find that we actually have a notion of absurdity for social meaning, just like we do for standard truth-conditional meaning, i.e. contradiction, or, for dynamic notions of meaning, ending up in an empty information state. Even better, though, it lines up with how we think dogwhistles should work. In an absurd truth-conditional state, the listener knows that something has gone wrong. The conversational context must be repaired. The same is true when a listener finds herself in an absurd conversational state with respect to social meaning. More importantly for dogwhistles, the listener knows that the speaker is sending social messages to groups of listeners she is not a part of. In the case the dogwhistle fails because it is no longer deniable. As discussed in the introduction, there is experimental work, mostly in the advertising literature, that confirms this effect. In particular, listeners punish brands when they can detect they are not the target audience of an advertisement, even if they would otherwise like what is being advertised (e.g., Aaker et al. 2000). We can model these kinds of effects in the RSA framework, and they make clear that an appropriate identifying dogwhistle must make $P(u|p)$ non-zero for some p. This means that in-group slang can be a dangerous choice unless it is also used in other ways across the wider population of listeners.

These considerations show that completely novel, in-group coinages do not make good identifying dogwhistles. We believe this negative result is quite important, and shapes the kinds of identifying dogwhistles we do see. First, returning to our ur-example of Bush's *wonder-working power*, we see that the first strategy to get around opaque in-group language is to use quotation. Quotes are ideal, especially snippets of larger works, because they can be composed of entirely ordinary language, yet gain immediate significance to a population that recognizes the quote. This is exactly how Bush's dogwhistle works. There is nothing special from a social-meaning perspective about the phrase *wonder-working*, nor *power*, nor in their combination. This kind of socially inert language would be modeled by taking the average listener to have a uninformative prior over personas—that is, $P(u|p)$ would be uniform, and crucially, non-zero. The fact that socially inert language is, for the average listener, consistent with all live personas makes it ideal as a potential identifying dogwhistle. What turns it into a dogwhistle is the fact that this language is immediately recognizable to evangelical Christians through quotation. In the late 1800s, a Moody Bible College student,

Lewis Jones, wrote a hymn called "There is Power in the Blood." The hymn's iconic refrain is:

There is power, power, wonder-working power in the blood of the lamb

It cannot be overstated how well known this hymn is in the Protestant evangelical community. It has been covered by, essentially, every gospel group and even pop singers in gospel mode, like Alan Jackson. In fact, most evangelicals would have sung those words themselves multiple times in their life. There is thus, through quotation, a tight connection between a community and a phrase that to the average listener is uninformative with respect to social personas. The result is a powerful identifying dogwhistle, which Albertson (2015) was able to confirm experimentally.

We have seen that quotation is a powerful tool for creating identifying dogwhistles because they can easily accrue their social meaning through repetition within a community. The fact that repetition is something separable from words themselves means that the quote as words can be socially inert for the average listener, while clearly marking the speaker as a member of the group who uses the quote. This idea of expressions accreting social meaning through repetition is closely related to the idea of memes. In fact, memes on social networking platforms have been a source of identifying dogwhistles. Memes are highly complex, and many are visual in nature (see the final section of this chapter for discussion of non-linguistic identifying dogwhistles), but reoccurring characters in memes can accrete social meaning, at which point those named entities can be used as dogwhistles.

A recent illustrative example of this process involves Gritty, the furry orange, googly-eyed mascot of the Philadelphia Flyers hockey team. Gritty was introduced with a series of mishaps, including the first time on the ice when he slipped and fell multiple times. This spawned a series of memes about Gritty as a relatable hero who bumbles around and messes up just like the rest of us. The idea of Gritty as an "everyman" mutated again when the socialist magazine Jacobin tweeted that "Gritty is a worker." This was the starting point for a series of leftwing memes that resulted in the widespread consensus on left social media that Gritty was, in fact, Antifa—that is, an antifacist, anticaptialist activist committed to militant direct action. This history in memes lays the groundwork for an identifying dogwhistle, because in the wider culture, Gritty is just the mascot of a hockey team, but in far left social media he is their own mascot. The result is that speakers are able to now use Gritty to make center left or even completely centrist claims while marking themselves as far left. The following tweet illustrates this point.

(3) [Retweet of Gritty jumping through a March Madness college basketball bracket]
    @Brian_E_Smith: Gritty says pay the players.

Paying college basketball players is a completely centrist position. Many on the right as well as the left hold it. The speaker, in using Gritty to express a centrist opinion, is able to simultaneously construct for himself a far left persona that would not be recoverable for the average listener from the truth-conditional content of this utterance.

While memes are a special case, the accretion of social meaning to named entities is a much broader phenomenon. Communities are built around people and places as much as ideas, and so if quotes provide a way to signal a persona through the latter, we expect that named entities can be used as identifying dogwhistles as long as those entities have purchase in the wider culture. We have lots of examples of named entity-identifying dogwhistles, even in examples we have already seen. Consider the case of the Subaru add campaign discussed in the introduction. Recall that Subaru had, post-hoc, admitted that the ad campaign had been explicitly constructed to contain dogwhistles that only members of the gay community, and lesbians in particular, would understand. In particular, the Subarus depicted in the commercial bear the license plates P TOWN and XENA LVR. The first references Provincetown, Massachusetts, a well-known LGBTQ vacation destination. The second references "Xena the Warrior Princess", a 1990s sitcom about a person called Xena and her poet sidekick (and obvious girlfriend), Gabrielle. The show was a major cultural touchstone in the lesbian community. Welsh (2016) writes about how she was afraid to search online for the word *lesbian*, so instead she would search for *Xena* in order to find other people like her online.[7] Next to each other, these two license plates clearly mark the drivers as gay, and do so by referencing people and places that are themselves associated with that community.

It is unlikely that there is a strict definition, in morphosyntactic terms, of what kinds of expressions are allowed or even predisposed to be dogwhistles. As we have seen, though, the theory we have proposed makes some predictions. Identifying dogwhistles emerge when we find expressions where there is sharp disagreement in a speech community about the likelihood that speaker bears a persona given their use of that expression. This means that very high frequency phrases are unlikely to make good dogwhistles—it won't be possible to establish a large differential in their usage frequency between the average speaker and speakers bearing a specific, distinguished persona. Additionally, our theory of identifying dogwhistles predicts that novel expressions make poor dogwhistles because for some listeners, the use of these expressions will be sociolinguistically infelicitous, rendering the dogwhistle attempt no longer covert. Against this backdrop, the fact that quotes and named entities are fertile ground for identifying dogwhistles makes sense. They are all likely to be low frequency expressions. Moreover, they provide natural protection in keeping the dogwhistle attempt covert. If a listener does not recognize a quote as a quote, it is no big deal. Quotes, in the main, are constructed from ordinary language, and so the unaware listener will be able to assign the speaker a persona based on the

---

[7] This is actually a beautiful example that lays bare the logic of identifying dogwhistles, which we have argued follow once we allow for members of a population to have different likelihoods for $P(u|p)$. Here the author is using her belief that there is a high probability that someone utters *Xena* given that she is a lesbian in order to find an online community. This would have failed had she been wrong about her Bayesian likelihood, but in fact, she found her fellow lesbians.

ordinary social meaning of the expressions that constitute the quote. Named entities provide a different sort of cover. Unlike other expressions, it is common to hear about novel people, places, brands, etc. Hearing an unknown person or place is thus less likely to provoke suspicion that secret social meanings are being sent, unlike novel slang, which is in-group language by definition.

4.5 Non-linguistic identifying dogwhistles

The analysis of identifying dogwhistles developed in this chapter has two foundational assumptions: (i) dogwhistles involve a novel kind of meaning, social meaning, which concerns the way expressions are linked to personas a speaker can adopt in a conversation, and (ii) listeners enrich the meanings conveyed by expressions a speaker uses through recursive Bayesian inference. The latter is a clear virtue of the analysis. We can use the same machinery to model dogwhistles, which operate in the social meaning domain, that is used to model classic Gricean inferences, which concern the truth conditional domain of meaning. The former assumption, though, that dogwhistles operate in the domain of social meaning, is perhaps more controversial. Why not have them bear propositional content, perhaps in an alternative meaning dimension in a multidimensional semantic framework (e.g., Potts 2005)?

We have already seen one argument against this approach, and thus for an account in terms of social meaning, which is that speakers do not merely report their social personas, but actively construct them in concert with the listener throughout a conversation. Another way of saying this is that it is not right to think about social meanings as the kinds of things that can bear truth values. Another argument that identifying dogwhistles do not traffic in propositional content is that we can find completely non-linguistic examples.

We are interested in cases like the Fred Perry Polo shirt, a simple black one with yellow stripes at the sleeve and laurels at the breast. The brand has a long history of being associated with working class, subculture music scenes in Great Britain (Spencer 2020). The issue is that many of these music scenes have had overlap with racist / fascist political subcultures as well. The complex history of the polo makes it a perfect dogwhistle because one can wear it to indicate that one is a skinhead, but if called out, deny it by saying you just like punk music, pointing out that Amy Winehouse liked to wear one, etc. In the lead-up to the 2020 presidential election the black polo became the de facto uniform of the Proud Boys, a far-right neo-facist organization famed for engaging in violence at political rallies. A young, white man wearing a Fred Perry polo anywhere near a political event in 2020 would be sending a strong signal about their social persona, as well as political ideology, but one that would be undetectable to the average citizen. That is, they would be engaging in political dogwhistle communication, but non-verbally.

We do not want to say that, for instance, a piece of clothing can bear propositional content, but it would completely natural to claim that it bears social meaning.

Clothing, hairstyles, and other aspects of physical presentation have been taken in the sociolinguistic literature to work alone, as well as in concert with linguistic variants, to convey speaker personas—that is, to bear social meaning (Eckert 2012, who dubs this phenomenon *bricolage*). Once something bears social meaning, we expect that it will be usable to dogwhistle as long as the association between the bearer and the persona at issue is stronger in some populations and not others.

The important point is that the fact that we find non-linguistic identifying dogwhistles forces us to a non-propositional, social meaning account. Such an account should then obviously be used for the linguistic cases, as we have done in this chapter. The result is a unified account of dogwhistling across linguistic and non-linguistic modalities.

4.6 Conclusions

In this chapter we developed a comprehensive account of the first class of dogwhistles that we treat in this work, namely identifying dogwhistles. We show how dogwhistling emerges in RSA signaling games when messages are differentially linked with controversial personas across an audience of listeners. In such situations it can be optimal for a speaker to use a dogwhistle, which will partition the audience into groups that will more likely assign the speaker a different, utility-maximizing, sociolinguistic persona. Ultimately, because these dogwhistles concern the speaker's identity (for the purposes of the conversation), we can call these identifying dogwhistles. This chapter has also considered what linguistic (and non-linguistic) signals make good dogwhistles.

Note that throughout this chapter we have focused on the speaker. We have asked when might it be optimal for a speaker to dogwhistle, but not considered how listeners do/should react upon receiving a dogwhistle message and detecting it as such. In the current formal system all a listener may do is infer the speaker's persona and assign an affective value to the speaker in virtue of whether the persona is approved of or not. In the next two chapters we begin to take the listener's perspective as we further develop our account. In particular, we build an analysis in the next chapter of what we call *enriching* dogwhistles—dogwhistles that also convey some kind of propositional content to the listener in addition to signaling the speaker's sociolinguistic persona. We will be concerned with what the listener will be able to conclude about the ideological basis of the conversation on account of detecting a dogwhistle. Then, in Chapter 6, we will consider the implicatures a sociolinguistically aware speaker will be able to draw on hearing a dogwhistle, which we call vigilance implicatures. We will see that these are very much like standard implicatures we find in the truth-conditional domain, but instead operate over social meanings.

5
Enriching dogwhistles

In the last chapter, we considered the analysis of identifying dogwhistles. We treated such dogwhistles as signals that allow clued-in listeners to identify the social persona of the speaker (or, at least, a set of social personas compatible with the signal). In this chapter, we turn to another type of dogwhistle: the enriching dogwhistle, where the recognition of the dogwhistle alters the semantic content of the utterance that hosts it.

We looked in detail at several examples of identifying dogwhistles: George Bush's 'wonder-working power,' which tags him as an evangelical Christian or someone sympathetic to that worldview, and Jill Stein's 'big pharma,' which identifies her as someone familiar with anti-vaxx discourse. In these examples, the information acquired by a savvy interpreter is only the identities that Bush and Stein are projecting: the clued-in listener is able to figure out who they are, what their sympathies might be, and what kinds of discourses they are familiar with, though not (without further assumptions) whether they are genuinely part of the relevant communities. Thus, our analysis of the last chapter focused solely on how recognition of these identities proceeds and on how observing them affects the listener's attitudes toward the speaker.

Enriching dogwhistles do more. They change the truth-conditional content of the utterance in which they appear: the dogwhistle 'inner-city,' for example, no longer means just neighborhoods in highly built-up areas, but instead such neighborhoods inhabited primarily by people of color; this is a kind of enriched meaning, where content is added to the meaning of the dogwhistle as literally interpreted for truth-conditional content. Our aim in this chapter is to propose an account of dogwhistles of this type.

We begin by briefly reviewing the phenomenon and some previous accounts of it, focusing on Khoo's inferential account and on our own previous work. Both of these views are examined and found wanting, Khoo's account on grounds of—ultimately—a lack of engagement with the general theory of social meaning, and our own due to a lack of constraint because of its reliance on pragmatic enrichment in a general setting. Still, both of these views have attractive features. We draw the lesson that a proper account of enriching dogwhistles must handle enrichment in a way both consonant with theories of social meaning and which leaves the lexical meaning of the terms intact (and therefore, strictly speaking, the semantic content of the sentence).

The rest of the chapter proceeds as follows. We propose an account on which recognition of speaker persona invites certain kinds of inferences, which result in alterations of the meaning recovered by 'savvy' interpreters. Doing so requires some explication of the nature of personas and ideologies, and of the ways in which the recognition of someone's persona influences our views of the attitudes and beliefs they have; we address this set of issues in 5.1. We claim that certain kinds of personas, mainly those associated with ideologies and political stances, 'project' sets of beliefs and values.[1] Such projections enable certain kinds of invited inferences which, we claim, ground the phenomenon of enriching dogwhistles.

5.1 Personas and perspectives

Our account of dogwhistles so far has focused entirely on the domain of social meaning. This was a profitable strategy, for instance allowing us to account for the fact that dogwhistles are conventionalized as dogwhistles, but do not seem to bear conventionalized content outside their literal meanings. The insight is that their social meaning is what is conventionalized. While profitable, this strategy falls short when considering dogwhistles like *inner-city* that seem to convey more than just the speaker's sociolinguistic persona, as it fails to account for the kinds of enrichment that arise with them.

The question then becomes: how does the recognition of personas contribute to, or induce, changes in truth-conditional meaning? To answer that question, we must first consider what personas are, what they do, and how they influence the behavior and attitudes of those that identify them.

Suppose I hear someone use a dogwhistle. I'm a savvy listener, in this case; I identify the dogwhistle as what it is, and associate it with the relevant political position. Suppose that the dogwhistle in question is 'TRA' ('trans rights activist') which is used to signal trans-exclusionary political attitudes to savvy listeners. Upon recognizing the dogwhistle and associating it with the relevant ideology, I will draw conclusions about some of the attitudes and beliefs that the person using this term holds: in particular, I will take them to subscribe to some tenets of trans-exclusionary ideologies, with the degree of probability that I have assigned their association with the persona in question.

We argue that enriching dogwhistles acquire their enriched meanings via this process of persona recognition and drawing conclusions about the attitudes of the persona bearer, as derived via what is known about the ideology associated with the persona. Ideologies are associated with beliefs: in particular, on our analysis, generic statements about the properties people who are members of certain social groups and their activities, and value judgments associated with certain properties, activities, or attitudes. These, we argue, trigger enrichment when relevant conditions are met.

To spell this out, we need to say more about what personas *are*, and *do*. What does it mean to have a certain persona? It seems to us that there are at least two types of persona discussed in the literature. The first is exemplified by the Obama barbecue case discussed earlier: using the apical form of the gerund gives the impression of the speaker as a friendly person, and consequently as having personas like *cool guy* or *doofus*, while the velar version associates the speaker with the personas *asshole* and *stern*

---

[1] This picture, and social meanings in general, likely connect closely to the view of perspectives proposed by Camp (2013), though we will not pursue this connection further in this book.

leader. Such personas seem to us to mark the speaker as having certain kinds of social affect, liking certain kinds of people, and being open to certain kinds of discussion. The second kind of persona is more straightforwardly ideological or political in quality, and involves marking the speaker as subscribing to a particular ideology or having a particular kind of background, as with the evangelical association of *wonder-working power*. Such personas also indicate affect and (dis)approval of various actions or people, but also bring in more global assumptions about the world in the form of the beliefs associated with the ideology they project.[2] Thus, to understand what effects assigning personas to discourse agents has, we need to incorporate at minimum a way of valuating actions and individuals and a way of introducing beliefs and world knowledge to our models. This task is pressing because it underlines our analysis of how enriching dogwhistles work.

Our goal in this book is not to give an exhaustive formal model of what ideologies are and do, and what effects they might have on interpretation. Here, our aim is much more limited: to show how associating personas with speakers can have enriching effects on the content of what is said by those speakers, and how that interacts with dogwhistles, in those cases where personas are associated with ideologies. Consequently, we will give only the simplest possible formal model of ideology which allows us to show how this process works.

The formal model requires two elements, one to model the ways ideologies associate with approbation or disapprobation of various actions and persons, and one to model the association of personas with beliefs about the world. For the first, we make use of a function which assigns affective values, in a somewhat similar but more general way than what we have already done for personas themselves. For the second, we let personas associate with sets of world knowledge axioms (in the sense in which 'axiom' is used in the literature on commonsense reasoning; see, e.g., Reiter 1980; Lascarides and Copestake 1999 for discussion), which then play a role in the interpretation of those expressions whose meanings figure in background beliefs.

Recall the ν function from the last chapter, which is an agent-relativized function which maps personas to real numbers (positive numbers only for the speaker preference function ν_S and positive or negative for the listener function ν_L). The speaker function was already introduced by Burnett (2017, 2019), and the listener function turned out to be needed in order to model dogwhistles. But a similar sort of function can also be used to assign affective values to various things in a way dependent on personas, or, more generally, on ideologies. This is the tack we will adopt here for the first, value-assigning function of ideologies.

We need a function that can assign affective values to objects relevant to ideologies and personas; we proceed to define and discuss this now. We want to reserve the 'ν'

---

[2] These two categories probably don't exhaust the field of personas in any sense. What about indexical signals which indicate the social group the speaker belongs to, in e.g., the high school burnout vs. jock factions discussed by Eckert (1989)? These presumably are mainly signals of non-ideological identity, but they still have some ideological content associated with them in the sense we discuss below: burnouts don't like school, for example, while jocks believe that participation is important. We can conclude that either there's a cline or there are more categories than the two we focus on.

notation for the functions we use to assign preferences to personas, so we will use ρ ('rate') for our new function. This function takes individuals as input and yields real number as value: we allow both positive and negative real numbers here, as with the listener valuation function v_L on personas.

What are the individuals which are the input to this function? Particular ideologies can, of course, assign affective values to particular individuals: MAGA ideology highly values Donald Trump, for instance, while antifascist ideologies don't rate him quite so much. These ideologies themselves also assign low affective values to each other, which, assuming that we view ideologies themselves as individuals in a formal model, can be straightforwardly handled by ρ. But more generally ideologies tend to incorporate attitudes toward behaviors, groups of people, and properties, which are in turn adopted by those who adopt the ideology.

We can treat these as individuals by making use of the kind-mapping function '∩,' used to provide a semantics for nominalizations by Chierchia and Turner (1988) and for some interpretations of bare nominals in languages like Chinese and Japanese by Chierchia (2004), though with rather different underlying formalisms.[3] In (1-a), a predicate is applied to its nominal version, which Chierchia analyzes as involving an application of the predicate to the object-type associated with niceness; in (2-a), the kind-mapping operator is used to derive the kind of dogs from the bare nominal *inu* 'dog.'

(1) a. Being nice is nice.
    b. $\text{nice}(^\cap \text{nice})$

(2) a. inu-wa hoeru
       dog-Top barks
       'Dogs bark.'
    b. $\text{barks}(^\cap \text{dog})$

We will use this operator quite generally to derive individual-typed objects suitable as input to the valuating ρ function.

In personas, we find affective values assigned to all sorts of things. Burnett, in work on slurs and ideologies (Burnett 2020), introduces a valuation function which plays a role in the construction of ideologies, which are construed within conceptual spaces theory (Gärdenfors 2004), i.e., vector spaces of the same sort used to ground formal models of cognitive lexical semantics. On this view, ideological structures have the form $\langle D, \text{sim}, \text{PERS}, \mu \rangle$, where $\langle D, \text{sim} \rangle$ is a $|D|$-dimensional vector space and sim a similarity function on points in such spaces. PERS is a set of points which correspond to personas in this ideological space. Finally, μ is a function partitioning personas into positively and negatively valued ones. Ideologies for Burnett thus amount to valuations of personas, which themselves are positionings along various property vectors.

---

[3] Thanks to Barbara Partee for reminding us of Chierchia's analysis of examples like (1-a).

Burnett's intended application is to slurs, or, more generally, to thick terms which derive their thickness from affective judgments about social elements. The idea is that particular words can interact with ideologies, which themselves are assignments of value to points on certain dimensions relevant to the ideological stance. Burnett's main examples are *lesbian* and *dyke*: she claims that *dyke* is associated with a kind of radical or punk stance within a same-sex attracted community of women, which is then assigned various valences: positive by people who like such a stance (feminist punks) and negative for more 'mainstream' women within the community. Here affective values are assigned to the relatively specific anti-authoritarian stance conveyed by *dyke* for those speakers with access to its use within the lesbian community.

We are sympathetic to this view, but we are not going to adopt it entirely, because we are unsure that it is sufficiently general to account for certain ideologies, or at least if applied to them it comes with certain commitments which we are reluctant to take on. Consider the cases of *dyke* and *lesbian* once again. Burnett takes these personas to be set within three dimensions (vectors): masculinity, same-gender sexual desire, and radical stance. Each of these has two endpoints: masculinity and femininity, more or less same-gender desire, and pro- vs. anti-mainstream. We are already somewhat unsure how to understand these dimensions: how are masculinity and femininity defined? What are the correlates of strength of desire? Where do we place personas which don't seem to fit cleanly into these scales, which are ultimately derived from binaries?

For instance, this analysis, where sexuality is derived via strength of desire as placed on a binary scale, makes it non-obvious to us how to understand bisexuality. One might respond that we just have multiple scales: one for same-gendered and one for different-gendered sexual desires; but does this mean that, ontologically speaking, bisexual identities are literally more complex than straight or gay identities (gay in the sense of purely same-sex-desiring)? And what happens to desire for people who don't fit the gender binary? These questions can be given answers, and presumably arise in part as an artifact of the particular example Burnett chooses, though it does seem to us that other examples are going to raise possibly similar problems of their own. In any case, the answers these questions require seem to us to require theoretical commitments that are far beyond what looks strictly speaking needed to make sense of the meanings of slurs, or of bigotry more generally. But our main worry is elsewhere anyway: this way of constructing ideologies appears to us to put all its weight on personas, but we think this method is not universally applicable.

Consider the homophobic ideology Burnett discusses, which has a strong negative affect for same-gender sexual desire. But how can a bigot know whether someone genuinely has such a desire? This is just a standard epistemological problem arising in a new setting: what access does an external observer have to someone's internal states? And here it does seem to make sense to link this affect to persona, broadly conceived: it is the external expression of such desire that creates negative affect in bigots toward those who show their desire. We thus have to tie negative affect to the external expression of persona in order to make sense of how the theory is to work. The problem is that it doesn't seem that everything bigots hate is persona-based.

An obvious example is race. There are, of course, conversations to be had about what (and, ontologically, if) race is, and the debate is intense and ongoing (see Mallon 2016 for a fairly recent overview of some of this discussion). But race, despite being at least in part socially construed and so legible from one's social or linguistic behavior, is also read directly from the body. We typically think of bigotry about race as directed at abstractions (or caricatures) of individuals with certain kinds of bodies and skin colors, and of racist ideologies as having hateful and discriminatory positions ultimately directed at people with certain kinds of racialized bodies. But bodies are not in themselves social positions, and they are not personas. Racists don't hate 'Black social personas,' whatever that might mean: they hate Black people.

For this reason, we are reluctant to let personas mediate all ideologically based affect. We instead simply use the kind-deriving function and ascribe to bigots a hatred for certain kinds, for instance toward Black people, which will be modeled in the formal theory by giving $\rho_i(\cap \text{black\_person})$ a negative value. This function can also be used to give values to the kinds associated with the properties Burnett describes in the context of *lesbian* and *dyke*, for instance $\cap \text{lesbian}$. As with race, precisely what this kind amounts to can be outsourced to auxiliary definitions, if indeed definition is the right method for making sense of categories like race and sexuality.[4]

It is somewhat more difficult to pick out the object of evaluation for the anti-authoritarianism associated with *dyke*: should we take a positive affect to be assigned to $\cap \text{antiauthoritarian\_attitude}$ or to $\cap \text{antiauthoritarian\_person}$? It seems obvious to us that punks like both antiauthoritarian concepts and people who act on these concepts, but the way these categories relate to each other at the level of value ascription associated with ideologies is less clear. We think this is an aspect of the general problem of effability which is often found around concepts with affective content, as discussed in different ways in the literature on expressive content (e.g., Potts 2007; McCready 2010) and on thick concepts (e.g., Väyrynen 2013). As such, we will put the general question aside here, assume that both kinds of things are in play as the object of affective attitudes, and return to linguistic applications.

Before we do, though, we should add one caveat about the whole project of assigning affective values.[5] Isn't the project of trying to define attitudes in terms of real numbers excessively reductive, or even impossible? It is, clearly, reductive, something not disputed by anyone who employs numerical values in the linguistic analysis of attitudes, or even real-numbered intervals, as with Potts (2007) on expressive meanings, or McCready (2019), who aims to model the formality of contexts; all these authors, to our knowledge, concede that the sharpness of real numbers fails to coincide perfectly with the blurriness of attitudes, and so that there's an element of arbitrariness to

---

[4] See in this context the literature on conceptual engineering, e.g., Haslanger (2000); Cappelen (2018), where some of the limits of the conceptual analysis method of using definitions to make sense of concepts and, by extension, words and categories become clear, particularly perhaps for the case of social categories.

[5] Thanks to a reviewer for pressing us on this point.

the values they give, something we would also readily concede about our own analysis (and already have, in the discussion of utility values assigned to personas).

It might be illustrative to look at one such model to see how much water the numbers are meant to hold. McCready (2019) is an analysis of honorific expressions in several languages, where each honorific expressively introduces an interval in [0,1]; the context also contains a similarly structured interval understood as a parameter indicating the formality of the speech situation. For contexts, McCready derives these single intervals from a multidimensional space corresponding to aspects of the relationship of speaker and hearer and the current speech situation. This is straightforwardly done by taking the average of the parameters considered. In this sense, it's clear that the intervals, though one-dimensional, are derived from multiple dimensions; the same likely holds for the kinds of affect we discuss here (and can be derived from multiple parameters in a similar way), though we won't go into detail, both because we aren't fully sure of what affective parameters are in play and because doing so is somewhat orthogonal to the work we want affect to do in ideologies. The general question of how affect is derived is, however, an important one, and one we hope to engage with more closely in the future.

The second piece of the puzzle is the kinds of beliefs associated with ideologies. Ideologies, as we saw above, assign positive value to certain behaviors, practices, and groups of people, and negative value to others; they also are, themselves, sets of beliefs about how the world is: the kinds of things that comprise it, the properties of kinds of people, systems, and objects, and the causal elements that induce and condition change. Beliefs like these are easily modeled as propositions; the truth-evaluable elements which make up an ideology are then modelable as sets of such propositions. We call each set of this kind the *basis* of an ideology. As we will show, ideological bases are the drivers of enrichment by dogwhistles.

What sorts of propositions form the basis of ideologies? The answers to this question are as various as ideologies themselves, but, for cases relevant to dogwhistles, involve beliefs about aspects of the world. For instance, anti-vaxx ideology takes it as a given that vaccines have negative effects, and that they are promoted by pharmaceutical companies as a part of exploitative capitalist strategies. QAnon ideology assumes the existence of a conspiracy with bizarre goals. Racist ideologies involve beliefs about the relative value and superiority of ethnic groups, and so on. All these beliefs can function to bridge gaps in reasoning and connect things that would be otherwise non-obvious: for instance, it might not seem plausible to the nonsubscriber to white supremacist ideology that when a nonwhite person is hired for a university position, the reason must involve affirmative action, but to the white supremacist, it will be obvious, because of the beliefs they hold as a result of subscribing to the white supremacist ideology. We argue that it is these sorts of beliefs, and ideological bases in general, that trigger enriching dogwhistles.

Turning to formalization, let us use the notation $\mathcal{B}$ for ideological bases. The upshot of the preceding discussion is that the ideologies related to personas have the form $\iota = \langle \rho, \mathcal{B} \rangle$ and so consist of pairs of affect-assigning functions and ideological bases.

Since the propositions comprising the basis of an ideology can be somewhat indeterminate and vary from individual to individual depending on where they have acquired their ideological beliefs, we must think in terms of related but possibly non-identical ideologies, which we can view as ideological equivalence classes: we thus define the basis of an ideology as the set of beliefs common to all its variants (here Π is a projection function, which we use a slightly non-standard notation for in order to avoid confusion with personas, which are written with the more standard lowercase π).

(3) $\Pi_2(\iota) =_{df} \bigcap \Pi_2(\iota')$, where $\iota' \sim \iota$.

We need to make one assumption about the relation between persona and belief for the analysis to go through, however. Fortunately, it's an independently necessary one. It starts with the question of what personas are available for an individual. That is, in a linguistic context, what kinds of personas can a speaker assume or signal? We assume here that speaker personas are required to be sincerely assumed. By sincerity we mean that when a speaker signals an ideological persona, ie one which comes with a basis, the basis of that persona correlates with the speaker's actual beliefs. This is an analogue of Gricean Quality for the domain of social meaning, which we will call *Social Sincerity*; this principle in turn means that speakers can only signal personas which have a basis in beliefs they actually have.

Formally speaking, this amounts to requiring the personas compatible with the speaker's utterance, **emf**(u), to associate with bases which have some relationship to the speaker's beliefs. The strength of this relationship is open to question, partly because of the indeterminacy of ideological content mentioned above, an issue we will say more about in a moment. For the purposes of our current project, we define a sincerity principle for social meaning-borne ideologies which requires the speaker to believe most of the propositions in the basis of each ideology compatible with their utterance.

(4) *Social Sincerity*
$\forall s, u, \pi[\text{utter}(s)(u) \wedge \pi \in \mathbf{emf}(u) \wedge \iota_\pi \rightarrow \text{MOST}(p \in \Pi_2(\iota_\pi))(\text{Bel}(s,p))]$
'If a speaker utters a sentence compatible with persona π, they believe a significant number of the propositions comprising the basis for π.'

Three comments on this principle, followed by one application. It is relatively weak in the sense that it simply requires the speaker to hold most of the beliefs associated with the ideology. It could easily be strengthened by using a different quantifier, or by moving over to an underlying theory which took sincerity to depend more directly on context, for instance by using a contextually determined parameter for sincerity in the manner of Kennedy (2007) on vague predicates or McCready (2015) for reliability of information source. It also treats all beliefs in $\Pi_2(\iota)$ identically, but likely some of these beliefs are more 'core' to the ideology than others: this can be modeled by weighting them in something like the manner found in the belief revision literature on entrenchment (e.g., Gärdenfors 2004), itself a way of understanding the work of

Quine on 'webs of belief' (Quine 1951). For present purposes we will not introduce these complexities.

A third, thornier issue involves personas that aren't associated with ideologies. Such personas won't have an ideological basis, so there won't be a way to apply Social Sincerity to them. But presumably we want them to be sincerely projected too. Can a speaker just willy-nilly signal any old persona, as long as there's not an ideological basis associated with it? Here though we can turn to the basic structure of our model, which implicitly already answers this question. Speakers choose what persona to project on the basis of their utility functions. They won't pick personas that don't maximize utility for them. A person who's neither friendly nor informal just won't want to project the *Cool Guy* or *Doofus* personas via use of apical gerunds, because they won't want to come off that way, which is something that will be reflected in the way their utilities are assigned.

One might think at this point that Social Sincerity isn't needed for ideology-associated personas either, because the utilities will ground sincere use in just the way discussed in the previous paragraph. But we think there's a crucial difference here. Personas like *Cool Guy* are constructed through active negotiation between speaker and hearer; using an apical variant will lead to looking like a cool person in the best case, but if the hearer's priors don't support that, one might end up judged to be a doofus instead. But more importantly there isn't (socially) a fact of the matter about whether one is a cool guy or a doofus, persona-wise: social facts like this are put together in discourse in a dynamic process, which is why Social Meaning games look the way they do as opposed to standard Lewisian signaling games, where communicating the facts is paramount (Lewis 1969).

Put in another way, there's no objective correlate of personas like this, or of the jock/burnout personas discussed by Eckert: placing yourself in the category, if successful, places you in the category. This isn't the case for all personas, though. In particular, it doesn't seem to be the case for ideology-associated personas. I might have reasons to signal adherence to ideologies that differ from my actual beliefs in a particular context, and indeed it happens every day with people who have reason in some situation to hide their political beliefs, gender, or sexualities, among many other categories. Otherwise put, utilities might not always track belief, which we can think of as a verifiable correlate of persona given Social Sincerity, but not without it. For this kind of case, then, Social Sincerity looks to be needed after all.[6]

One issue we have not addressed directly is exactly how speakers come to associate ideologies with particular personas. This point relates closely to the question of how dogwhistles arise as linguistic phenomena, and by extension (assuming, as we do, that dogwhistles correlate with social meanings): how does a particular piece of content—a persona—become associated with a lexical expression? We think an answer can be

---

[6] One could also think of Social Sincerity as pushing some persona-related content back into the truth conditions. If the speaker doesn't actually have the relevant beliefs, the content of the utterance will fail to be truth-tracking, and so game players will fail to maximize utility because the full state of the world won't be communicated, just as with other games that enforce maximal information transmission.

found in the idea of communities of practice as discussed for instance by Quaranto (2022). A linguistic community of practice is essentially a community in which a practice of using a particular expression in a certain way has developed over time. For Quaranto, dogwhistles rely on the existence of multiple communities who use a given expression in different ways, so that it starts to have multiple meanings. Quaranto doesn't stress this point, but we don't think we need to think of these as conventional meanings in the truth-conditional sense. Rather, they can be differences in how expressions are associated with social positioning in those communities: essentially, social meanings in the sense we've given of associating personas with the expressions. Once an expression has multiple personas associated with it (within different communities of practice), those in the know about practices in those multiple communities can extract information about ideology from it, given that they assume sincerity in the speaker as described above.

With this machinery in place, we are ready to turn to our account of enriching dogwhistles. Before we do, though, we want to briefly discuss one point that arises in the context of *Social Sincerity*: is it really right to assume that all signals of personas are properly correlated by the speaker with the beliefs comprising the relevant ideology? Consider, for example, a case in which an agent becomes familiar with political discussions of some issue via a particular community, for instance within some 'bubble' on Twitter, and that in the course of following the discussion she acquires some relevant terminology. In many cases terminology learned in this way will include dogwhistles, or even slurs, which signal certain kinds of ideologies in ways much more direct than dogwhistles do. But it can still be the case that the speaker doesn't hold the relevant ideologies. An example might be a speaker who is deeply pro-vaxx but also watches a lot of anti-vaxx discussion on the internet and learns the term 'big pharma' discussed in the previous chapter, but just parses it as equivalent to 'pharmaceutical industry.' Such a speaker might well use 'big pharma' without any kind of intention of dogwhistling. We might fault a speaker like this for being bad at figuring out the meanings and associations of the terms they observe, but we wouldn't fault them for being anti-vaxx. This line between vigilance and hypervigilance in dogwhistle detection is a difficult issue which we consider in detail in Chapter 6; for now, we put it aside.

This does point up a problem with *Social Sincerity*: simply put, it overgenerates sincerity. But we think this is not so much a problem with the principle but with the way in which people interpret the social meanings of utterances. The issue is closely related to one well known in variationist sociolinguistics: is it really the case that intentionality can be ascribed to all indexical variables or are some produced without the intention of the speaker? How does intentionality interact with the ascription of identities? This issue has recently been discussed extensively from a more formal perspective by Acton (2022). We don't want to go deep into this complex issue here. Rather, we want to understand *Social Sincerity* as a default principle which makes explicit the heuristic by which we assume that people are sincere in their social presentation, and aware of it; sometimes this turns out to be wrong, but we think the basic heuristic assumption is as natural as Gricean Quality, and as useful, which helps us to understand why (also like Quality) the principle may tend to be overapplied.

5.2 Proposal: Personas induce enrichment

We are now in a position to return to enriching dogwhistles. It might already be clear in outline how the machinery just introduced plays into the enrichment process we observe there; this section begins by sketching this process, and then turns to working through a pair of examples to show the action of the theory. We then provide some supporting evidence for our view from experiments on racial bias and language, and also compare the account to Khoo's view and to our own previous work; finally, we turn, in the next section, to some brief comments on standpoints and close this chapter.

The flow of interpretation goes as follows. The speaker produces an utterance which includes an enriching dogwhistle. Enriching dogwhistles, on our view, function via the communication of personas. The savvy hearer recognizes the persona, just as with identifying dogwhistles; but here the persona is associated with an ideology and consequently with an ideological basis. Further, suppose that there is some relevant proposition in the basis, which interacts with the (other) content of the utterance, generally its truth-conditional, at-issue content, and allows the computation of an inference. All this together allows enrichment to occur.

5.3 Application and comparison with other views

Recall our previous discussion of enriching dogwhistles. Our leading example there was *inner-city*, as drawn from Paul Ryan's utterance. This dogwhistle indicates a sort of quasiracist persona to savvy listeners, which is, of course, associated with a quasiracist ideology ι. Suppose that $\Pi_2(\iota)$ ('Π_2' again a projection function here picking out the second element of the tuple ι) contains the proposition

$$\text{live\_inner\_city}(x) > \text{black\_person}(x),$$

i.e., that people living in the inner-city are generally Black ('>' here is a conditional in a default logic, cf. Reiter 1980). Together with the at-issue content of Ryan's statement, that people living in the inner-city lack a culture of work, this proposition allows the interpreter to derive the inference that such people are also Black, which constitutes and further contributes to a racialized and negative view of Black people. Thus, given the analysis of ideologies we have proposed and the way in which the recognition of personas induces associations with ideologies, we end up with a straightforward account of enriching dogwhistles.

It can easily be seen how this view improves on our own previous work, and on that of Khoo. In our previous work, we treated enriching dogwhistles as simply inducing a kind of pragmatic enrichment along the lines of what is found with (5), taken from Recanati (2003). This sentence, spoken by a mother to her young child on the playground who's just fallen and skinned her knee, is strictly speaking false, since (as far as we know) we're all going to die; but in context it is interpreted as stating that the cut won't kill the child, which is presumably true. This process can be understood as simply allowing context to make the statement into a sensible one.

(5) You're not going to die (*from that cut*).

But this isn't completely parallel to what we see with enriching dogwhistles, where enrichment is crucially mediated (on our view) by the recovery of a persona. In our previous work, we had no principled answer to the question of how enrichment relates to particular dogwhistles; the current picture, on which enrichment depends on persona recognition, is a clear improvement, especially because the analysis becomes a straightforward extension of our account of identifying dogwhistles.

It is also a clear improvement on Khoo's account. Recall that Khoo presents a deflationary view on which enrichment in dogwhistles is the simple result of an inferential process. On this aspect, Khoo's account is similar to our own; but ours differs in its tie to persona, which allows us to overcome the problem of inferences from extensionally equivalent terms that we argued in Chapter 2 to be a crucial issue for Khoo's view. On a pure invited inference view, coextensive expressions should induce the same enrichments even when only one functions as a dogwhistle, but this is not the case; on our view, this falls out directly from the fact that it's the recovery of personas from particular expressions and consequent recognition of speaker ideologies that allows the inference to be triggered, instead of the pure semantic meaning of the expression itself.[7]

Finally, our account allows us to better understand cases where dogwhistles seem to trigger Relevance-like implicatures. We take George Bush's reference to the *Dred Scott* decision as a canonical case. Recall that Bush was asked about who he would choose to fill a Supreme Court vacancy. His response was that he would appoint justices who would enforce the constitution and not rule based on personal opinions, like justices did in the *Dred Scott* case. While *Dred Scott* was a decision ruling that enslaved people (and their descendents) had no claim to US citizenship and so had no standing in federal court, it is widely known as an anti-abortion dogwhistle. The reason is that in anti-abortion rhetoric *Roe vs. Wade*, which established the right to an abortion, is consistently referred to as a decision as equally bad (and deserving to be overruled contra precendent) as *Dred Scott*.

Both Saul (2018) and Lo Guercio and Caso (2022) argue that this additional anti-abortion content is a Relevance implicature. The idea is that Bush's reference was not

---

[7] Breitholtz and Cooper (2021) also propose a means of getting around the coextensionality problem, but their proposed solution which utilizes hyperintensionality within type theory with records, while it does solve the problem, fails to provide a principled explanation of why particular expressions trigger the relevant patterns of inference (topoi). In this sense, it's similar to our own previous theory in Henderson and McCready (2017), which we argued earlier to be insufficient in a way that's solved by the analysis in the current chapter.

relevant to the question of which modern judges to appoint because *Dred Scott* is an century-old decision that no longer has the force of law. A listener who assumes the speaker is following Relevance must enrich what was said in order to establish the relevance of the speaker's contribution. In particular, an anti-abortion listener will enrich *Dred Scott* to be *Dred Scott and Roe vs. Wade*.

We objected to this account because it seems to mix up who should be computing Relevance implicatures. For listeners who are intimately familiar with anti-abortion rhetoric the discussion of *Dred Scott* is not irrelevant at all. It is perfectly relevant. In this worldview, *Roe vs. Wade* is a decision on par with *Dred Scott* and abortion abolishonists are the moral equivalents of the slavery abolishonists who fought against *Dred Scott*. No Relevance-based implicature is needed, and none should be generated. In contrast, it is precisely those people who would not hear the dogwhistle who need to enrich the meaning of *Dred Scott* in order to ensure that the speaker is conforming to the maxim of Relevance.

Our account of enriching dogwhistles allows us to understand how anti-abortion activists interpret George Bush's answer without appealing to a Relevance implicature, which we think does not correspond to the contours of how listeners reason in this case. For us, *Dred Scott* would bear social meaning by virtue of being a common phrase used in anti-abortion rhetoric. A savvy listener would be able to assign Bush a sociolinguistic persona based on its use—namely as an anti-abortion evangelical. This is a kind of person that is clearly linked to an ideology with a basis rich in propositional content. In particular, that ideology bears a deontic proposition asserting the necessity of overturning *Roe vs. Wade* if it is necessary to overturn *Dred Scott* (given that they are moral equivalents).

$$\Box\text{overturn}(\text{dred\_scott}) > \Box\text{overturn}(\text{roe\_vs\_wade})$$

This proposition is enough to drive the enriched meaning of what Bush said, without appealing to a Relevance-based implicature. It simply follows as an entailment from what was said and common ground established by the ideology. George Bush wants to appoint judges who do what they should do (interpret the constitution), unlike what those judges did in *Dred Scott*. That is, he will appoint judges who agree to the proposition $\Box\text{overturn}(\text{dred\_scott})$. Given the ideological background induced by persona, they must also agree that $\Box\text{overturn}(\text{roe\_vs\_wade})$. This is precisely the inference we hoped to account for. Crucially, we did not need to appeal to Gricean maxims, like Relevance, nor did we have to enrich the meaning of *Dred Scott*. We only have to realize that personas can be linked to ideologies.

5.4 Other evidence: Experiments on bias

Our theory provides what we take to be a convincing explanation of the way that enrichment arises in certain dogwhistles as an extension of the process of identifying speaker personas. But this is not the only reason to adopt a theory which involves the recognition of ideology in the way that ours does. The gap between invited inference and persona-based computation can also be seen in experimental results presented in Hurwitz and Peffley (2005) in work on racial dogwhistles.

These experiments show a difference in the kinds of biases that people of different racial backgrounds exhibit on post-tests after exposure to racial dogwhistles. White people were found to unconsciously assign stereotypes to racial minorities after such exposure, but this didn't arise with Black people, despite them knowing that the terms in question are in fact racial dogwhistles. For white people, further, it was shown that if they were informed prior to exposure that the expression was a dogwhistle, the new biases didn't arise.

We conclude from this study that hearing the dogwhistle and recognizing it as one, together with the persona that it signals, doesn't directly cause interpreters to make the enriching inferences that it enables. But it's also possible for the ideology associated with the persona to 'bleed over' into a person's epistemic states, or at least factor to some degree into their judgments, perhaps not to the level of inducing overt inferences or enrichment but at least to the degree that bias and stereotypes become subconscious factors in making judgments (the 'poisoning of the well' discussed in Saul 2018). Black participants in these studies aren't susceptible to this, because the ideology that these racial dogwhistles convey is one that's inimical to them and which they are therefore already primed to resist.[8] White participants, too, once made aware of the negative nature of the dogwhistle are similarly primed for pushing back. But without these prior cues or sensitivity, the ideology the dogwhistle conveys appears to become salient enough to affect attitudes, regardless of the attitudes the person takes themselves to have (at least in some cases).

What this means is that one can recognize the dogwhistle and what it means to do in terms of enrichment without actually performing the enrichment or adopting any elements of the ideology associated with the conveyed persona. This fact shows again that a deflationary theory like Khoo's is too simple to account for the full range of phenomena associated with enriching dogwhistles, or, of course, dogwhistles in general.

5.5 Conclusions

With this section we have essentially finished the first part of this book. We have a complete account of how dogwhistles work, and how dogwhistled meaning is related

---

[8] A reviewer brings up the interesting issue of *stereotype threat*, where potentially conforming to negative stereotypes affects individual behavior/performance. This is, of course, a large topic, but stereotype threat plausibly arises via a different mechanism than being (un)consciously guided to accept certain background propositions via dogwhistles. We assume that inoculation against dogwhistles is successful when the listener recognizes the speaker wants to have a conversation on certain ideological grounds, but the listener refuses to admit the offensive propositions of that ideology to the common ground. Note that stereotype threat could still occur, even if a listener is, in our terms, successfully inoculated against the dogwhistle that tried to smuggle stereotypes into the common ground. The listener would still learn the speaker believes in those stereotypes, and so worry about fulfilling them, giving their interlocutor confirmatory evidence.

to other kinds of meaning. The main takeaways are the dogwhistles do not traffic in truth-conditional meaning, but instead bear social meaning. Social meaning is determined interactionally, which we modeled via signaling games over social meanings. This chapter has allowed us to link up social meanings to truth-conditional content, though without conventionalizing this truth-conditional content. This was needed because dogwhistles do seem to convey more information than just who their user presents themselves to be. We dubbed this the enriching aspect of dogwhistles and showed that it follows once we allow social personas to be linked to ideologies, which is a natural extension. Ideologies, in virtue of containing propositional content—beliefs endorsed by the ideology—means that listeners, on detecting a dogwhistle, can use the speaker's detected persona, and their ideology, to enrich the truth-conditional content of what was said.

With this account in place we can now extend the account in various ways, which is what we will do throughout the remaining chapters. We begin in the next two chapters to consider the pragmatics of dogwhistles. The next chapter, Chapter 6, returns to questions of implicature. If dogwhistles bear social meaning, instead of truth-conditional meaning, then what kinds of implicatures over social meanings can be drawn by listeners detecting a dogwhistle? This discussion of how listeners should react to dogwhistles in discourse will then open a broader discussion of the sociopragmatics of dogwhistles, which will be the concern of the final chapters of this work, where we will ask (among other things) how the use of dogwhistles should affect our assessment of the speaker's testimonial reliability, and when is it optional to abandon dogwhistles for overt appeals, even if taboo.

6
Vigilance and hypervigilance

We emphasized in laying out the formal apparatus in the first half of this book that dogwhistles support the idea that the construction of personas is interactional. Speakers balance their desire to be assigned a particular persona with how the audience will (dis)approve of that persona. We have then asked under what conditions it is optimal for a speaker to dogwhistle, and what kinds of messages, ideological or otherwise, are sent by dogwhistles. In this chapter we will continue to explore how listeners do/should react to dogwhistles, given that persona construction is interactional. In particular, we return to the core RSA framework developed in Chapter 4 and consider the behavior of L_1, the sociolinguistically aware listener. How should a listener optimally reason about a speaker's persona, assuming a speaker that is attempting to maximize their social utility relative to an audience?

The answer to this question, from a formal perspective, is an easy one. The heart of the RSA framework is a recursive reasoning process with listeners reasoning about the messages that speakers would send to less sophisticated listeners. Optimal behavior for a sociolinguistically aware listener is thus immediately given as follows, where, as we have discussed in detail, $P_{S_1}(u|p)$ is based on the social utility of attempting to use message u to receive persona p in speaking to some audience.

$$P_{L_1}(p|u) \propto P_{S_1}(u|p) \times P(p)$$

The sociolinguistically aware listener is thus determining the speaker's persona given their message by modeling how that speaker reasons about their message choice relative to the audience (which includes the listener themselves).

The more interesting question is whether this formal model successfully captures the observed behavior of such listeners. Here we are at a slight disadvantage compared to the situation of formal models of 'standard' pragmatics because the RSA framework was developed against the backdrop of a large pragmatic literature that had already identified a wide range of phenomena that a successful theory of pragmatic listeners should account for. In contrast, the literature on dogwhistles has focused more on the expressions themselves, their covert content, and how speakers deploy them (e.g., in the service of propaganda). There is essentially no literature on how a rational listener should behave in conversations where dogwhistles are likely, which the sociolinguistically aware listener can determine by modeling the speaker computing the social utility of various messages in the context.

This chapter begins to look at this question and identifies two strategies that we see in actual listeners, which we dub *vigilance* and *hypervigilance*. The first follows from the RSA theory we have developed in previous chapters, and, in fact, we will see that it involves a standard kind of implicature familiar from the RSA literature on implicatures in the truth-conditional domain. What we find is that a sociolinguistically aware listener should be more likely to detect a dogwhistle than the literal listener in conversational contexts where dogwhistling is utility-maximizing for the speaker. This is what we dub a *vigilance* implicature.

The second phenomenon concerns listeners who are quick to call communicative acts dogwhistles—i.e., they are being hypervigilant against dogwhistling. To model hypervigilance we have to move outside the core RSA framework developed thus far, but we remain in the realm of signaling games. We show that hypervigilance is related to the credibility result for cheap talk games of Farrell (1993), where a neologism is credible to the degree that the interests of the sender align with those of the receiver. In particular, identifying some expression as a dogwhistle—a deceptive neologism—is related to the extent that speaker and listener interests are misaligned, which we model in terms of the affective values for the sociolinguistic personas at play.

6.1 Vigilance

When observing a speaker using an expression we know to be a dogwhistle, what is the proper reaction? For a moment we want to back away from what our formal model predicts and ask about our intuitions concerning how agents should and do react. The problem, of course, is that upon hearing a dogwhistle, it is possible that the expression is being used innocently, an issue also discussed in earlier chapters. For instance, speakers often hear dogwhistles without recognizing them—in fact, that is how a good dogwhistle should work—and so one may pick up expressions from certain discourses, especially political discourse, without knowing their dogwhistle quality.

Note that this does not make the dogwhistle not pernicious. Saul (2018) talks about the negative effects of non-intentional dogwhistles on the discourse, context even in quoted speech, say, in new broadcasts that replay soundbites with dogwhistles. That work, though, does not consider how the listener should appraise a speaker that uses a dogwhistle non-intentionally. Our intuition is that intent matters, and so we should be less likely to assign that speaker the sociolinguistic persona associated with that dogwhistle. Additionally, following the discussion in Chapter 5, we should be less likely to ascribe beliefs to such a speaker which follow from an ideology associated with the persona.

The conclusion that intent matters means that the 'literal listener' approach, in RSA terms, cannot be right. We cannot simply compute the probability a speaker bears the persona associated with the dogwhistle from the raw frequency association between the dogwhistle and that person (and our prior for the speaker). Instead, we must consider more fine-grained facts about the local discourse context, for instance whether it is likely to be utility-maximizing for the speaker in the current context to use an intentionally deceptively dogwhistle. If so, we should be even more likely to assign the speaker the persona they are attempting to conceal than the raw frequency of association between persona and message should suggest. That is, we need a sociolinguistically aware listener that draws implicatures in the domain of social meaning, just as a standard pragmatic listener draws implicatures in the truth-conditional domain of meaning. A major result of this work is that the RSA-style account developed in the previous two chapters immediately predicts such vigilance implicatures, which confirms the unity of pragmatic reasoning across meaning domains.

6.1.1 Implicatures in RSA

Recall that in RSA accounts of implicature calculation, listeners (beyond the literal listener), take into account the process that generated the speaker's utterance in determining the meaning, rather than just literal utterance meeting. In particular, if it is more likely, for whatever reason, that the speaker will choose a message to convey a state than the raw semantic probability that the message conveys that state, a pragmatically aware listener, reasoning that the speaker will do this, will also assign the same linkage between state and message a rate higher than raw semantic probability.

Frank and Goodman (2012) illustrates this process especially cleanly with a simple reference game. In this game, the speaker is shown a blue square, a blue circle, or a green square, and is asked to send a message—*blue, green, square, circle*—so that a listener will correctly select the observed object. In this game, the literal listener takes any objects that satisfy the predicate sent by the speaker to be equally likely. Thus, on hearing *blue*, given that there are two blue objects, the literal listener will guess that that speaker is referring to the blue square half of the time and referring to the blue circle the other half of the time. Reasoning in this way, we get the following values.

Literal Listener

	blue square	blue circle	green square
blue	.5	.5	0
green	0	0	1
square	.5	0	.5
circle	0	1	0

Putting ourselves in the speaker's shoes, we can ask how a pragmatically aware agent should talk to the literal listener to improve their chances of successfully referring. Let's focus on our blue shapes. Note that on observing a blue circle, we should prefer saying *circle* over *blue* because, in the latter case, there is a 50% chance the literal listener will incorrectly pick the blue square. Assuming a temperature of 1, the speaker will generate messages at the following frequency, which, as we can see, follows our intuition that *circle* should be preferred over *blue* when presented with a blue circle.

Speaker

	blue square	blue circle	green square
blue	.5	.33	0
green	0	0	.66
square	.5	0	.33
circle	0	.66	0

This asymmetry between *circle* and *blue* in the case of blue circle alone is already enough to generate an implicature for an agent listening to such a speaker. We can consult our intuitions about how we would react to hearing *blue* from such a speaker. Now, if we didn't know what kind of speaker we were listening to, on hearing *blue* our best guess would be to flip a coin and pick the blue square or the blue circle. They are both consistent with the literal meaning of *blue*, and this is what the literal listener would do, as we see in the table above. The calculation changes, though, if we know we are listening to a pragmatically aware speaker. This speaker prefers *circle* when seeing a blue circle. This depresses the frequency they use *blue* for blue circle and so increases the relative frequency of using *blue* on seeing a blue square. Thus, when hearing *blue* from this speaker, we should not flip a coin, but guess blue square. It is the more likely referent.

This calculation is precisely what a pragmatic listener does. We see the results in the table below. Note the bump in probability for blue square when hearing *blue* over the literal listener. This is the result of pragmatic enrichment.

Pragmatic Listener

	blue square	blue circle	green square
blue	.6	.4	0
green	0	0	1
square	.6	0	.4
circle	0	1	0

The listener reasons about how the speaker would communicate with the literal listener, and so generates an implicature that certain meanings are more likely for certain forms because of a preference, in the context, for the speaker to use that form for that meaning. We can now see that implicatures with the exact same structural origins are generated in the social meaning domain. In the case of dogwhistles, for listeners acquainted with the dogwhistle, the result is what we call a vigilance implicature.

6.1.2 Social meaning implicatures in RSA

The structure of the Social Meaning Games for dogwhistles developed in Chapter 4 for identifying dogwhistles is analogous to the reference game presented in the previous section. In particular, none of the messages semantically entail any other, but just as with the reference game, the speaker's type—their desired persona—is consistent with multiple messages, just like both *blue* and *square* are consistent with reporting the observation of a blue square.[1] The implicature is generated in terms of mutual attention. The speaker reasons that certain expressions in the local context, while perhaps semantically equivalent to other expressions in terms of consistency with the referent, are more likely to get the literal listener to guess the referent, and so prefers them. The pragmatic listener reasons about this speaker's preference, and so even more so than the literal listener prefers the message–referent pair the speaker was attracted to.

Analogizing to the case of dogwhistles, imagine a speaker considers the audience (of literal listeners), and reasons that it is utility-maximizing to use a dogwhistle in an attempt to bear a controversial/taboo persona with respect to a subaudience, rather than use another, more widely known message consistent with that persona. A savvy listener—one who knows about the dogwhistle—when reasoning about this speaker will also see dogwhistling as likely in the local context, in virtue of being utility-maximizing for the speaker, and so will also increase, over the literal listener, their likelihood of assigning the speaker the controversial/taboo persona associated with the dogwhistle.

The pragmatic listener was vigilant for dogwhistles by reasoning about whether the speaker would profit from dogwhistling. In doing so, the pragmatic listener is more likely than the literal listener, even a savvy one, to assign the speaker the dogwhistled persona. This difference is a vigilance implicature in the social meaning domain on par with the implicatures we see in the simplest RSA reference games. We can now show that such implicatures follow formally in precisely the way described.

We start with a slightly simplified version so as to show the connection to implicatures in reference games we have just seen. This can be carried over to the full example where more assumptions have been made, including informative priors for the various kinds of listeners and a more variegated set of affective values for personas.

To make the simple example easier to uptake, let's reuse the social meanings we used in Chapter 4 when we explored the example of Jill Stein considering whether to use anti-vax dogwhistles to an audience of literal listeners. Recall that in this game Stein is choosing between the messages *big pharma* and *corporate scientists*, which are linked with personas in the following way due to *big pharma* denoting anti-vax and anti-corporate features and *corporate scientists* denoting pro-vaxx and anti-corporate features.

Expressions and Their Consistent Personas

big pharma	{anti-vaxxer, anti-corporate}
	{anti-vaxxer, pro-corporate}
	{pro-vaxxer, anti-corporate}
corporate scientists	{pro-vaxxer, anti-corporate}
	{anti-vaxxer, anti-corporate}
	{pro-vaxxer, pro-corporate}

---

[1] In fact, it doesn't even make sense to talk about entailment in the social meaning domain. It is nice, then, to have this kind of reference game example, which is quite different from, say, the structure of a game in which scalar implicatures are calculated.

In the example in Chapter 4, our hypothesized Stein was speaking to an audience of three different types of literal listeners, whose proportions potentially varied, and whose propensity to associate messages with personas varied. This makes the computation we must do for a pragmatically aware listener a bit complicated because we must do the group computation. There is a way to simplify, though. Suppose the speaker is speaking to a group of literal listeners with the same priors for the speaker and the same likelihoods for messages (given personas). We can average the affective values for the personas at issue across those listeners and model the group as a single listener. This is because with the same priors and likelihoods, the listeners will all assign the speaker the same personas at the same rates. The only question is the expected utility the speaker will receive for being assigned those personas, which is equally weighted across all listeners.

The Stein example from Chapter 4 affords us the possibility to simplify in this way. The reason is that we treated savvy listeners, both pro- and anti-vax, as being equivalent except for the affective values they assigned to personas. The idea was that the committed pro-vaxxers are aware of the rhetoric of their ideological enemies.

So, let's assume we have the following likelihoods for the two messages at issue, which will be the same for all listeners, who are uniformly savvy. The idea is that 'big pharma' is linked to anti-vax discourse in particular, but could possible be used in anti-corporate speech. The phrase 'corporate scientists' is less well known. We will assume that listeners know it is not associated with anti-corporate, anti-vax speakers, but that otherwise its use by different types of speakers is uncertain.

Likelihood of 'Big Pharma' for Savvy Listeners

personas	$\Pr(m|p)$
{pro-vaxxer, pro-corporate}	0
{pro-vaxxer, anti-corporate}	.5
{anti-vaxxer, pro-corporate}	.75
{anti-vaxxer, anti-corporate}	.75

Likelihood of 'Corporate Scientists' for Savvy Listeners

personas	$\Pr(m|p)$
{pro-vaxxer, pro-corporate}	.5
{pro-vaxxer, anti-corporate}	.5
{anti-vaxxer, pro-corporate}	.5
{anti-vaxxer, anti-corporate}	0

We further assume that listeners have uniform priors over the space of possible personas for Stein.

Priors for Stein's Persona

{pro-vaxxer, pro-corporate}	.25
{pro-vaxxer, anti-corporate}	.25
{anti-vaxxer, pro-corporate}	.25
{anti-vaxxer, anti-corporate}	.25

The final ingredient is a valuation function for each kind of listener. Once again, we are assuming that all listeners have a relative dislike for pro-corporate personas, but that anti-vaxxers also dislike pro-vax personas and pro-vaxxers dislike anti-vax personas.[2]

$v_L(p)$ for Anti-vaxxers

personas	Values
{pro-vaxxer, pro-corporate}	1
{pro-vaxxer, anti-corporate}	2
{anti-vaxxer, pro-corporate}	19
{anti-vaxxer, anti-corporate}	20

$v_L(p)$ for Pro-vaxxers

personas	Values
{pro-vaxxer, pro-corporate}	19
{pro-vaxxer, anti-corporate}	20
{anti-vaxxer, pro-corporate}	1
{anti-vaxxer, anti-corporate}	2

From these two types of listeners we can construct a listener that represents the average of the audience. We are considering a situation where it is rational to dogwhistle, so let's assume that the anti-vaxxers outnumber the pro-vaxxers 2 to 1.[3] This gives us the following average listener affective values.

$v_L(p)$ for the Average Savvy Listener

personas	Values
{pro-vaxxer, pro-corporate}	7
{pro-vaxxer, anti-corporate}	8
{anti-vaxxer, pro-corporate}	13
{anti-vaxxer, anti-corporate}	14

---

[2] Note that we use positive values and a smaller range of affective values in this example compared to the example in Chapter 4 in order to ease the computation. Again, this doesn't have any substantive effect on the results, because what matters is the relative order of values, not their absolute value.

[3] Once again, we could work in unsavvy listeners, but this complicates the calculation. In addition, their effect is negligible. By assumption such listeners are not likely to detect the dogwhistle. As long as there are enough anti-vaxxers Stein could reach, taking into account how likely she is to be detected, it becomes rational to dogwhistle. Whether she is detected by savvy or unsavvy listeners is moot, it is just that the latter are more likely to detect.

We can now compute the effects for our three kinds of interlocutors. The literal listener L_0, in a by now familiar way, just rebalances after ruling out those personas that are simply inconsistent with the message. In this case, the message *corporate scientists* rules out an anti-vax, anti-corporate persona, while the message *big pharma* rules out the pro-vax, pro-corporate persona.

Literal Listener

	+vax,+corp	+vax,-corp	-vax,+corp	-vax,-corp
corporate scientists	.33	.33	.33	0
big pharma	0	.25	.38	.38

The speaker, who is pragmatically aware, will use messages at a certain frequency aimed at maximizing utility given the speaker's preferences for certain personas. Given the particular cost structure we imposed, what we see is that pragmatically aware speakers will be preferring *big pharma* for all anti-vax personas, even pro-corporate ones, and *corporate scientists* for all pro-vax personas, even anti-corporate ones.

Speaker

	+vax,+corp	+vax,-corp	-vax,+corp	-vax,-corp
corporate scientists	1	.72	.34	0
big pharma	0	.28	.66	1

The reason is that a pragmatically aware listener will know that a pragmatically aware speaker will be using *big pharma* to signal anti-vax personas at a higher rate than we might otherwise think because it is utility-maximizing for the literal listener. This means that the pragmatic listener should assign anti-vax personas to speakers that use *big pharma* at a rate greater than we should expect given the literal social meaning of the phrase. This is exactly what we see. Compare the following to the chart for the literal listener.

Pragmatic Listener

	+vax,+corp	+vax,-corp	-vax,+corp	-vax,-corp
corporate scientists	.48	.35	.17	0
big pharma	0	.14	.34	.52

In particular, the overall probability mass assigned to anti-vax personas shifts from .76 to .86, and in particular, the probability that a pragmatic listener decides that the speaker is anti-vax and anti-corporate on hearing *big pharma* jumps from 38% to 52%. This is the vigilance implicature. The listener who knows the speaker maximizes utility by dogwhistling is more likely to dogwhistle, and so should be more likely to detect the whistle.

This result is quite striking. Bayesian RSA was not originally created to analyze implicatures in the social meaning domain, but once ported to this domain, we see that the predicted implicatures do, in fact, arise. Vigilance implicatures have never been discussed in the literature, but they are quite natural, and they are an immediate consequence of assuming an RSA-style account. We take this as strong evidence that interlocutors use the same kinds of reasoning mechanisms across both social and truth-conditional meaning dimensions, and that the recursive Bayesian reasoning used by RSA captures important aspects of this shared mechanism.

6.1.3 Vigilance and intention

In the previous section we show how a pragmatically aware listener is more likely to detect a dogwhistle than a literal listener in those cases where she believes the speaker will get a utility payoff by dogwhistling. The converse is also true. A pragmatically aware listener will be less likely to assign the speaker the taboo persona associated with the dogwhistle if the speaker is less likely to get a payoff for dogwhistling in the present context. In this section we consider what this model can say about the contrast between intentional and non-intentional dogwhistling, a distinction first discussed by Saul (2018). In particular, we have to ask whether we need intentionality in our model, or, phrased differently, how much of the phenomenon that Saul identifies can be covered by pragmatically aware speakers making vigilance implicatures in the kinds of games we have developed over the past two chapters.

To begin, we should immediately discard the idea that intentions and payoffs can be identified. Intending to do something is clearly distinct from the payoffs one may receive for doing it, and we cannot say that an agent intends to do something if and only if the agent will receive a payoff. That said, they are also intertwined. The fact that someone would receive a benefit for doing something, paired with the fact that they did it, is evidence, though not of course conclusive evidence, that they intended to do so. Moreover, when it comes to assigning censure (and the amount of censure)—which in our models is expressed by the listener's affective value for the speaker's persona— an agent's motives clearly matter. People who do bad things for good reasons may get off lightly, but those who do bad things for bad reasons are the worst of all.

There is a large many-centuries-old literature in law and philosophy of law concerning the relationship between intent (*mens rea*, in their terminology), and motive (*utility*, in ours). Examining this literature will help us sharpen some of the considerations that Saul (2018) raises about the intentional vs. non-intentional use of dogwhistles. Moreover, it will clarify how vigilance implicatures relate to the question of intention in dogwhistling.

In classical legal thinking, a criminal trial involves making two determinations: (i) whether the defendant did what was alleged, and (ii) whether the defendant had the necessary state of mind, or *mens rea*. While the relevant mental states come in various shades, at the heart of this test is intent—did the defendant intend to do the act forbidden by law? Note that motive is not mentioned. It is not constitutive of guilt, classically speaking.[4]

---

[4] We must add the modifier because, as Hessick (2006) notes, it is becoming more and more common for lawmakers to write statutes with motive written into the forbidden act. We discuss this more below, especially with respect to so-called *hate crime* legislation, which is perhaps especially relevant to the topic of racial dogwhistles.

While motive is not constitutive of guilt when considering canonical crimes—murder, theft, etc.—motive plays a larger role than is sometimes recognized in legal proceedings. Following the review in Hessick (2006), (i) motive can be used as evidence of intention, (ii) motive can be used to determine the degree of culpability at sentencing, and (iii) while not constitutive of crimes like murder, many crimes do, in fact, have motive built into the definition of the forbidden act—e.g., hate crimes. If we think of the pragmatic listener as trying to determine whether the conversational crime of dogwhistling has been committed, as well as how to react, then the first two aspects discussed by Hessick (2006) are captured by vigilance implicatures. It also allows us to establish a link between motive, which we model through expected utility, and intention, as discussed by Saul (2018). The third aspect is perhaps the most interesting, though. Is dogwhistling actually a conversational crime of this sort? The answer could force radical changes to our theory as presented here as well as Saul's.

We begin with the fact that motive can be used as evidence of intention. Once again, we should not confuse motive and intention, but motive is clearly relevant for determining intention. Hitchler (1931, p. 112) puts it well:

> As an evidential fact motive is always relevant, but never essential. When a motive of the accused for the commission of a crime is discovered, it is easier to believe that he committed it than when no motive is apparent. For this reason it is always relevant to prove the existence of a motive. But though the discovery of a motive helps to prove the guilt of the accused, there may be ample proof, independent of motive, of his guilt. It is not necessary therefore for the state to prove the motive as an evidential fact.

Game-theoretic reasoning is essentially a motive machine. All moves are made against the backdrop of maximizing utility. Vigilance implicatures are no exception, and we can think of the pragmatic listener in our social meaning games computing such an implicature as doing Hitchler's style of always relevant, but never essential, reasoning. By reasoning that the speaker will receive a payoff by dogwhistling, the pragmatic listener is more likely to conclude that the speaker committed the offense of dogwhistling—i.e., used a message in order to get a sub-audience to assign them a certain persona that another segment of the audience would not approve of.

This is all well and good, but what about the determination of intent itself? Intent is not explicitly part of the model, and so we must bite the bullet and say that we cannot directly model the distinction between intentional and non-intentional dogwhistling. That is, we cannot say that some listener in our social meaning games determines the probability that one speaker has a certain persona given they sent a particular message, and intended to do so, while another speaker has that persona on sending the same message, but did not intend to do so.

While we do not explicitly represent intent, there are still ways to work the concept of intent into our model. The clearest is through the prior, and in particular, how the prior is initialized. Let's consider the case of an unintentional dogwhistle in reported speech, a case that Saul (2018) considers. Imagine a newscaster reporting controversy over a politician's use of a dogwhistle who in doing so uses the dogwhistle themselves. Should a listener assign the newscaster the taboo persona associated with the dogwhistle? Our intuition is that we should not. The fact that the newscaster is not intending to use the dogwhistle to project the persona in question means that we should lower the probability that we assign the newscaster the taboo persona, even though the dogwhistle was part of their message. We can model this situation through the prior. In this situation, where the newscaster is not likely to be intending to construct a taboo sociolinguistic persona, we should have a low prior that the newscaster has the taboo persona in question. With this low prior, it will be unlikely that a listener will assign the speaker the taboo persona given their use of the of dogwhistle, and so they will not be detected as dogwhistling. Thus, the determination of intent, which helped set the prior, can have a direct effect on whether the speaker is determined to be dogwhistling.

To summarize, while intent is not explicitly represented in our model of dogwhistles, it can be play a role in the determination of priors, which has downstream effects in terms of whether agents are determined to be dogwhistling. Additionally, just as in legal proceedings, motive, cast here as utility, can play a role in determining whether the speaker is taken to be guilty of dogwhistling—i.e., using the dogwhistle to surreptitiously hold a taboo persona. Vigilance implicatures capture this kind of reasoning, where the likelihood of a payoff for a move is evidence that the agent intended to make the moves they did in order to receive that payoff. We see, then, that while not represented as such, intent can play a role in our model, and the agents in our social meaning games are reasoning the way we hope that they would around issues involving intent.

The careful reader, though, may have noticed that we are perhaps sliding around an issue. In the discussion above, we show that a lack of intent, or a lack of motive (or both), can affect whether the listener assigns to the speaker the taboo persona associated with the dogwhistle. But, is the speaker still considered to be dogwhistling in these cases, even unintentionally so? What does it mean that the listeners in our models are not likely to react to the speaker's message in the same way as a bona fide dogwhistle attempt?

This matters because Saul (2018) makes the strong case that unintentional dogwhistles can still have a deleterious effect on the conversation. In the newscaster example there is the clear effect of, what she calls, *amplifying* the dogwhistle, which helps achieve the conversational goals of the original, intentional use of the dogwhistle. For instance, replaying and discussing a political advertisement that contains dogwhistles can shape the common ground on which the political discussion is taking place so that it contains toxic propositions associated with the dogwhistle.

We believe that we can model the amplifying effect of unintentional dogwhistles. Additionally, we make good predictions about how a rational listener should react to a speaker, like a newscaster, who unintentionally dogwhistles. First, though, let's address the question about whether such speakers are dogwhistling. Saul (2018) takes the position, precisely because of unintentional dogwhistles, that to dogwhistle is to use an expression that could be used to intentionally dogwhistle, and in doing so, affect the conversation in ways that an intentional dogwhistle would. Thus, if we can show that we can model the effects of unintentional dogwhistles that Saul (2018) discusses, then these agents can be said to be dogwhistling under Saul's definition. This is good because, recall, that agents in our games do not determine that a speaker is dogwhistling per se. They don't label messages as such. Instead, dogwhistling is a label that we impose from the outside for particular configurations in such games. It is nice, then, that we can find games with configurations that conform to Saul's definition.

Let's return to the canonical case of unintentional dogwhistling, namely the newscaster using dogwhistles in reporting the speech of another agent. We want to take the position of a savvy listener—i.e., one that is aware that the dogwhistle is linked to certain taboo personas, and so, in principle, can *hear* the dogwhistle. First, we immediately can make sense of amplifying. Listeners compute the social meanings of messages sent by speakers. In reported speech, there is no reason why a listener cannot attempt to infer the persona of the original speaker, in virtue of their message, as well as the persona of the speech reporter, in virtue of their speech report. If the listener approves of the persona transmitted by the dogwhistle, or is receptive to the ideology associated with the dogwhistle, then in the case of enriching dogwhistles, the original sender will have met their goal in intentionally dogwhistling, for any enriching effect of the dogwhistle will take place as usual.[5]

Perhaps more interesting is how the listener should react to the speaker who transmitted the unintentional dogwhistle. It makes sense to consider the position of a savvy listener who does not approve of the persona transmitted by the dogwhistle, or its associated ideology. As discussed above, if the listener thinks the speaker is not likely, in the current context, to bear the persona associated with the dogwhistle, and so not likely to intentionally dogwhistle, this should lower the listener's prior for the speaker to bear that persona. The result is that the speaker is not likely to be tagged with the taboo persona, but it does not completely eliminate that possibility. This is critical. It means that the expected utility of using a dogwhistle expression in conversation with a savvy, non-approving listener, even unintentionally, will be degraded relative other strategies. Additionally, the posterior likelihood that the unintentional dogwhistler does, in fact, bear the taboo persona will be increased.

These two outcomes seem correct. Using a dogwhistle, even unintentionally, is not a completely blameless activity. Saul (2018) notes that in the case of amplifying unintentional dogwhistles, in particular, that such speakers need to "pay attention to the effects of what they say, and to the careful manipulation that has caused them to say these things."[6] A speaker who habitually unintentionally dogwhistles may, over time,

---

[5] It is interesting to consider that speakers, in calculating the utility of sending a dogwhistle to an audience, must take into consideration amplification. That is, their message may be received by a larger audience than that of the original communicative act. Amplification, depending on what kinds of audiences received the amplified message, could backfire, making the move not utility-maximizing. In normal conversation, this is probably not a huge issue, but is something to take into account for mass communication, and in political campaigns in particular.

[6] While this may seem correct in the case of journalists, politicians, etc., who are expected to be informed and speak carefully, one might worry that this is too strong. What about people who use a dogwhistle legitimately not knowing it as such? Perhaps they speak a different dialect, which is exactly how we would handle such cases, again construing 'dialect' as relating to social meaning. Remember, a critical aspect of dogwhistles is that they

come to bear the taboo persona associated with the dogwhistle because careful listeners' priors will change on being repeatedly sent the same dogwhistle messages. 'Unintentional' uses may not look so unintentional anymore.

This discussion shows that our model can capture aspects of unintentional dogwhistles, as first discussed by Saul (2018), but it also relates to the discussion of the role of intention in legal proceedings. In particular, recall the second point, which is that intent plays a critical role in determining culpability at sentencing. In our model, we can think of sentencing as the affect score the listener assigns to the speaker based on the persona they are deemed to have in virtue of their message choice. Although different from sentencing at trial due to being stochastic, the result is the same. A speaker who is seen to be intentionally dogwhistling (i.e., there is a high prior that the speaker bears the persona associated with the dogwhistle), and who has a strong motive to dogwhistle (i.e., dogwhistling, given the audience, is utility optimizing), will receive a larger expected negative affect score from a savvy listener who disapproves of the dogwhistle than a speaker who is unintentionally dogwhistling. This is because affect scores are weighted by the posterior probability the speaker bears the persona associated with the dogwhistle, which will be lower when the speaker is unintentionally dogwhistling (and has no motive to dogwhistle).

We turn now to the third and final question raised by our discussion of motive and its place in legal practice, though we have partially addressed it—or at least, we have settled the position of previous authors on this question given their stance on intentionality. What we are interested in is the fact that certain crimes have motive built into their definition. That is, one must not just do the act and do it with the right kind of intention, but one must do it for a particular motive. So-called 'hate crime' legislation us the canonical case. For instance, the supreme court ruled in *Virginia v. Black* (2003) that it is consistent with the First Amendment for the state of Virginia to ban cross burning when the motive is to intimidate any person or group.

The parallel definition of dogwhistles would require that the speaker send a message with the intent to conceal their sociolinguistic persona to a sub-audience (in order to maximize utility). This motive to conceal is an interesting idea, but we think that it cannot be made definitional. First, it is inconsistent with the distinction we have drawn, following Saul (2018), between intentional and unintentional dogwhistles, especially the amplifying type. It is clear that a newscaster reporting a second party's words is not attempting to conceal something about their own persona, yet this communicative act can have a dogwhistle effect, which we have shown that we can model.

---

are probabilistically linked to their social meanings. Agents know some conditional probability P that a speaker bears some persona given that they used a particular message. If this is high for some agent, and near zero for another, they are speaking radically different dialects (as far as social meaning is concerned). In extreme cases like this, the use of a dogwhistle expression begins to look less like an unintentional dogwhistle and more like a genuine miscommunication, and so the question of culpability is moot. Once again, we can handle this situation through the prior. One aspect of communication is figuring out how alike we are to our interlocutor. If it is clear that the answer is quite different, then we should be conservative about how we interpret the social meanings of their messages. In the most extreme case, their sociolinguistic persona may just be *foreigner* or *outsider* no matter what they say. It just might not be possible to have a more fine-grained negotiation of social identity due to lack of shared social meaning conventions.

Given the solid grounding we have for the idea of unintentional dogwhistles, we simply cannot build intent to conceal into the definition of dogwhistling. That said, there is another role of that motive plays in hate crime legislation. Instead of being built into the prohibited act, motive can be used as a sentencing enhancement (Hessick 2006). In these cases otherwise unlawful conduct is required by law to be more gravely punished when done with the motive to harm an individual based on the victims' race, ethnicity, religion, gender, abledness, or sexual preference.

The parallel in the case of dogwhistling would be for the speaker to receive a larger negative affective value score when a listener catches them using a dogwhistle meant to conceal their sociolinguistic persona to a sub-audience. We can fairly cleanly model this, and in fact, have already done so through vigilance implicatures. Recall that vigilance requires a listener modeling a speaker's computation of what message maximizes their utility when sent to the audience at hand. If there is a motive to send a dogwhistle to conceal their identity to a sub-audience, modeled via a large utility payoff, then a savvy listener will be more likely to identify the speaker as dogwhistling than otherwise. That higher likelihood, which acts as a weight on the negative affective valued assigned to the bearer of the dogwhistled persona, will result in a large negative affective value. Thus, when speakers are determined to be dogwhistling, and to have a pernicious motive to do so, they will receive a greater punishment. This is analogous to the motive-based sentencing enhancement we see for certain kinds of crimes, including hate crimes.

6.1.4 Side-stepping intent

Having established the existence of vigilance implicatures, which arise of the course of vanilla RSA reasoning, we might quickly consider other approaches to detecting a dogwhistling speaker without reference to intent or the speaker's payoff for using a dogwhistle. This would be useful, for instance, if a listener does not know about the audience receiving the message. Without knowledge of the distribution of savvy and naive listeners, it is not possible to compute the payoff a speaker will receive for using a dogwhistle.

One interesting option would be just compute the probability of message

$$P(m)$$

which can be computed via marginalization (see Scontras et al. 2021 for applications in RSA-based pragmatics).[7]

$$P_S(m) = \sum_s P(s)P(m \mid s)$$

Note that this quantity can be computed for different spaces s, yet are still comparable. This means that we can ask, for some polarizing persona p, the probability a (dogwhistling) speaker would use m to communicate p

---

[7] We need to thank Michael Franke (p.c.) for raising this possibility.

$$P_{dogwhistler}(m) = \sum_{p} P(p)P(m \mid p)$$

This could be compared to the computation of the base rate of using m, which would be the probability a (naive) speaker would use m in some neutral state s.

$$P_{naive}(m) = \sum_{s} P(s)P(m \mid s)$$

A listener could then use the likelihood ratio

$$P_{naive}(m)/P_{strategic}(m)$$

to determine how much the use of m would suggest they are talking to a dogwhistling speaker versus a naive speaker that had a random slip of the tongue. While not an implicature that directly arises out of RSA reasoning, an agent making use of all probabilistic information at hand to make pragmatic inferences could still draw vigilant conclusions about whether their interlocutor is dogwhistling, even without information about the audience structure.

6.1.5 Summary

In this first section we have provided a thorough introduction to vigilance implicatures, which emerge when taking the perspective of a pragmatically aware listener reasoning about how a pragmatically aware speaker sends messages to convey social meanings. We began by showing that vigilance implicatures in the case of dogwhistles are the formal analogue to so-called reference implicatures, as commonly discussed in the Bayesian RSA literature, and emerge just like standard Gricean implicatures do in the framework, but in the social meaning domain.[8] In showing how vigilance implicatures arise, we saw that they arise because speakers have motive, in terms of expected utility, to dogwhistle in certain contexts.

We then turned to explore idea of the role of motive in dogwhistling, and in particular, how motive, cast as payoffs, works in our model. In particular, we saw that motive can be used as evidence for intention when we are trying to determine whether the speaker is intentionally or unintentionally dogwhistling. Additionally, we saw that motive leads to larger negative affective value scores assigned by listeners who detect the speaker is dogwhistling. These were good predictions in that they accord with our intuitions about how to react to a speaker that is dogwhistling (either intentionally or not), and we saw that motive plays analogous roles in legal reasoning about other kinds of unscrupulous behavior.

---

[8] Michael Franke (p.c.) points out that we can take the implicatures generated in reference games to be a generalized kind of quantity implicature, one that is not based on entailment but a probabilistic notion of "more informative". Under this view, both reference implicatures and the vigilance implicatures we have identified would be examples of traditional Gricean Quantity operating in this probabilistic pragmatic setting.

6.2 Hypervigilance

The previous section investigated the concept of vigilance implicatures, which we have shown are a social meaning version of the standard reference implicatures obtained in the truth-conditional games of Bayesian RSA. As we have seen, they arise when pragmatic listeners consider which moves are utility optimizing for the speaker when communicating with the literal listener. The pragmatic listener infers that these utility optimizing moves should be even more likely given that this is the best play for the pragmatic speaker. In terms of dogwhistling, then, the pragmatic listener determines that a speaker who would profit from dogwhistling, given the audience, is more likely to be dogwhistling than they might otherwise think given the raw social meanings of the message sent.

Note that in this discussion the focus is entirely on the speaker's interests. The listener's affective values for the speaker's range of personas plays a role, but only as a part of the broader audience, and weighed against the speaker's own affective values for those personas. In this section we turn to a phenomenon we dub *hypervigilance*, which we think emerges from a more direct comparison between speaker and listener personas, and not just from considering the speaker's utility for various messages. We will see that this effect is related to a particular result by Farrell (1993) for cheap talk games, which considers when it is possible for a listener to take speaker messages to be credible.

First, though, let's consider what we mean by hypervigilance. What we are interested in is a phenomenon often observed especially on social media, where people are quick to label expressions dogwhistles. This can cause a lot of rancor, especially because to accuse a speaker of intentionally dogwhistling is to accuse them of deception and manipulation.

A recent possible example of this concerns the leader of the British Labour Party, Keir Starmer, and the 2021 pamphlet he released to set priorities for his party into the post-COVID mid-2020s (Starmer 2021). Starmer, as the head of the Labour Party, is on the left, but he is seen as being on the right side of the party. This has put him in opposition with the left flank, especially those that supported the previous leader Jeremy Corbyn, who is seen as authentically leftist. With this backdrop, an interesting dynamic emerged with online sleuths combing through his pamphlet for conservative dogwhistles, which they see as revealing Starmer's true identity.

For instance, one of the pamphlet's 10 principles is to put "hard-working families and their priorities first," which the internet has seized on as an anti-LGBTQ dogwhistle. The result is that when Starmer mentions families on social media there are replies accusing him of dogwhistling. For instance, on January 11, 2021 Starmer tweeted "I'm calling on the Government to put families first during this lockdown," paired with a video calling for pay raises, a stop to tax hikes, and cuts to social security payments.[9]

---

[9] @Keir_Starmer: https://twitter.com/Keir_Starmer/status/1348629025888083968?s=20&t=ZvkleDruOkwnEUmLKnaPng

The first reply calls Starmer out for using the word *family*, someone replies to that defending Starmer, and then there is a reply saying "Wow, that's one of the more twatty defences of a Lab leader going pastel blue tradfam dogwhistle I'm likely to see today...."[10]

This is not a one-off. There is a lot of discussion on Twitter about on this point, and it has even worked its way into opinion pages, e.g., Barrett (2022). Is Starmer really using *family* as a Tory (i.e., pastel blue) trad dogwhistle? These disputes are hard to adjudicate precisely because dogwhistles are deniable, but we believe this is a likely case of hypervigilance. In particular, the fact that Starmer is seen as being to the right of his party has made co-partisans hypervigilant. They expect him to be dogwhistling and so they are motivated to hunt out possible examples.

As evidence for this, we note that the former Labour Party leader Jeremy Corbyn has made direct appeal to supporting *families* in tweets over the same period, but is not receiving replies that he is excluding single people, people in non-traditional families, is dogwhistling to the right, etc. If pressed why not, people would surely say that this is because Corbyn can't be a shadow Tory because he's Jeremy Corbyn, a true socialist. This is precisely the point, though. Co-partisans have no motive to closely scrutinize Corbyn's language. They are not in hypervigilance mode with him as speaker.

This example shows the major contours of hypervigilance. The calculation to determine whether the speaker is dogwhistling seems to include very little about determining the speaker's payoffs for doing so, and more about the relative social/political/sociolinguistic positions of the speaker and listener. In this case, Starmer and his critics, while in roughly the same ideological camp, are on opposite sides. They each see the other as opposing them in an ideological battle (or at least the critics do), and that provides motivation for rooting out dogwhistles. In such a hypervigilance scenario, the result is that the threshold for determining an expression to be a dogwhistle goes down. Interlocutors come to see dogwhistles everywhere.

In the next subsection we consider how to model hypervigilance, recognizing that it is not the standard kind of implicature we see in RSA, unlike the vigilance implicatures we considered in the previous section. Instead, we will take our cue from work on establishing coordination on novel meanings in cheap talk games. Then, in the following subsection—section 6.2.2—we ask about the effects of hypervigilance in discourse. While hypervigilance may be rational in certain kinds of conversations, it can lead to major breakdowns and preclude the possibility for productive communication to take place.

6.2.1 Modeling hypervigilance

The example with Starmer showed that hypervigilance results in listeners aggressively identifying expressions as dogwhistles. At first pass, this seems difficult to model in the

---

[10] @A_48er: https://twitter.com/A_48er/status/1348742214042660874?s=20&t=ZvkleDruOkwnEUmLKna Png

formal system developed over the past few chapters. The reason is that, in the course of the games as presented, listeners do not determine expressions to be dogwhistles at all. They come to the table believing that certain expressions are linked with certain personas, and then, on receiving a message, determine the speaker's persona and consider ideologies linked with that persona. A listener detects dogwhistling, not by determining some expression is a dogwhistle per se, but by determining the speaker's in-group persona based on some message, when out-group members would fail to do so.

For us, then, the locus of hypervigilance must be in how messages and personas are linked. Recall that listeners compute the probability that the speaker bears a certain persona given the message they sent according to Bayes' rule.

$$L_0(p|m) \propto P(m|p) \times P(p)$$

The critical parameter for dogwhistle detection is $P(m|p)$, or, equivalently, the likelihood of the message given the speaker has some hypothesized persona. It is this likelihood parameter that varies across the population for particular messages, allowing some but not all listeners to detect when a speaker is dogwhistling. Our proposal is that hypervigilance is the result of a shift in this parameter across a broad swath of messages when talking to particular speakers, and to possible (perceived) ideological enemies in particular.

To see how this would work, let's put ourselves in the position of a hypervigilant listener, like a British Labour Party member skeptical of Keir Starmer. The hallmark of hypervigilance is believing 'everything is a dog-whistle'. We can reach this state in two steps.

First, we become skeptical—i.e., we no longer believe we understand the social meanings our interlocutor is sending. This is comparable to the first step in belief revision where we must back off certain beliefs in order to update in light of new information. In our terms, this means adjusting the value of $P(m|p)$. In the most radical case, it could be set to a fixed value for all messages.[11] For instance, one natural setting would to be to let the value be 1 if the persona is consistent with the conventionalized social meaning of the message, and 0 otherwise, as in the standard Social Meaning Games introduced by Burnett (2017, 2019).

Having become skeptical, we can now take the next step and become paranoid. What should a listener do when they become uncertain about the social meanings of the expressions being used in a discourse? Here, we have guidance from a credibility result by Farrell (1993) in cheap talk games, which we want to use to think about how agents might behave in social meaning games for dogwhistles.[12] Farrell is interested in so-called *cheap talk* games, like ours, where there are no penalties for

---

[11] In practice, though, we likely only back off some set of low frequency expressions that appear at a relatively high frequency in the discourse at hand. These expressions *stand out*, and so are good targets to bear special social meanings.

[12] We need to make an important caveat here. We do not have a formal implementation of Farrell credibility in RSA because Farrell is working in very different kinds of games than RSA. Instead we need to use a different notion of credibility, one that is appropriate for the games in question. For instance, Franke (2008) provides

sending messages. In particular, games with cheap talk have trouble with neologisms—i.e., messages not expected at equilibrium. The reasons are two-fold. First, how do we know the neologism has meaning? We must rule out that the speaker is just babbling. When sending messages is costless, the latter is always a possible strategy. Second, even if we can reconstruct a meaning for the neologism, we have the problem of determining whether the neologistic message is credible, namely, whether the listener should believe it.

While we will not completely review Farrell's results here, he shows that when interlocutors share a language with conventionalized meaning (like the social meaning games we consider here), communication with neologisms is possible to the extent messages are credible. Furthermore, credibility is deeply connected to shared interest. In a zero-sum game, for instance, a recipient should not believe a neologistic message m if they believe the sender wants them to believe m. To the extent sender and receiver have shared interests, that is the extent to which a neologistic message should be taken seriously.

We take hypervigilant listeners to be operating in this space where interests do not align (or at least perceiving them as such). As in Farrell's signaling games, communication should break down in concert with shared interest. We can model shared interest in the following way. Recall that, as Chapter 5 discusses, personas are linked to ideologies, which are treated as sets of beliefs. We can thus measure the distance between ideologies on the interval between 0 and 1 using one of many standard such measures.[13] In virtue of the link between personas and ideologies, we can then compute the distance D between two personas as the distance between their ideologies. We take this distance between ideologies, and thus personas, as a measure of the alignment between the interests of speaker and listener. More precisely, a speaker with persona p_S has more shared interest with a listener with persona p_L than a second listener with persona p'_L just in case $D(p_S, p_L) < D(p_S, p'_L)$. The latter listener is more ideologically distant.

We propose that hypervigilant listeners, when speaking to assumed ideological enemies, are using this distance metric for the probability of a message (given a persona). That is, if a particular persona is ideologically distant, then the listener assumes that a message consistent with that persona is being used to signal that persona with a probability equal to the ideological distance. To implement this analysis, recall that we proposed that the first step to hypervigilance is to back off from beliefs about how various kinds of speakers prefer particular messages. This is because such a listener needs to revise their beliefs. From this state where the probability of m

---

a definition of credibility using Iterated Best Response (IBR) reasoning. A full formalization of hypervigilant listeners would take place by taking insights from Franke's IBR work and defining credibility in RSA. We think this will be a challenging, though fruitful problem. For now, though, the critical point is that credibility and preference alignment are related, both in Farrell credibility and notions of credibility developed in Franke (2008). The same should hold in any credibility result for RSA.

[13] For example, the Jaccard index $J(A, B) = \frac{|A \cap B|}{|A \cup B|}$.

given p is 1 just in case m and p are consistent, the listener can revise their beliefs as follows

$$\text{HypervigilantL}_0(p|m) \propto ([m](p) \times D(p_{L_0}, p)) \times P(p)$$

Note that for the hypervigilant listener L_0, we have returned to the notation $[m](p)$, where we predicate p of the social meaning of m, which will return 1 just in case p is a persona m denotes. In the case in which p and m are consistent, the result is equivalent to saying that $P(m|p)$ is just the listener's ideological distance from the speaker.

This is quite radical, and in the extreme case likely not rational (if the goal is to extract the maximum information about what our interlocutor is saying, a point we return to below), but this is precisely what is observed in examples of hypervigilance. Let's return to the case of Keir Starmer and his tweets about families. Recall that this involved Labour partisans calling out Starmer, a co-party member, for using anti-gay dogwhistles, in this case, the word 'family.' Of course, dogwhistles can have many sources, but on par, high frequency words are not likely great dogwhistles. They will be used too much by out-group members to make them a solid signal of in-group membership. Hypervigilant listeners, though, can turn any expression consistent with the personas of their ideological enemies into dogwhistles of those personas.

To see this, consider the most extreme case. Suppose a hypervigilant listener has a prior of 1 that Starmer has a secret Tory persona. Additionally, assume that that persona is associated with a distance of 1 from the listener's ideology—that is, they are maximally ideologically distinct. Such a listener will take any expression that is not immediately inconsistent with a Tory-linked persona as perfect confirmatory evidence that speaker bears that persona. On the use of any such expression the hypervigilant listener will conclude with probability 1 that speaker bears this persona in virtue of using that expression. This is a ridiculous case, of course, but it shows that we can capture the proverbial 'liberal that thinks everything is a dog-whistle.'

While ridiculous in the extreme case, the effect of hypervigilance is felt even with moderated parameters. Assume we have a hypervigilant listener who is agnostic about Starmer's precise persona—and so has uniform priors about his persona—but suspects he is an ideological enemy. The result is still the kind of uncharitable confirmation bias we see in the most fractious discourses. In particular, the result is that such a listener will be more likely to assign the speaker personas that connected to enemy ideologies at a frequency directly proportional to the distance that ideology is from the speaker's. That is, if you use a term that is plausibly linked with an enemy ideology, then the probability you are, in fact, that kind of person scales directly with how much the hypervigilant listener dislikes that ideology.

Critically, this kind of uncharitable scrutiny is not present when conversing with non-ideological enemies. Bringing it back to our example, this is why Corbyn can use a word like 'family' without being called a closet Tory. Crucially, we think it is not just because of priors about Corbyn's sociolinguistic persona (and linked ideology). Rather, the manner of discourse is completely different. Interpreters, when listening to Corbyn, are simply not trying to root out dogwhistles. They are not taking any expression consistent with an enemy ideology and then using it as evidence the speaker bears a persona consistent with that ideology, which is what we claim hypervigilant listeners do, as we model above.

6.2.2 Hypervigilance and discourse breakdown

In analyzing hypervigilance we had to move fairly far away from the standard recipe we have used so far to deal with dogwhistle inferences. Unlike vigilance implicatures, which emerge from naturally from our RSA-based account by considering higher-order listeners, hypervigilance required doing away with the standard way of computing the probability of a persona given a message. Instead of using empirical observation to determine the likelihood of the message, the most rational procedure, we instead used ideological distance to give that likelihood. This is clearly perverse. It means, all things being equal, assigning your interlocutor the persona you least prefer that is consistent with what they said.

We believe, though, that the perversity of the account is actually a virtue in that the phenomenon itself has a perverse quality (from the perspective of cooperative communication). Hypervigilance, especially in the extreme case modeled here, leads to fairly serious breakdowns in discourse. In a real way these are not normal interlocutors (in both normative and descriptive senses). It is good, then, that we have had to change our model so drastically to deal with hypervigilant listeners. Their behavior does not emerge naturally from our standard account of dogwhistles, which assume at least a partial kind of cooperativity on the part of discourse participants. With this in mind, we want to consider the effect on a discourse when it contains hypervigilant listeners.

Once against, it is helpful to consider the most extreme case of hypervigilance. These are listeners we explicitly model with $HypervigilantL_0$, who take the likelihood of all messages (given a persona) to be proportional to the ideological distance between the listener and speakers bearing that persona. These are essentially bad faith listeners in the following sense. If the goal of social meaning games is for speakers to pick messages in order to receive a sociolinguistic persona that maximizes affective value across all interlocutors, then the presence of hypervigilant listeners creates a situation in which any message that could possibly be construed as negative will be read as negatively as possible. The speaker must walk on eggshells, so to speak. Every message must be conventionally inconsistent with personas that the listener does not approve of or they will be taken as strong evidence that the speaker bears that persona, whether or not, purely empirically, those messages are good signals of speakers with that persona.

Speakers who find themselves in such a game are in a lamentable position because messages that would be safe to send to an average interlocutor will incur large utility penalties, and only increase the listeners' priors that the speaker bears the persona the listener does not like, making any subsequent misstep even greater confirmatory evidence that the speaker bears that persona. The speaker's best move in this situation is most likely not to play.[14] This is what we mean by discourse breakdown. If most messages, whatever their truth-conditional content, will be interpreted as essentially taboo, then communication cannot proceed.

We want to emphasize that this discussion is not merely hypothetical. Say what you will about the merits of the concept 'call out culture' or 'cancel culture', a common aspect of high-profile social media missteps around race, gender, sexuality, politics, etc.—realms of life around which we have taboos, and rich sociolinguistic practice connected with ideologies—is for people to comb through the social media posts of the person in question for evidence to presage their speech in question, and to carefully scrutinize any subsequent apology, for evidence that they are actually doubling down. Of course, in some cases the scrutiny is warranted, and we do not mean to say that all such behavior by listeners is in bad faith, but we clearly see the signature of hypervigilance. The result is conversational breakdown. The goals appear no longer to transmit truth-conditional information while collaboratively constructing our sociolinguistic personas. The primary goal in such conversations is to root out linguistic evidence that the speaker bears a persona (and associated ideology) that the listener does not like.

It is important to note that hypervigilant listeners are not necessarily the only ones at fault for such conversational breakdowns. Intentional dogwhistling is not exactly good faith conversational behavior. It is duplicitous to send covert messages to a sub-audience, and as we have discussed, dogwhistles can poison the common ground by slipping propositions into the conversational background through ideologies they are associated with. Thus, rooting out such speakers in a way that ends the conversation is defensible. One should not be a good faith listener in a conversation with a bad faith speaker. Perhaps there should be no conversation at all.

There are other virtues to the hypervigilant listener, especially in less extreme forms. We have considered a hypervigilant listener that becomes agnostic about the social meaning of all messages, caring only about whether the message is strictly consistent with the personas at issue, and using ideological distance to determine the likelihood that certain messages will be used given those personas. There are, of course, weaker versions of such hypervigilant listeners that only use this strategy for certain messages or classes of messages, perhaps related to some topic, for instance. These listeners, in virtue of following a different strategy than standard listeners, could play an important role in detecting dogwhistles, or potential dogwhistles, and diffusing that information throughout a population. This is because they aggressively associate terms that could in principle be used as dogwhistles, with personas that could potentially be signaled via those dogwhistles. There will be many false positives, but having an ecosystem of listeners with different sociolinguistic backgrounds and pursuing different strategies is more likely to be able to, in aggregate, better detect dogwhistles, just as with

---

[14] Another strategy, of course, especially if the speaker were actually dogwhistling, would be to lean into the persona the hypervigilant listeners do not like—that is, to abandon dogwhistles entirely in favor of messages that explicitly index the persona in question for all listeners. We call these *mask-off moments* and discuss them more in Chapter 8.

the standpoints discussed in the previous chapter. From this perspective, the moderately hypervigilant listener could even perhaps be viewed as having a special kind of expertise that's useful to the broader epistemic community.

6.3 Conclusions

While the first part of this work focused on the speaker, in particular, the conversational configurations in which dogwhistling is a profitable strategy, this chapter has begun to address the question of how a listener should react to a possible dogwhistle. We started with the most conservative extension of our account, which perhaps does not even count as an extension because it merely involves considering listeners of a higher type, implicit in the RSA framework we have adopted. We showed that such listeners generate implicatures in the social meaning domain, which we dubbed vigilance implicatures. The core result is that listeners who determine that a speaker could receive a utility payoff by dogwhistling are more likely to assign the speaker the persona signaled by the dogwhistle.

The discussion of the listener reasoning about speaker payoffs raised the question of whether the speaker's awareness of those payoffs should affect listener behavior. That is, we wanted to know how a listener should react to intentional vs. unintentional dogwhistles, and whether our account could model this listener behavior. While we cannot directly model intentionality in our framework, and believe we do probably need intentionality to accurately account for all aspects of the dogwhistles, we showed that tweaking parameters like priors allows us to indirectly get at listeners reasoning about speakers intentionally dogwhistling (or unintentionally doing so, as the case may be).

In the final section of this chapter, we diverged even further from our account as developed so far. We introduced a novel way for listeners to compute the probability that a speaker bears a certain persona given their message using the idea of ideologies linked to personas, which we introduced in the previous chapter. This new account was used to model what we called hypervigilant listeners. If vigilant listeners are more quick to identify dogwhistling when there is a payoff to the speaker, hypervigilant listeners are even more aggressive in identifying possible dogwhistles. They do so at a high frequency proportional to the assumed ideological distance between speaker and listener. This aggressive strategy likely leads to conversational breakdown, which we discussed. Still, hypervigilance has its virtues. Perhaps one should not converse with an interlocutor intentionally using dogwhistles.

The next chapter will continue this focus on listener reactions to dogwhistles. Instead of the adversarial case of listeners looking to detect dogwhistles in order to punish the speaker, we will consider the case of speakers and listeners using social meaning, and dogwhistles in particular, to build trust. What we will see is that trust can be built, even when a speaker's utterances are not truthful, if the social meaning signal is strong enough.

7
Dogwhistles and trust

Questions of trust are often discussed in linguistics, though usually not by precisely that name. For example, we are advised to provisionally believe what other people say because we can (normatively) take them to be following the Gricean Maxim of Quality, which instructs them not to speak falsehoods. Together with the assumption that people have minimal competence about the domains they talk about (Sauerland 2004), it follows that people's words can be taken to have epistemological significance for us, and that it's rational to allow them to affect our beliefs (e.g., Lackey and Sosa 2006; Lackey 2008). In Chapter 5, we proposed a different notion of trust under the name *Social Sincerity*, which has it that we should, again provisionally, assume that people project social personas which they sincerely hold, in the sense that they believe the ideological content associated with those personas.[1]

Both of these notions rest on the idea that people are sincere in what they convey. This sincerity grounds rational acceptance of what others say, and of the personas they (choose to) project. But problems arise for this kind of view when particular speakers, or people in particular social contexts more generally, are believed and trusted despite being well-known to play fast and loose with the facts in the things they say. This is the case with many politicians, for example, at least in the context of propositional content, and perhaps in a lot of political discourse that involves people who aren't professional politicians. Donald Trump is perhaps the most prominent case. Many people – journalists and various others – have devoted a great deal of time to exposing the false claims he routinely makes in his speeches and comments, but his supporters seem to trust him nonetheless. On standard views of the evaluation of information sources in epistemology, this is a surprise. Given that someone is consistently untruthful and is known to be so, why should we ever trust them?

This chapter uses the tools presented in this book so far, augmented with existing work on reliability and trust, to address this puzzle in three parts. First we spell out and contextualize the starting puzzle in a theory of source evaluation based on interactional histories and heuristics for judgments of reliability (McCready 2015), which is used to spell out the puzzle and as an exemplar of truth-based views on trust. This is done in section 7.1. The second is a theory of how ideological considerations are valued alongside truth-conditional content, in 7.2. We have of course discussed this topic in some detail in previous chapters, but here we wish to push it further. The

---

[1] Social Sincerity could perhaps be extended to a more general, strategic notion, in a way similar to the way in which cooperative behavior in other settings has been tied to 'selfish' considerations using insights from how the evolution of cooperation has been modeled in game theory (e.g., Bowles and Gintis 2011). This question closely relates to the discussion in Chapter 5 concerning the idea of using utilities in Social Meaning Games to model sincerity without recourse to a dedicated principle, where we argued that there are reasons to have an explicit statement of Sincerity for social meanings.

main idea involves methods of valuating personas via the ideologies they project, i.e., ways of spelling out the function ν which we've used to represent speaker and hearer attitudes toward personas. This is then used together with temperature parameters on truth-conditional content and social meaning to model the degree to which each is valued in particular contexts.

We claim that considerations about social meaning are what makes people trust messy testimonial agents like Trump: fundamentally, because in certain contexts people value similar ideological beliefs more than they value true-speaking, a surprisingly rational mode of behavior for political settings, given the way politics works, and maybe in other contexts too. Finally, the theory of reliability in repeated games is extended to cover cases of trust that aren't founded on truth-conducive speech, but instead are grounded in expectations about what a speaker exhibiting a particular ideology is likely to do, and how that is likely to affect the person making the decision to trust or not. We close with several conclusions, first the descriptive claim that trust in Trump-like agents can be rational depending on one's preferences, and second a set of prescriptions for how oppositional political discourse must proceed to be effective, given the foundations of ideologically based trust.

7.1 Evaluating information sources

The theory of reliability in terms of truth-conduciveness developed by McCready (2015) addresses the question of how one can determine whether content obtained from a particular agent, or other information source, should be believed. This is a longstanding and controversial issue in epistemology, and has been extensively addressed in thousands of works; our goal in this section is not to present a solution to this question, but simply to use one approach to the issue to make the question of trust in social agents more precise. For the reader who already finds the question precise enough and who isn't interested in the formal modeling of reliability or evidence-based belief update, this section can be passed over without too much loss of readability, though it will serve as the basis of the formalization to follow.

McCready (2015) in her book aims to address two empirical questions: the function of hedges and the ways in which evidential factors play into reasoning and information update. She proposes a two-factor theory of source reliability for both agent testimony and other evidence sources and applies it to dynamic update with evidential constructions in formal semantics/pragmatics. Here we consider only the case of testimony, as the more general theory is not required to clarify the main question we are interested in: the relationship between reliability/truthfulness and trust.

On the view of McCready (2015), the determination of reliability has two parts: a method of assigning initial judgments about whether a particular source is going to be reliable, and then a method for updating those judgments. An agent first uses a set of heuristics to determine whether a particular testimonial source has properties associated with reliability. Sample properties that might be taken into account by these heuristics include the source's profession, personal presentation, gender, race, etc.

Of course, some of these properties are genuinely useful for determination of reliability and some are not. For example, an agent's profession is relevant to deciding whether that agent is going to be reliably truth-tracking for assertions about content domains relevant to that profession: we might believe a linguist on issues of linguistic practice, for example, or a farmer on the question of the right time to plant a crop of barley. Conversely, some professions might lead us to downgrade those who work in them in our judgments about likelihood of truth-tracking: learning that someone spends all their time trading cryptocurrency might lead us to stop listening to them when they give investment advice. (This downgrade might also relate to the identification of a 'cryptobro' social persona.)

However, some choices of property lead to *epistemic injustice* (Fricker 2007), such as gender and race, which aren't in general relevant to evaluation of reliability, but are nonetheless taken into account by (some) agents in making judgments about whether to believe a piece of testimony (see McCready and Winterstein 2017, 2019 for a detailed investigation of the case of gender, which shows via experimental methods that at least for some domains men are assigned higher baseline degrees of reliability than women). Still, application of these heuristics leads to a probability that the source is reliable. This is an initial determinant of whether it is a rational move to accept content proffered by the source.

The initial probability assigned using the heuristics is only a starting point which is subsequently modified by interaction with that source. Each observation of a discourse move by the source, together with verification of whether its content is truth-tracking, alters, via conditionalization, the probability that the source is reliable. In particular, following McCready 2015, suppose that each information-transmitting discourse move by a source of testimony contributes to a history of discourse moves, understood as iterations of a repeated game of information transmission. Such moves are modeled, simplifying slightly from the original system, as tuples $\langle \varphi, V \rangle$, where V is a value in the set $\{T, F, ?\}$ reflecting the truth value of the proffered content. Here, '?' indicates that the move cannot be evaluated for whatever reason: that its truth value is unknown, for instance, or that its value is otherwise indeterminate, as in utterances containing only non-truth-conditional content or more controversial cases such as sentences expressing subjective judgments ('Life is beautiful.').

Records then have the form $\text{Hist}_g = \langle a_1, ..., a_n \rangle$, for a game g with n repetitions. The basic probability of reliability across this discourse sequence is then interpreted as the frequency of T-valued moves, so the result is a real number in [0,1] where each T-valued move induces an uptick in value (unless the frequency is already 1). In this setting, the degree of reliability assigned to an agent R_a is defined as, where $t_a = \Sigma_{i \in 1,...,n} \text{val}(\Pi_2(a_i)) = T$ (where 'Π_2' is as before a projection function picking out the second element of the tuple) and $f_a = \Sigma_{i \in 1,...,n} \text{val}(\Pi_2(a_i)) = F$,[2]

$$R_a =_{def} \frac{t_a}{t_a + f_a}.$$

---

[2] This formulation is simplified from that in McCready 2015 and follows the discussion in McCready and Henderson 2020.

The result is that each truth-tracking move raises (possibly very slightly) the perceived likelihood that the source is reliable, and each move that fails to track truth lowers it. The basic model is thus entirely frequentist. This simple treatment can be made more sophisticated in various ways (e.g., by weighting more recent interactions over older elements in the history, as we'll do shortly for valuation of histories that integrate social meaning, or by introducing awareness, or by putting in place other ways to deal with question-valued elements), but it is sufficient for our purposes to note that all such modifications will still be restricted to judgments about truth-tracking and leave out social meaning entirely.

But how should reliability relate to belief? That is, how should an agent incorporate information from a variety of sources of varying reliability? Furthermore, when should an agent be willing to say they believe a proposition based on information from these various sources? Once we understand how reliability affects belief, we can model the fact that in general people discount unreliable sources, and begin to address the puzzle that some unreliable sources continue to be believed.

We can link reliability and belief using a flavor of dynamic semantics (Groenendijk and Stokhof 1991), following work on dynamic updates in Plausibility Models (e.g., Baltag and Smets 2008). In this literature, slightly simplified, a frame σ is a set of worlds ordered with a 'plausibility ranking' reflecting epistemic preferences on states, which is enriched into models in the usual way. In Reliability Dynamic Logic (McCready 2015), these structures operate at several levels. While we have a global model σ, most of the action happens in indexed submodels (hereafter *information states*), each of which represents a source whose reliability we mean to track.

$$j \in \text{Source} \cup \mathcal{A}$$

where Source is the set of non-testimonial evidence sources and $\mathcal{A}$ the set of agents.

These information states are ordered by a total ordering $\preceq_a$ satisfying the following, where a is the agent tracking reliability, and $\text{Rel}_a(i)$ is the probability that source i yields reliable information according to a–i.e., a's index of reliability derived from their history with this source.

$$i \prec_a j \text{ iff } \text{Rel}_a(i) < \text{Rel}_a(j)$$

Updates on information states are of the following form, where the subscript i marks the source of the evidence of φ. For cases of testimony, as we discuss here, i ranges over $\mathcal{A}$, the set of agents. The idea is that an update indexed with an information source affects the information state associated with that source, and leaves the rest of the information states untouched.

$$\sigma[E_i \varphi] = \sigma' \text{ where, for all } \sigma_j \in \sigma, \begin{cases} \sigma'_j = \sigma_j[\varphi] & \text{if } i = j \\ \sigma'_j = \sigma_j & \text{if } i \neq j \end{cases}$$

Note that a sentence $E_i \varphi$ always induces the standard update of state σ_i, namely $\sigma_i[\varphi] = \{s \in \sigma_i | s \in \varphi\}$. At this level, update with φ always takes place—but this is *not* the same as coming to believe φ at a global level.

To determine global beliefs, we unify the information of all tracked substates σ_i via lexicographic merge.

$$R_{a \text{\scriptsize ⋒} b} := R_a^{\prec} \cup \left(R_a^{\cong} \cap R_b\right) = R_a^{\leq} \cup (R_a \cap R_b) = R_a \cap (R_a^{\prec} \cup R_b)$$

The core idea is that merging σ_i ⋒ σ_j will result in state where all non-contradictory content survives, and in case of conflict, information from the higher-ranked source overrides the lower-ranked source—i.e., $i \prec_a j$ will privilege content from j. Recursively applied, the global state σ_T on which belief is defined will almost never exhibit conflicts.[3]

With the link finally established between reliability (encoded in $\prec_a$) and belief (propositions that follow from σ_T), we are now in a position to more precisely state the problem of trust encountered in political discourse. Each information-transmitting discourse move affects the perceived reliability of a source in a way dependent on the properties of the source and whether it is truth-tracking. Thus, an agent that is consistently non-truth-tracking will rank lower on $\prec_a$ with each non-truth-tracking discourse move. As these agents fall on $\prec_a$-rank, the content this agent provides will be less likely to survive lexicographic merge and appear in σ_T. Thus, the content such an agent provides will not be believed, as belief is defined on the global information state. This seems right in the general case.

But now the puzzle is clear: what about politicians who are known to consistently ignore the truth, but are still trusted by their supporters? What about Trump? And what about other non-politicians who choose to transmit information that's dubious but who people somehow seem to trust anyway? The answer, we think, lies in a different, thicker way of making sense of the general notion of trust: one that takes into account social meaning and ideology.

7.2 Ideology and trust

The analysis of dogwhistles and of social personas in the previous chapters (and also in Burnett 2019) assumes that we have a way to assign affective values to personas, as realized in the function $v_{S/L}$. What is the basis of this value assignment? As of this point, we haven't said much about this; here, we've mostly followed the literature, which is fairly quiet about how exactly affect comes to be assigned in the context of social meaning. We now want to explore several methods by which this kind of assignment might be made, and how they relate to issues of trust.

Agents can have various reasons to assign positive (or negative) value to a given persona. There are obviously many options, some involving personas and some not, for instance the degree to which the persona instantiates some value independently held by the agent such as originality, rebelliousness, safety, or conformity to some social

---

[3] We will forego giving further details of the formal model here; the interested reader can find them in McCready (2015).

norm.[4] Here, though, we will make use of a very simple metric, namely *similarity*, as already used extensively in the last chapter. Our route here is to assume what's called *homophily*, where similarity induces a positive reaction: as Lazarsfeld and Merton put it in a classic paper on the topic: "common values make social interaction a rewarding experience, and the gratifying experience promotes the formation of common values" (Lazarsfeld and Merton 1948: 36). The intuition behind this criterion is that there is intrinsic value in discovering other individuals who share our core values, ideologies, and personal styles. We could paraphrase this as 'I like people who are like me,' or, in this context, 'I like people who have social personas which are like mine.' A homophily-based method of assigning value is widely used and indeed forms a portion of the basis for the algorithms driving social media, though here it has the negative effect of driving individuals into bubbles separated on the basis of social or ideological identity where they are free to express their views, and also where those views get reinforced, as discussed in detail by Chun (2021). We will return to this point at the end of the chapter.

Using a similarity criterion means we can assign affective values on the basis of similarity metrics between speaker and hearer personas. There are many candidate metrics depending what we choose to base the relevant notion of similarity on; as discussed in the last chapter, any simple similarity metric is fine given that we use personas, which seems the obvious choice for both our purposes here and for more general uses of homophily across computational and political domains. Personas themselves as used in sociolinguistics are extremely various and we want to focus on the cases at hand, ie. the personas associated with ideological content which are relevant for dogwhistles. Since ideologies for us consist of pairs of rating functions and ideological bases, we can use either of these elements, or both, to compute similarity. As already observed in Chapter 5, though, ideological bases influence the way we rate people and properties, and the affect we hold toward particular individuals in turn influences the kinds of propositions we're willing to admit into our ideological bases. Consequently, we define similarity only using ideological bases, as already done in the last chapter.

With all this, we are in a position to enrich the analysis of reliability in McCready 2015, which was predicated on truth-tracking alone. The core idea is to let hearers determine trust through a mix of truth-conditional and social meaning, with different mixes leading to different kinds of listener utilities in the repeated game setting. Just as we've set things up so far, speaker payoffs rest on two fundamental aspects of meaning: first, for truth-conditional meaning, the successful transmission of true information about the world, and, second, for social meaning, successfully transmitting information about speaker personas together with the hearer's evaluation of that persona. We treat hearer payoffs identically because (for truth-conditional meaning) clearly the hearer cares about learning the truth, and (for social meaning) as social

---

[4] Such valuation could be understood as persona-based but need not be; it could also be understood via the similarity mechanism discussed immediately after this, but again it need not be.

agents, we value finding individuals who share our values and social groupings, as already discussed.

We follow Henderson and McCready (2018) and weight the two components of the utilities with values δ, γ, giving the following formula. Here $U_S^{Soc}(m, L)$ is the utility of the social meaning and $EU(L, Pr)$ is the value of the truth-conditional meaning, a value given by computing the expected utility of sending a message m, which amounts to the likelihood with which the hearer can recover the true state of the world on the basis of that message, following van Rooij 2008.

$$U_S(m, L) = \delta U_S^{Soc}(m, L) + \gamma EU(L, Pr)$$

Thus δ indexes the value placed on the social meaning, while γ indexes the value of the truth-conditional meaning. Setting $\delta = 0$ gives a style of communication where social meaning is disregarded, for instance "science" as traditionally construed, i.e., as a completely objective enterprise where social aspects of the identity of the agents (scientists) involved are irrelevant. At the other extreme, setting $\gamma = 0$ gives "post-truth", a style of communication in which facts are irrelevant and only social persona matters, in the sense that only social meanings contribute to utility computations, as any utility derived from factual communication yields no payoffs.

This mechanism can be exploited for an analysis of reliability in the face of countervailing evidence as in the case of Donald Trump. When $\delta >_! \gamma$,[5] we end up with Trump-voter-style confidence and trust, because considerations of truth are vastly undervalued compared to persona signaling. Indeed, enriching the system of McCready (2015) with social meanings means that perceived reliability can increase in repeated game settings in virtue of social signaling alone, given that social meaning is allowed to play a role in the 'vetting' process. Here, 'reliability' is best understood not as truth-conduciveness, as in the original work of McCready (2015), but rather as a high (probability of a high) degree of similarity of social persona which induces homophily.

Combining these setups, it becomes possible to judge an individual unreliable in the sense of section 7.1 – in that their statements don't consistently track the truth – but still trust them, in the sense that one takes them to have similar goals and thus judges them to act in a way consistent with one's interests. The idea then is that if an agent has a similar enough persona to oneself they can be *trusted*, without precisely being *believed*.

Let us now be slightly more precise about the way in which similarity can be defined. In the last chapter, we discussed the use of similarity metrics to make sense of the phenomenon of hypervigilance. The idea there was to base utilities on (dis)similarity of the personas of speaker and listener. Using the same general set of assumptions, it is easy to see how to incorporate a notion of trust: once the persona expressed by the signaler is extracted by the interpreter, a similarity metric is used to compare the personas of signaler and interpreter, yielding a value in the real-numbered interval

---

[5] Where '$>_!$' indicates a vast difference in value.

[0, 1]. Given a sufficiently high degree of similarity, the interpreter will be justified (in terms of closeness of interests) in trusting the signaler; the formal mechanisms for making decisions about trust then work in essentially the same way as which reliability was handled by McCready (2015), though the overall mechanism makes reference to additional parameters.

To extend this model to discourse-level phenomena and thereby make the actions of agents across the lifespan of testimonial interaction genuinely dependent on both social meaning and reliability, we now integrate our view on social meaning with the histories of McCready (2015). Game iterations are now of the form $\langle \varphi, V, \pi \rangle$, where φ and V are as before and $\pi \in$ PERS. The degree of trust assigned by the interpreter to the signaler a in the initial state is just the degree of similarity between the persona π_1 expressed by a in their first interaction, i.e., the first game iteration.

$$\text{trust}_a^1 = \text{sim}(\pi_1, P)$$

As interaction continues, trust is assigned as follows by averaging the trust assigned before the current iteration with the similarity of the interpreter's and the agent's currently expressed personas.

$$\text{trust}_a^{i+1} = \frac{\text{sim}(\pi_i, P) + \text{trust}_a^i}{2}$$

This system is extremely simple and gives a high degree of importance to the latest interaction of the two agents; this is easy to modify, but we find it intuitive to let the latest interaction of agents be highly determinative of how they judge trustworthiness via social aspects of persona and ideological communication.[6]

This kind of approach to 'reliability,' while prima facie aberrant from the perspective of the epistemology of testimony, can be rational in terms of maximizing utility in a variety of scenarios. One case would be in scenarios where social signals are more easily interpreted. In a political campaign where voters may not know much about certain policy domains, sending a true message about those policies may not actually help the listener much in picking the true state of the world. Listeners in such a situation would do well to downgrade truth-conditional content in favor of social meaning, for doing so helps them more to make choices about their voting behavior, and speakers who recognize this situation would do well to focus on the social personas they are communicating. If these message are additionally uninformative in terms of social meaning, then it would be rational in terms of payoffs to pick an alternative message that is false, but which clearly sends a message about the speaker's persona/ideology. In the extreme case of this strategy, which we've been taking Trump to exemplify, over a conversational history interlocutors become ever more sure of each other's sociolinguistic personas and attendant ideologies, but do so by discounting truth-conditional considerations.

---

[6] Note the difference here to McCready 2015, which uses a much more gradual method of integrating new information about testimonial reliability.

While setting $\delta >_! \gamma$ discounts truth conditional information, note that this setting does not necessarily lead to perverse truth-conditional outcomes. Remember that on first interaction with a speaker, a listener must fix a prior for reliability based on a heuristic which evaluates interlocutors' perceived reliability. One thing that must be taken into account here is of course the speaker's persona as indicated by non-linguistic social cues, as well as any social meanings recoverable from their first utterance. We expect that one viable strategy to evaluate a speaker's trustworthiness is to, early in the conversation, set $\delta >_! \gamma$ so to better alight on their persona and likely ideological commitments. Crucially, this can be truth-conditionally virtuous. Recall, for instance, that certain dogwhistles only get their enriched meaning once a listener has identified the persona of the speaker. This means that social meaning can affect the truth conditions of messages, and so having an accurate picture of the speaker is crucial. Further, as Stephanie Solt (p.c.) points out to us, it can be useful for hearers to learn speaker personas even when they do not share them, for instance when the persona in question is highly objectionable or when it might otherwise impact judgments about the reliability of the speaker in a truth-conditional sense; we will return to this issue in the next chapter. As these considerations show, focusing on social meaning by setting $\delta >_! \gamma$ early, and then switching to $\gamma >_! \delta$ in order to monitor the truth-tracking of an agent whose persona/ideology has been sussed out is thus a viable strategy to maximize payoffs in both communicative domains.

We have shown how focusing on the social meaning domain is a viable strategy for maintaining high payoffs in repeated communication, and thus can be used to establish trust. This chapter has formalized these insights by integrating the model of testimonial reliability of McCready (2015) with the model of trust of Henderson and McCready (2019) via notion of persona similarity, weighting of social meaning versus truth-conditional content, and setting the result in repeated games. This integration brings together notions of reliability in terms of truth-telling and reliability in terms of common interests and ideological similarity, on the assumption that the latter is to be understood in terms of personas.

7.3 Social hedges: Fake news and fig leaves

We now turn to several communicative moves that can be used by speakers who are employing this strategy or their supporters, in the first case we discuss. The first signals that, indeed they are pursuing this strategy: this is the framing of taking someone 'seriously not literally.' The second, crying *fake news*, kneecaps alternative strategies. The third aims to hedge social meanings with truth-conditional content; this is the use of discursive fig leaves.

The first case is the simplest. In discussing Trump's communication style, multiple pundits and partisans have said that we must 'take Trump seriously, not literally.' What could this mean? In our account, the meaning is clear. It is an exhortation to set $\delta >_! \gamma$, or even to set $\gamma = 0$. The idea is that we should not pay attention to the literal truth-conditional content of his utterances, but to instead take him seriously. But take him seriously as what? We think we are being instructed to take his social persona as a billionaire, as a businessman, as a fighter, as a nationalist, etc. seriously. This rhetorical move immediately makes sense in the framework we have developed, and shows that social meaning and truth-conditional meaning are separable, and that we can prioritize one or the other.

The second case also shows the utility of the picture we've set up here. In some conservative/right-wing discourse, taking a statement and calling it *fake news* is a signal to remove it from truth-relevant consideration. We see several different ways to model this within the present setup. The first is to view it as a call to set $\gamma = 0$ in its payoff evaluation. The interpreter then considers only similarity of persona (ie. politics) in the utility calculation. With this, if the fake news move is accepted, considerations of truth become completely (though temporarily) irrelevant to political discourse. This is initially plausible, but it has several shortcomings. First, since it eliminates any utility stemming from the recovery of truth-conditional information, it leads to generally lower utilities for 'fake news' content; while this may be part of the intended effect, it is not clear to us that this way of computing utility properly tracks the way in which we value such content. Even if something is deemed to be fake news, there is a sense in which the truth-conditional content still provides some value to the interpreter, specifically that she comes to believe that the content is *false*, which is already useful in a way that should be reflected in utility calculation.

We thus think that *fake news* is best viewed as a kind of hedge which functions as a denial operator. Simultaneously, it has a pragmatic effect as an invitation to the hearer to ascribe themself a persona in ideological opposition to whatever agent made the original claim, which we write below as π_r ('the persona of the reported individual'). Given the way in which we tie opposition and thus negative affect to lack of similarity, the ascription of low similarity will result in a negatively viewed persona. We use the following definition.[7]

(1) $\text{FN}(\varphi) = $ (i) $\text{Deny}(\varphi)$
      (ii) $\neg\text{Low}(\text{Sim}(\pi_r, \pi_h))$

The fake news operator works as follows: first, the truth-conditional content of the original utterance (factual claim) is denied. Because it's said to be false, any utility stemming from recovery of the truth-conditional content of the utterance is set to zero, if the denial is accepted. Second, the persona of the original speaker is claimed to be at odds with that of the listener. If so, this persona will be assigned a low value or even a negative one. The combination of these two factors works to destroy trust both from truth-conditional (reliability) and social meaning perspectives.

The utility of this operator can be motivated in various ways, but here is our preferred take. Imagine you're playing a Trump strategy in which the goal is to gain favor

---

[7] As with the work of McCready (2015), the precise way in which hedges behave compositionally is left underdetermined here.

via the use of social meaning rather than being a reliable communicator in a truth-conditional sense. You would want to tell people that other news is fake so that they can't play a strategy which maximizes truth-conditional meaning: the explicit denial of a bit of content means that one won't be able to extract utility from it on the truth-conditional side of the utility calculation, so it will only be sensible to try to extract value from the social meaning side. As a result, the hearer (who accepts this discourse move) has to play the social meaning strategy-maximizing game you're playing, which is your preferred outcome, whether because you are better at the social meaning side in general, or because it is better for you to avoid strategies which pay attention to truth-conditional content in the particular case in question.

The second phenomenon we consider here is the case of fig leaves. Fig leaves are defined by Jennifer Saul as bits of content which are 'tagged onto' other uttered content with the aim of 'thinly veiling' some objectionable attitude expressed. For example, a speaker might say 'I'm not racist, but ...' and follow it with a racist statement, or 'I have nothing against trans people, but ...' and follow it with the expression of a support for removing rights from trans people. Another, more complex, kind of example is provided by Saul (2017), and comes from a comment made in a speech by Donald Trump, which we quote here in full:

When Mexico sends its people, they're not sending their best. They're not sending you. They're not sending you. They're sending people that have lots of problems, and they're bringing those problems with [them] ... They're rapists. And some, I assume, are good people.

Both of these types of example can be thought of as hedges of a special kind which aim at deflecting the inference of a particular social persona, namely a racist or transphobic one for the examples above. Since the work of McCready (2015) on reliability we make use of in defining 'social trust' above was originally intended as a treatment of both reliability and hedging, the current framework is well suited for the analysis of this aspect of fig leaves.

According to McCready, the function of hedges is to keep some particular aspect of an utterance from going into the 'permanent record.' As already discussed above, she uses histories of actions in repeated games to define such records: they are just sequences recording the actions taken by a given agent in a given game. Reliability is then computed from these histories by taking the proportion of actions with the property of being truth-tracking, or, for social trust, that proportion together with the similarity of the social persona/ideology projected by a given utterance with that of the speaker. McCready develops an analysis of truth-oriented hedges in this framework by simply postulating that hedges indicate an intent of the speaker to keep the hedged discourse move from going into the computation of reliability. Hedges are thus viewed as requests that the hedged utterance be excluded from computation of the proportion of truth-tracking utterances that leads to judgments of (un)reliability. We have not yet considered in this book how this kind of analysis can be adapted to judgments about ideological similarity of the kind that lead to trust, mostly because we haven't yet seen hedges of the relevant kind; but, since (we think) fig leaves have precisely this character, we now extend McCready's view of hedges to this situation. Fortunately, the project is straightforward.

As we've shown in detail in previous chapters, the mechanism by which personas and by extension ideologies are assigned to discourse agents is as follows: the speaker utters some bit of linguistic content which makes available, as part of its meaning, a range of possible social personas the speaker might be projecting. The hearer chooses one on the basis of Bayesian reasoning and assigns it to the speaker. If the hearer takes the speaker to be communicating sincerely about their social persona, she will, via Social Sincerity, take them to also subscribe to any ideology associated with the persona, ie. some set of beliefs. The persona itself, or the ideological basis thereof, can then be compared with the hearer's own persona and ideology to see how similar it is, at which point the hearer will recalibrate the degree of social/ideological sympathy they have for the speaker. The aim of the fig leaf hedge is to eliminate the last step in this process.

We can view the action of this hedge in several different ways. One is to adopt the view of McCready (2015) for truth-oriented hedges, where the action of the hedge is metalinguistic and simply removes the game iteration from the computation of reliability. But the current framework makes available a simpler method. Given the two parameters δ and γ, which respectively weight the values of truth-conditional meaning and social meaning for the current utterance, the hedge can be viewed as resetting the parameters. In particular, fig leaf-style hedges for social meaning can be thought of as setting γ to 0, and thereby eliminating the contribution of persona to the meaning of the utterance entirely for those who allow the hedge. If the hedge has its intended effect, then, the hearer won't engage in persona recovery for the utterance. For the case of racist fig leaves, then, racist personas won't be derived, and the question of impact on (social) trust won't arise at all; rather, the hearer will simply consider the remaining content of the utterance on its truth-conditional merits or lack thereof.[8]

Of course, it doesn't always go quite this smoothly, from the perspective of the fig leaf user. Commonly, the hearer will reject the attempted hedge and instead compute the speaker as projecting not just a racist and xenophobic persona (for the case at hand) but a disingenuous one, where the racist content is disavowed in a way that still in theory allows it to be expressed in contexts where standard antiracist norms are in effect. In many cases, indeed, this outcome is in line with the intent of the speaker: often people use hedges of this kind to try to play down the consequences of their actual beliefs, as already indicated by the name 'fig leaves,' which in art conceal the observable fact of genitalia without actually calling into question in any way the existence of the physical organs in question. This strategy is exploited by agents who want to say racist things,

---

[8] The same could be done for the truth-conditional side; if δ is set to 0, any truth-conditional content would be removed from the computation as well. We won't explore the changes doing this would require in the formal model further, however.

and signal their actual personas, while making transparent attempts to shield themselves from consequences. This presumably is the intent of the fig leaf in the Trump speech above.

An interesting aspect of fig leaves is that truth-conditional content is used to try to deflect the inferring of speaker persona. This makes sense, of course: social meanings themselves don't have the requisite Boolean structure to negate, or attempt to negate, further social meanings (cf. McCready 2014 for discussion of the expressive power of expressive content).[9] But it raises further questions. What is the relationship between personas/social meaning and truth-conditional content? And what kind of additional content can social meanings generate? Are there social implicatures? Are there differences in social meanings parallel to what we find with nonprojective and projective content in the truth-conditional domain? These questions are large and complex and we cannot fully address them here; still, see the next chapter for some discussion and speculation.

7.4 Conclusions

This chapter has considered how trust interacts with social persona. As we have seen, trust is distinct from reliability, which is concerned strictly with truth-tracking; we can trust the testimonially unreliable, and not trust the testimonially reliable. We implemented this observation in an extension of McCready's (2015) model of reliability, and extended the result to the 'fake news' effect, where particular truth-oriented utterances are diminished in force via the expression of incompatible social personas, and to fig leaves, which we analyzed as a kind of social meaning-oriented hedge.

We close with a final point. While trusting people who consistently lie might look like a bad life strategy, it turns out that in certain contexts where social similarity is valued over truth it is likely a rational way to behave. One such context might be the case of political speech. When we ask ourselves which politician we want to support, it is arguably rational to care most about what kind of policies a politician might want to implement, as opposed to whether they consistently speak the truth in debates and speeches. Certainly we see this in the case of Trump, as we have discussed in some detail; his supporters aren't concerned with whether he is conveying facts so much as that he does, in some sense, what they want, and that they feel sympathy for him. In general, any context in which homophily in a social sense is more important than fact will be one where $\gamma > \delta$ to a degree sufficient to make ignoring reliability in favor of social trust a rational strategy.

A consequence of this observation is that it doesn't make sense to try to sway people – in the political case, voters – away from a politician or other agent who relies on a social trust-based strategy by fact-checking their speeches or trying to show that

---

[9] Expressive content also lacks Boolean structure but is still more manipulable than social meaning as expressed in personas, as can be seen from the fact that expressive content can be modified by other expressive operators, as in expressions like *fucking asshole* (Gutzmann 2011) or *fuck, man!* (McCready 2010).

they play fast and loose with the truth. The people who are swayed by such an agent are already in a strategy space where truth is devalued via low settings for δ. Trying to change people's minds in such contexts requires a method that calls into question the agent/politician's social personas. Analogous to showing that an agent is unreliable via showing that they speak falsely, one must try to show that the agent's social persona is presented insincerely, so that their actual persona is different from the one they try to project, or to show that the persona and its projected ideology itself has pernicious effects on the person whose mind one is trying to change. This kind of picture explains the fact that exposing the lies of certain kinds of populist politicians doesn't have an effect on their bases of support: at best, the untruths they speak are waved off by supporters as irrelevant to the main political project.

The result is, perhaps, a general lowering of the tone of political discourse: effective counteraction requires populism and appeal to social persona and ideology, which many people in the political sphere would be loath to resort to. Given all this, the general prognosis, if our conclusions in this chapter are correct, is not so favorable for a fact-based rational politics, at least in the short term.

The situation is compounded by the way in which democratic systems work, which don't line up well with the situations which ensure various kinds of cooperative behavior. Within game theory as applied in economics and theoretical biology, as well of course as linguistics and philosophy, various mechanisms for ensuring cooperation been established (e.g., Gintis 2000; Bowles and Gintis 2011). These basically boil down to repetition, as in McCready's work on reliability discussed earlier, and supervision (threat of punishment) by an external agent. But both of these mechanisms require that there is a clear way to determine whether a particular game agent has violated cooperative norms or not. Sometimes this is straightforward. In the standard Prisoner's Dilemma case, it's easy to figure out who has chosen to defect; in the case of communicative acts aimed at truth-conveyance, it's also easy: we just see if someone's words track the truth.

All this is unproblematic, except that in the case of political speech in democratic contexts, it's less obvious what the utterances of politicians are meant to do. Even in the case of truth-conditional communications, not keeping campaign promises (for example) doesn't necessarily appear to be grounds for not being re-elected.[10] Further, the way in which electoral processes work in, e.g., the US mean that not being viewed as consistently truth-telling might not be a problem for re-election, as voters may not have other candidates available when it comes to the point of selection (e.g., in the case of incumbents, where that advantage might be viewed by primary voters as being more important than whether or not someone has always told the truth). This means that reliability might not be the most compelling consideration in the choices of the electorate, which already reduces the need for politicians to work hard at being judged as truth-tracking.

---

[10] This sentence assumes that a truth-conditionally based account of promises is available, which seems to us unproblematic at least at the level of content, where we suppose that they would look something like self-committing imperatives.

But our results in this chapter suggest that in many cases politicians' utterances aren't necessarily meant to be truth-conducive at all, but instead primarily to signal the persona of the politician. We suggested above that it's hard to argue against this kind of strategy, as such arguments, if sincerity-based, have to target the projected persona, which is non-trivial. If persona projection is primary, it potentially becomes unclear how to hold politicians accountable, for the ideologies we associate with them are the result of inference and association rather than direct statement. If this is right, it makes the state of political discourse look even more muddy than before, and, in the worst case, opens the possibility of politics being a noncooperative context in which the interests of politicians and voters are opposed. How this situation can be overcome is a question far beyond the scope of this book, and beyond linguistics in general. We hope that the present work at least helps to clarify the structure of the problem.

8
Beyond dogwhistles

8.1 Summary

Let us briefly summarize what we've done in this book before moving to some extensions and consequences of the theory.

This book has provided an analysis of dogwhistles, first situating them in the broader pragmatic landscape and then giving an account in terms of persona projection. In Chapter 2 we discussed the notion of dogwhistle and the way in which we define it and divided the class of dogwhistles into two: identifying dogwhistles, which indicate something about the (political) views and persona of the speaker, and enriching dogwhistles, which also alter the literal meaning of the sentence. We then showed that dogwhistles occupy a liminal space between conventional and nonconventional meaning, and that previous accounts of dogwhistles in linguistics and philosophy fail to properly capture the phenomenon in that they either steer too closely to conventional, lexical meaning, as with treatments in terms of conventional implicature, or too far away from it toward abstracting away from particular lexical items, as with purely inferential treatments. The rest of the book, particularly Chapters 3 through 5, showed how to steer a middle course between these two extremes.

The theory we proposed uses tools from Rational Speech Act theory and from discussions of identity in sociolinguistics, together with their formalization by Burnett (2019) in a game-theoretic setting. Chapter 3 introduced those toolkits. We applied and extended them in Chapter 4 to identifying dogwhistles, claiming that dogwhistles of this type are coded messages which allow clued-in listeners to draw inferences about the speaker's social persona in addition to communicating the literal content of the utterance, which it does to all interpreters. Chapter 5 extended the analysis to enriching dogwhistles. Such dogwhistles crucially rely on the kind of persona identification found with identifying dogwhistles in order to induce the inferences which alter the literal content, which takes place via association of an ideology with the persona the listener has found, and inferring enrichments based on this content. These chapters together comprise the core analysis of dogwhistles in the book.

Chapter 6 considered vigilance and hypervigilance. These terms refer to states of awareness of the kind of pragmatic content that dogwhistles involve: extending the RSA terminology, sociolinguistically aware listeners. Vigilant listeners are aware of personas, their utilities, and how they are expressed, and consequently work harder than the sociolinguistically unaware literal listener to draw conclusions about the personas of speakers. Here we also discussed the question of intentionality in dogwhistling, and concluded that a kind of intentionality can be encoded into our model via prior probabilities that a given individual has a particular persona, which in turn relate to utility calculations. Hypervigilant listeners are a kind of extreme case of vigilant listeners who quickly conclude that dogwhistles are being used. They consequently systematically put aside the idea that expressions which are actually dogwhistles might be used innocently, or nonintentionally. We related these two ways of listening for social meaning and personas to credibility results in signaling games, showing that the common point between the two is the degree of alignment of utilities between sender and receiver; hypervigilance itself we modeled as reassignment of priors to be a function of ideological distance.

In Chapter 7, we turned to the notion of trust as it relates to both dogwhistles and to social meanings. We began with the observation that people trust politicians even when they are shown to consistently ignore the truth, an unexpected fact in the light of epistemologies of testimony like that of McCready (2015) which link trust in the reliability of speech to past experience with particular speakers, the leading idea being that speakers who don't tell the truth end up judged untrustworthy. After reviewing McCready's model and situating the initial question of political trust within it, we proposed a theory of trust in testimony which takes into account both truth-tracking trust of the usual kind and also the kind of trust that comes from recovering ideological social meanings, namely one that relies on learning that a particular speaker is ideologically similar to the interpreter. We took this notion of trust to be the one at issue in political speech, at least political speech of the populist kind exemplified by Donald Trump. The rest of the chapter considered several consequences of the model, and some related issues: the notion of 'fake news' and the function of fake news claims as discourse moves, and the phenomenon of 'figleaves,' which lightly veil ideologically questionable speech, treated by us as a kind of social-meaning directed hedge. We closed the chapter with some discussion of implications for political speech and debate in general.

The rest of this chapter is dedicated to considering some additional phenomena and questions that arise with respect to our analysis.

The book so far has been about dogwhistles: when speakers might choose to dogwhistle, how listeners identify those dogwhistles, or not, and how that affects their behavior and interpretation, how care about detecting dogwhistles is rational but can lead to communicative disaster, and how trust can be built on social meaning – the signaling of personas – rather than facts. The following section, 8.2, considers a kind of opposite case: situations in which speakers choose *not* to dogwhistle, but rather to say objectionable things flat out; we show that these can be given an explanation within our model as certain parameters move toward extreme settings. Dogwhistling, then, turns out to be a signal of a kind of discursive health, in that to the degree that those parameters remain within a 'normal' range,

Section 8.3 turns to questions about how to situate social meanings in other aspects of pragmatics, the form of social meaning domains, and the question of how and whether they interact with truth-conditional content. Section 8.4 is a discussion of the relationship between personas, perspectives, and standpoints in the sense of standpoint epistemology, which shows some advantages of treating things in this way but also some potential pitfalls. We show that these can be overcome by treating standpoints as depending both on the sincere use of personas by speakers and on their uptake by interpreters. Section 8.5 invites reconsideration of the scope of our model beyond dogwhistles to other kinds of coded speech and covert communication. We argue that all speech, at some level, is coded speech, and so our theory has applications far beyond dogwhistles; this claim concludes the book.

8.2 Mask-off moments and discursive health

In previous chapters, we have explained speaker behavior with respect to the choice of using dogwhistles, together with some aspects of their listener pragmatics, focusing on vigilance, hypervigilance, and trust. One conclusion was that the pragmatics around both vigilance and trust lead to strategies which are potentially bad news for truth-oriented communication and dialogue, in that attention to social meaning can lead to privileging it over truth-conditional content. It does not address why a speaker may choose to abandon the use of dogwhistles and instead make an overt appeal that, without a doubt, allows listeners to detect they bear the taboo persona.

We call situations where speakers put dogwhistling aside 'mask-off' moments. They require a novel explanation, for the theory so far leads us to expect that it's rational to dogwhistle quite generally, as doing so can be expected to lead to better results for the speaker given the presence of a mixed audience, which, after all, is the usual situation in political discourse. What would cause a speaker to stop dogwhistling?

Our strategy in answering this question is to give a typology of unmasking, understood as a specification of the various situations in which a speaker may choose to abandon dogwhistles, and then show that our model predicts this typology as certain model parameters are set to extreme values. As we'll see, these parameter settings are likely to emerge under political polarization. The theory thus provides an important prediction about political rhetoric, namely that polarization should lead to an abandonment of dogwhistle politics in favor of explicit extreme appeals. In particular, we propose that unmasking tracks several factors related to political polarization involving changes in speaker beliefs about how their use, or lack thereof, of dogwhistles is going to affect their payoffs from particular linguistic choices.

On our analysis, dogwhistle use is prompted by the attempt to maximize utility with respect to a mixed audience. As we saw, the results can lead to various kinds of pragmatic effects, but in the core case the key idea is that the dogwhistle allows persona recovery by more listeners that hold positive views toward that persona than negative ones. There are several situations, however, in which utility maximization would push the speaker toward the abandonment of dogwhistling.

We think that mask-off moments come from three general sources. The first is changes in the speaker's beliefs about the way their audience is understanding their social persona: if one thinks dogwhistling isn't going to be effective, there's no reason to do it. The second comes from beliefs about who is in their audience, ie. who they take themselves to be addressing: if no one susceptible to dogwhistling is in the crowd, there's no point in it, and if no one who's listening cares if one masks one's unpalatable ideologies, there's no point in dogwhistling either. The last case involves changes in the value the speaker assigns to presenting with that persona: the more important it feels to them to clearly have a persona, the less they'll want to disguise it. The conclusions of this discussion have implications for diagnosing the health of a particular political discourse or speech situation.

The first situation resulting in a mask-off moment arises when the speaker no longer believes that dogwhistling is going to be effective. One way in which this can happen is when the speaker's audience already believes that she has the persona in question, or when the speaker believes that they do, or, more technically, in cases where the priors the audience has for the speaker's personas (or that she believes they have) are unbalanced enough that they will assign her the one she's trying to hide regardless of whether she used the dogwhistle. In such a case, the speaker will think the dogwhistle is going to be ineffective.

The speaker might come to think this for various reasons, but in the modern (e.g., internet) context a common cause is being called out for more subtle signals of negatively viewed social personas or ideologies, which leads to increased scrutiny of further speech. This of course relates closely to the discussion of hypervigilance in Chapter 6. The drive to monitor and expose ideological adversaries which results in hypervigilance is one which we take to be an effect of political polarization. The result of being aware of hypervigilance is that speakers often seem to conclude that they might just as well double down. In a slogan: 'if I'm already canceled, I'll just speak my mind (= not dogwhistle anymore).' Ultimately, this is rational behavior, just as with the other two cases we discuss below: if my probability assignment leads to the belief that I'm going to be assigned negative utility by some discourse participants based on what people take my persona (ideology) to be no matter what I say, it's best for me to focus on appealing to the people who I know approve of my views. This is so even if only a small amount of utility is extracted from making an overt appeal when compared to using a dogwhistle, which those sympathetic will also likely detect.

A second reason for 'doubling down' also results in the abandonment of dogwhistling. One might change the way one assigns value to the presentation of social personas, or to the value of the specific social persona one aims to project, by increasing the affective value assigned to the persona associated with the dogwhistle. As $v_{S_1}(p)$ for some persona p tends to ∞, dogwhistling becomes non-optimal. It is better to make an overt appeal and ensure all audience members assign you p, even if they don't like p. The speaker's own affective value for p will swamp whatever the audience values. A speaker like this cares more about (to put it kindly) being honest than being liked.

For the case of social personas that aren't associated with dogwhistles, like Burnett's cases of the cool guy and the asshole, the speaker values presenting whatever they take themselves to be like over what they think will make them attractive to their audience; for personas which are associated with ideologies, the speaker wants to present their actual views come what may, no matter how awful those views might be or how dark a situation they result in for the speaker in terms of social approval. Such a speaker's slogan is 'I don't care what you think of me if you don't think like me.' This evaluative shift results in the formation of communities in which extreme and explicit speech is valued, and represents a move toward overt extremism and consequent polarization around the topics associated with the ideology in question.

Finally, another possibility with a somewhat similar effect is for the speaker to change her take on the audience. If she comes to view the group she is addressing as one composed of same-believers (that is, individuals who have positive views of her preferred ideology), she won't have an incentive any longer to use dogwhistles. One can compare here shifts in the group used for determining the truth value of epistemic modals in the literature on philosophical contextualism (e.g., DeRose 1991), where changes in the group alter what possibility claims are taken to be true or false, with consequent modifications in the behavior of cooperative speakers. Of course, changes in one's beliefs about who is listening also can result in ideological polarization when one takes one's audience to become more homogeneous.

This situation arises easily on the internet where one can't see who one's statements are reaching (slogan: 'I'm not talking to you anymore'). Social media like Twitter are the paradigm case where one can project content into the void without having a clear picture of who's seeing it; the structure of apps like these also likely supports this sort of shift, as one starts to pay more attention to likes (which are assigned mostly on ideological lines) than comments (which might be combative). Of course, the opposite situation, where one starts to believe that one's audience is more heterogeneous than one initially believed, also arises, but leads to the converse situation where one is more likely to prefer dogwhistle use, as the audience again has the requisite structure for the use of dogwhistles to increase utility.

We just saw that the resources made available in our model can help make sense of the abandonment of dogwhistling. One can think of dogwhistle abandonment as a defensive reaction similar to *backfire*, a phenomenon in which agent belief in a proposition is strengthened after it's shown to be false, which has as one of its effects the creation of polarized political communities (Nyhan and Reifler 2010);[1] the abandonment of dogwhistles indicates the speaker's belief that she's no longer addressing a mixed audience, and, as such, is a way of constructing and delimiting such polarized communities via linguistic methods.

Can we draw any conclusions about all this about how to judge political discourse? We think we can, and that the conclusions are somewhat counterintuitive. Ordinarily, people take dogwhistling to be completely out of line – it is taken to signal that people both hold ideologies they know are unpalatable enough that they should be hidden, and they take steps to do so, which is usually viewed as a deceitful move. And

---

[1] Backfire might be better described as a putative phenomenon, as the results of the original study haven't proven to be very amenable to replication. We expect our analysis to be much more replicable than the backfire effect, however. Perhaps the postulation and immediate popularity of the backfire effect itself indicates something about people's beliefs about the structure of current political discourse, but we will not consider this further here.

at the very least dogwhistling isn't cooperative even in the Gricean sense of conveying information transparently, at least not to those speakers who aren't clued in; it also isn't cooperative in that it indicates a desire to remain unaccountable for some of one's ideas. All this is obviously bad, and in an ideal political world we wouldn't see dogwhistles at all, for they wouldn't be needed – everyone would be on the same page in rejecting racism, homophobia, transphobia, misogyny, etc. But sadly this isn't the way the world looks at this point.

We think that, given the way the world does look now, we should be more concerned when people *stop* dogwhistling then when they dogwhistle – on the assumption that some people have something to hide in terms of views that are completely unacceptable in mainstream discourse. This might be a surprising view. But consider. If speakers dogwhistle, it means they care about what others with differing views think, and they think that those others haven't already written them off. They think they're not canceled, and they think other people are still listening. Conversely, ceasing to dogwhistle means they have given up on everyone outside their bubble. The three cases above show this: the belief that no one with different ideologies is listening anymore (case 3), or at least not listening with any kind of desire for dialogue (case 1), or, worst of all, just that the speaker doesn't care at all about anything other than broadcasting their ideology regardless of consequences (case 2). None of these situations is healthy for a political discourse. In this sense, one conclusion we draw from our theory is that, surprisingly enough, dogwhistles in politics have the potential to be signs of a relatively healthy discursive environment (emphasis: *relatively*), at least if they are likely to arise in the first place.

8.3 Lessons on social meaning

This book has taken the phenomenon of dogwhistles to crucially involve social meanings. But, from a formal semantic perspective, there are many puzzles around this domain. What kinds of interactions do we see between social meanings and truth-conditional meanings, if any? Are there implicatures that arise in the social meaning domain? We have already addressed this question for dogwhistles in particular in Chapter 2, where our conclusion was negative (for standard Gricean implicature anyway), but what about social meaning? Does something like Heim's Maximize Presupposition principle apply, which instructs us to use the most pragmatically rich expressions we can, all else being equal? Do social meanings come in different types, as other kinds of non-truth-conditional content do, for example presuppositions and expressives? What is the general structure of the evolution of social meanings: do we find structure in this domain analogous to the convexity found in color terms (Jäger 2010), and in general the Voronoi tesselations observed in truth-conditional predicates (Gärdenfors 2004)?

These questions are obviously too rich and complex to address in this small subsection of the conclusion of this book, and we have already considered some of them at various points in the preceding. But we can point to a few places that our analysis of dogwhistles can contribute further to answering them.

One thing that is already clear from the preceding discussion is that the kinds of social meanings that we've modeled via personas come in at least two types. Both signal the identity of the speaker, but one is associated with ideologies and one is not. Consider again Obama at the barbecue and his use of an apical variant of a gerund (*cookin'* as opposed to *cooking*) to signal his friendliness and approachability. These qualities have nothing to do with ideologies, or even arguably with propositional content at all, but the signal itself is a social meaning. Compare the speaker who chooses to use a racial slur. Such a speaker signals a social identity – racist – and also, via the social meaning analogue of Gricean Quality proposed in Chapter 5, their belief in various propositions relating to racist ideologies. Clearly, these two kinds of social meanings are different and require distinct formal treatments. This is a clear-cut distinction in the category of social meanings that stems directly from the present analysis.

Do social meanings interact with truth-conditional content? The answer is a clear yes, for at least the kind of social meanings that come with ideological commitments. Since dogwhistles as we have defined them require ideologically associated personas to function, they of course also have such effects. We have two cases in mind that exemplify this interaction.

First case. What happens when an interpreter recognizes a speaker as projecting a particular social persona? The information that the speaker has that persona is information like any other kind of information, and, like any piece of new information, will affect the way the interpreter thinks of the world. One way to think of this which is consonant with our analysis above is to make use of probabilities: acquiring new information leads us to conditionalize our prior probability assignments on the new information, and consequently assign new probabilities to various relevant things. One area which is of interest in the present context where communication is involved is trying to project what the speaker means: ie. what their communicative intentions are, in cases of ambiguity or underspecification, which arise both in trying to make sense of lexical items with this character (for example, the ambiguous *bank* or emotive adjectives like *fucking* which are underspecified for positive/negative interpretation, as discussed extensively in terms of probability in McCready 2012), and in trying to recover the speaker's intention in making various kinds of discourse moves.

In some cases, assigning a speaker a particular persona can change the likelihood with which we take them to have been trying to communicate certain propositions. If I think you are projecting a racist persona, I am more likely to interpret your subsequent ambiguous utterances in a way that gives them racist overtones (or straight up racist propositional content) than I would be if I knew you to be actively antiracist. The reason is just that I find it more plausible that you might be trying to say something racist, so I am less likely to rule this kind of interpretation out. One might argue about whether this is genuine interaction with truth-conditional content, because it operates in some sense at a pragmatic and interpretative level; but similar things could happen even in syntactic parsing once meaning is taken into account, for cases of attachment ambiguities and the like. At least in a broad sense, then, social meanings have clear impact on the interpretation of truth-conditional content.

Social meanings can also lead to the loss of trust. This is the second case. My observation of a dogwhistle that covertly conveys content that I have major problems with will lower the trust I have in the individual who used the dogwhistle, as discussed extensively in the last chapter. The kind of trust focused on there mostly concerned a general notion of 'trust in action' on which the evaluator takes themself to have common interests with the person being evaluated. But this kind of loss of trust might also lead to me ceasing to consider the person reliable with respect to truth-conditional content as well.[2] If I know someone has ideological sympathies which cause them to hold beliefs I deem irrational (flat-earthers, big-lie Trumpers, racists, etc.), I am less likely to believe them when they make factual claims to me, especially when those claims relate to their ideological beliefs. A statement made about voter fraud by a QAnon believer is not one I'm likely to take at face value. We saw a somewhat similar case in the last chapter: that of the person we learn to spend all their time trading cryptocurrency, though total loss of credibility might require a cryptobro social persona as well.

These kinds of changes in credibility can be cashed out in the formal theory presented in the last chapter by restricting reliability evaluation in the repeated game setting to utterances whose content relates to the content of the ideology, as done in McCready (2015) for domains of expertise; regardless of how one chooses to understand the phenomenon, though, it is clear that social meanings play a role in how reliable and trustworthy we find our interlocutors.

Let us turn to a second question. What is the structure of the domain of social meanings? For Burnett (2019), who we have followed here, social meaning denotations are selected from indexical fields, which are consistent subsets of some set of properties none of which subsume the others. The field is itself constructed according to current discourse needs within a community, which we can equate with a community of practice in the sense of Quaranto (2022). These fields shift in ways that depend on the discourse topic, the context, and what aspects of social difference the conversational participants choose to highlight. At this level of generality, there may not be much more to say about these domains, excluding standard observations about second-order logic and the structure of properties; for example, persona domains in the simplest case (where each persona is composed of a single property) presumably have the standard structure of a Voronoi tesselation, where the space is partitioned into spaces in terms of distance from a single point which is taken to be the 'center' of the property in a way interpretable as its canonical example or prototype (as in Gärdenfors 2004). This construction, of course, won't be so easily available as personas become more complex. But perhaps social meanings of more specific types have more articulated structure? Can something more general be said about any particular kind of social meaning?

For social personas which are associated with ideologies, perhaps something can. Ideologies by definition are relatively stable objects which don't vary so much across

---

[2] Thanks to Stephanie Solt for discussion on this point.

contexts. In Chapter 5, we defined ideologies as pairs of affect-assigning functions and ideological bases of the form $\langle \rho, \mathcal{B} \rangle$, where the latter is a set of propositions, essentially those that people subscribing to the ideology take to be true. Since the precise contents of what is believed can vary somewhat across subscribers, we also defined the core of an ideological basis to be those elements which are stable across believers in the ideology, ie. the generalized intersection of the ideological bases of particular believers. The notion of ideological basis, and in particular of the core of such bases, imposes some structure on the domains. Specifically, these bases can also be viewed as inducing Voronoi tesselations, assuming restriction of the base set of propositions to a finite domain (perhaps, for example, propositions related to social content). The core ideology would then function as the seed of a cell in the partition. We have already seen something like this in previous chapters when discussing similarity of ideologies/personas, in that we made use there of similarity functions over ideological bases, which is precisely what is required to induce tesselations of this kind.

Lastly, we turn to analogues with other domains of pragmatic meaning. Do we find something like implicature more generally with social meanings, as opposed to dogwhistles specifically? Is there a way something like Maximize Presupposition can apply (cf. Schlenker 2012)? We explore these questions now, with generally negative conclusions.

Consider first implicatures, restricting ourselves to the standard Gricean picture modified for the social meaning context.[3] Gricean Quality has already seen an analogue in the Social Sincerity principle introduced in Chapter 5. What about the other maxims? Relevance as stated by Grice is vague enough that it probably can apply to social meaning too; but it doesn't seem to do much extra in the social meaning context, instead just pretty much indicating that the speaker thinks it's relevant or useful to communicate the persona projected by the social meaning. Manner would require the ability to communicate the same, or extremely similar, social meaning content in multiple forms, where one carries substantially more cost than another. This seems like a situation that might in principle arise, but it's not clear to us at present what the effects might be. But Manner implicatures and how they work are a little opaque and contentious among linguists and philosophers even in the truth-conditional context, so it's perhaps not surprising that it's difficult to draw general conclusions in the social meaning case.

What about Quantity implicatures, which are easily the best-studied category of implicature barring perhaps Quality? The general structure of Quantity implicatures on a (neo-)Gricean account is as follows: there are multiple linguistic expressions of different strengths, where strength can be defined in various ways: positions on a scale, informativity, or what have you. We will use informativity here as the most general of the obvious possibilities. The speaker uses a less informative expression, which allows the interpreter to infer that the stronger expression was inappropriate,

---

[3] Note for clarity that we're interested in the question of whether the use of expressions that project social meaning, including dogwhistles, generate implicatures, as opposed to the question of whether dogwhistles can be treated in terms of implicatures, an idea we already rejected in Chapter 5.

ie. false, by combination with Quality. This general structure seems in principle applicable to social meanings.

We see several possible ways in which Quantity-type implicatures could arise in social meaning domains. The first involves competing expressions, both of which carry social meanings indexing social groups, in cases where the group indexed by one expression subsumes the other. This is essentially an analogue of informativity for social indexing, in the sense that if one is indexed as a subgroup member, one is also understood necessarily to be a member of the supergroup.[4] The idea then would be that using the expression indexing the supergroup would imply that the speaker isn't part of the subgroup, or at least doesn't want to present as being so.

At a theoretical level, this makes sense. Empirically, do we actually find these sorts of pairs of expressions? Certainly there are plenty of pairs of expressions where one signals identity in a group and the other signals a kind of cultural identity that's ordinarily connected with that group: for example, white people and identities associated with white supremacist ideologies. But a little thought shows these identities aren't really in the kind of informativity relationship required for a Quantity inference. Probably nearly all white supremacists are white, but some aren't, so the inference fails due to lack of group inclusion. Ultimately, we don't see any case of social indexing and group inclusion where the inclusion isn't more statistical than necessary, at least not in cases where the speaker unambiguously has enough freedom of choice to make the implicature computation relevant in the first place. Consider accents, which signal geographical origin in a broad sense. A Texan accent implies that one is from the US, but people don't necessarily have enough agency over their accents to make decisions about how to present themselves in terms of location of origin in the way we'd need for a Gricean account of implicature generation. We conclude that we need to look elsewhere if we want to find the necessary structure to support Quantity implicatures.

One possibility is to look to personas which are associated with ideologies, which have been the kind we have considered most in this book. The structure of ideological bases—sets of propositions—is ideally suited for our purposes: we need only find cases of 'ideological inclusion,' cases where one ideology subsumes another, and see whether we actually find Quantity inferences arising from them. The first step of this project is to find two ideologies such that $\Pi_2(\iota_1) \subset \Pi_2(\iota_2)$ which associate with social meanings which are carried by linguistic terms which can be used in sufficiently similar contexts (i.e., ones which are intersubstitutable enough to serve as pairs inducing Quantity inferences). The second is to determine whether an utterance which allows a hearer to conclude that the speaker means to present with a persona associated with ι_1 also yields an inference to the speaker either being unable to sincerely present with a persona associated with ι_2 (the blocking Quality inference, via Social Sincerity), or

---

[4] A similar situation would arise with property inclusion for cases where the social meaning indexes properties like the *cool guy* or *asshole* of Burnett, but it's not so obvious to us that the requisite kind of structure exists at the level of granularity that social meanings of this kind give us access to; Burnett's way of constructing personas also rules out the very possibility of property inclusion, which might or might not be sensible for the kind of persona that signals ideologies, as discussed below.

an inference that she doesn't want to so present, which is of course dependent on the assumption of speaker intentionality in social indexation and persona presentation.

Are the necessary conditions met? It turns out to be surprisingly (?) non-trivial. First, are there such pairs of ideologies at all? It seems like there probably are, at least at first glance, though it's a bit difficult to be sufficiently clear about the precise content of ideological cores to have full confidence in ideological inclusion. The situation is complicated, though, by the observation that, when it comes to similar ideologies, it's often the case that they are fairly explicitly differentiated by belief or lack of belief in specific propositions. For example, a political ideology ι_1 which supports armed insurrection is differentiated from one that doesn't but which otherwise has a similar ideological base, ι_2, not just in that $\Pi_2(\iota_2)$ doesn't include the proposition that armed insurrection is OK, but also that $\Pi_2(\iota_2)$ includes the proposition that armed insurrection is not OK. In other words, 'weaker' ideologies aren't necessarily neutral on the propositions that characterize 'stronger' ones, but rather actively deny them. If this is a correct characterization, it becomes very difficult to find pairs of ideologies that exhibit genuine inclusion.

Second, if there are indeed such pairs of ideologies, are there pairs of this kind which are associated with lexical terms of the needed kind, ie. which can appear in approximately the same contexts with approximately similar production and processing cost? This is an easier condition to meet, but, again, the range of social meaning bearers is so various it's difficult to make clear estimates, especially considering the issues of the previous paragraph. We have not found what we take to be any absolutely clear examples with the relevant structure, and so have to leave any definitive answer to the question of Quantity implicatures to future work.

Even before the empirical questions, though, our intuitions are a little unclear around the case. Does observing a speaker projecting a relatively weak version of an ideology lead one to conclude that they don't support a stronger version? Or are they just saying something they think will be relatively socially acceptable? How one answers this question likely correlates to some degree with one's the degree of (hyper)vigilance around a particular issue; the trans person with bad experiences with transphobia is more likely to consider extreme ideological possibilities when faced with someone 'just asking questions' about trans issues, for example. Perhaps the right way of thinking about Quantity here is that the generation of implicatures is extremely situation-dependent, and dependent on the agents involved, in ways that might approach the open-ended computation of Relevance implicatures, themselves quite different from standard Quantity implicatures, which have a fairly well-defined structure.

All this is not to say that no implicatures arise from the use of social meanings, or of dogwhistles in particular. Recall the discussion of Gricean approaches to dogwhistles in Chapter 2, where we made use of something like a 'safety principle' to derive implicatures about speaker beliefs about their audiences. Specifically, use of a dogwhistle implicates that the speaker thinks that someone in the audience would disapprove of their persona; this can be concluded on the basis of a desire not to self-incriminate as believing in a problematic ideology, which we discussed then as a kind of safety maxim. Dogwhistle use also implicates speaker belief that someone in their audience is savvy enough to recover the dogwhistle. It's not clear that this is an implicature in the Gricean sense though, and again it isn't something that can be derived for all social meanings, because some indices don't come with the required intentionality for Gricean derivations of implicature.

This observation also allows us to draw the conclusion that Maximize Presupposition doesn't have a social meaning equivalent. This principle states that one should pick the most informative expression in terms of non-truth-conditional content from one's available expressions, all else being equal (Schlenker 2012). Such a principle makes sense for presuppositions, for example, in that they function to tighten the connections between various elements introduced in discourse and among sequences of utterances. But such a principle doesn't make much sense for social meanings, for two reasons. First, as just observed, we don't really get to choose in general whether to use a social meaning; some indices, such as dialect, are not always within conscious control. Second, a principle requiring us to use social meanings if available wouldn't be reasonable, for it would require people to reveal their ideological commitments in every context, which would mean they had to either remove their masks as in the last section, or at the very least dogwhistle, which just isn't the case. We conclude that Maximize Presupposition is limited to other kinds of non-truth-conditional meanings, and possibly even just to presupposition.

Our aim in this book has been to analyze dogwhistles. But we have seen in this section that the analysis we have given speaks to broader questions about the nature of social meaning, the structure of the domain, and how it interacts with other kinds of content. As so often in linguistics and philosophy, detailed examination and analysis of one phenomenon leads to a greater understanding of the broader picture. Dogwhistles, in this sense, are no exception.

8.4 Standpoints

This book is not about epistemology, but we want to point out one way in which we think the theory we've presented could prove useful in an epistemological sense, perhaps even one which turns out to be relevant to linguistic interpretation. Specifically, we think that the work presented here, involving probabilities and personas, can be used to make formal sense of the idea of a standpoint in standpoint epistemology. However, the notion of standpoint we end up with is partial and relational, which has interesting consequences for both the notion of standpoint itself and for the kinds of personas which speakers can choose to present.

What is standpoint epistemology? The idea has many realizations, but the essential concept is that the position one occupies in society can give access to knowledge about the world, given that one is sufficiently attentive to one's positioning and how it makes one sensitive to certain things others might not be able to access. The notion of a standpoint itself is usually cashed out in terms of identities: gender, race, sexuality, and so forth. Having such an identity is by itself only a necessary condition, not a sufficient one; giving the right kind of attention is also key. The basic idea is not surprising, indeed it's almost a truism: of course people in certain social positions can see things people not in those positions can't! A club promoter can make a better guess about what partygoers are likely to be willing to pay for an event than many others, and people falling into a particular category (of, e.g., race, gender etc.) find it easier to identify language associated with ideologies that target them; expertise matters, in domains of race and gender as anywhere else.

In this context, we don't want to go deep into epistemological considerations or explore how the notion of a standpoint contributes to them, though there is of course a vast literature on these topics. Rather, we want to briefly sketch a way in which the theory we've presented can be used to formalize standpoints, and to also suggest ways in which standpoints themselves (especially as realized in the way we will indicate) can be used to help understand certain aspects of linguistic interpretation. The basic idea we want to propose is to think of standpoints as probability distributions resulting from the sincere use of certain personas which also require hearer uptake.

There are various ways to formalize the idea of a standpoint. One interesting recent method is suggested by Saint-Croix (2020), who proposes thinking of standpoints as certain kinds of evidential support relations within neighborhood models in modal logic, building on the work of Benthem and Pacuit (2011). Evidence in probabilistic frameworks is usually treated as conditional update of probabilities, but it also maps to conditions on prior probabilities. Consequently, the idea of evidential support in our framework corresponds to certain kinds of probability assignments: certain kinds of priors will sensitize people to things others can't access. Thought of in this way, a 'good' prior in the sense of one that allows extraction of knowledge that's not available on some other settings of priors turns out to be an epistemic advantage with respect to those areas it's good for, and certain standpoints will give information others don't. This is one way of cashing out the idea that standpoints and privileged viewpoints are like a kind of expertise that strictly improves people's intuitions about certain kinds of cases, just as found in eg. Devitt's defense of philosophical expertise in intuitions (Devitt 2012).

It's clearly not enough though to think of standpoints as just certain kinds of probability distributions, which after all can arise from a wide range of sources. The literature on standpoints makes a distinction between just being in a particular social position and occupying a standpoint: occupation of a standpoint requires being conscious of that standpoint and its effects. This is already present in some sense in probability distributions – if you aren't aware of the ramifications of where you stand you'll assign different probabilities to things than someone who is – but we have the resources in our theory to make things a bit more explicit, by thinking of standpoints as involving social personas.

But social personas as we've discussed them are things that discourse agents select and which are inferred from their utterances by other agents, not intrinsic properties of the agent. As we argued above, we need to treat them this way because social meanings of this kind aren't meant to match the world but rather to express the way the agent wants to place themself in the world, allowing the possibility of variation. These aren't quite the right kinds of objects to embody standpoints, mostly because they don't explicitly involve evidential bases. Better and more subtly, we suggest that standpoints comprise pairs of probability distributions and capacities to sincerely project particular personas. The Social Sincerity principle presented in Chapter 5 gives us the resources to make sense of someone presenting with a persona as something that almost necessarily involves some kind of awareness: one can't be sincere about something without being committed to it, and commitment in some sense requires one to be conscious of what one is committing oneself to.

Social Sincerity as we presented it only makes sense for personas that are associated with ideologies, for without an ideology the kind of sincerity we talked about—which requires the agent to believe a certain proportion of the propositions in the ideological basis—fails to be well defined. Classical standpoints, though, aren't political personas in the sense we talked about there, but relate instead to aspects of speaker identity relevant to marginalization or lack thereof: gender, race, socioeconomic class, and so forth. For such personas, we need to either find a different way to allow them to be sincerely projected, or not; or else we must allow them too to associate with ideological bases.

What if we go the latter route? There are two nice aspects to doing so. First, it's nice if the existing mechanisms and resources of the theory can account for this case without need to add extra moving parts, though of course the latter is sometimes necessary. All else being equal, though, we would prefer a simpler theory, and it's worth trying to work one out. Second, we don't find it outlandish to think that identities of this kind also associate with sets of background beliefs, which is after all what ideological bases are: perhaps there are beliefs about the world that a person who chooses to project a particular identity persona typically has, and there's no reason to think that they couldn't be modeled as sets of propositions.

The danger is that one has to be very careful here not to fall into a kind of 'belief essentialism' about identities. Obviously not all people of a particular gender or race (etc.) share any special beliefs, and it would be a reductio if the theory implied that they do. There seem to be two ways out. The first is to use the equivalence classes over individual ideology-holders already proposed in Chapter 5 to make sense of the fact that ideologies differ in their details across those who subscribe to them: not all libertarians think exactly alike. The idea would then be to limit the background beliefs associated with a particular identity to those shared by everyone with that identity. We think this is a strange approach, both because the beliefs shared by (for example) all women are likely to be few enough that there won't be enough left to do the epistemological work standpoints are meant to do, and because whatever is left as a universal residue of femininity is probably not very universal at all, in the worst case in the way pointed out by Lugones and Spelman (1983), where the content collapses to that associated with the most privileged.

8.4 STANDPOINTS

We conclude that using ideological bases to understand sincere presentation for identity personas is not the way to go. We will, instead, use a different notion of sincerity: an agent can sincerely project this kind of persona if they take themself to be of the identity that persona signals. We will understand 'being of an identity' in the simplest possible way: that the predicate associated with that identity can be truly predicated of the individual. Thus I am of the identity 'woman' if the predicate *woman* truly applies to me: $woman(C_a) = 1$, for Kaplanian contextual agent C_a (Kaplan, 1989). The possibility of this move didn't arise earlier. Ideological personas don't come with the relevant sort of predicatable identities, and neither do personas indicating dispositions such as friendliness and professionalism, as with the apical and velar gerundives discussed earlier.

All this is not to imply that there are in fact projectable personas which index bare identities. Taking, for example, gender identities, it's not so obvious to us that there are personas which have as their sole content the identification of the speaker as a woman; we here follow researchers like Ochs (1992), who takes gender identities to be constructed via a bricolage of more ambiguous categories. One of us in fact takes a similar line with Japanese first-person pronouns (in McCready 2019), which are often tied directly to gender identities, but actually are used in a much more nuanced way which can be tied to self-presentations which defeasibly imply a gender when taken together with social norms present in a Japanese context. Ultimately, we don't think there are personas which simply indicate gender; however, there certainly are personas which require a particular gender to be used, such as that involved with self-ascriptions of *dyke*, as described by Burnett (2020) and discussed in Chapter 5. In these cases, speaker belief that $woman(C_a)$ is true licenses the self-ascription of this predicate.

Is this enough? An immediate worry is that sincerity here is subjective. One can sincerely project an identity persona if one takes oneself to fall under the predicate. But surely one doesn't necessarily occupy a standpoint if one just takes oneself to have some property. This view opens the door to many undesirable results: to take an obvious and controversial one from the philosophy literature, Rachel Dolezal would have to be understood as occupying a standpoint associated with Black people, since she (apparently sincerely) took herself to be Black and so sincerely presented with that persona.

It would obviously be wrong to say that Rachel Dolezal occupied the standpoint occupied by Black people. But perhaps it's not so wrong to say that she did have access to some of the knowledge Black people have, given that she took herself (apparently sincerely) to be Black and that people treated her as if she was. If she was indeed treated as a Black person, she presumably experienced some of the racism that people of color face. At the same time, since she wasn't in fact Black, those experiences were only partial and started midway through her life, meaning that she lacked access to those experiences and whatever component of the relevant standpoint stemmed from them. Formally speaking, she experienced some things which caused change in her probability distributions in a way aligning them with some experiences that Black people undergo, but did not experience others, meaning that those aspects of her distributions went unchanged.

The case of trans people is extremely different from this one in very many ways, not least that one's gender is less dependent on external factors like family histories and genealogies than race and so exhibits a possibility of individual change (see also Kukla and Lance 2023 for discussion of this point). Still, in this discussion we do find some analogues of trans experience. Trans women don't experience the particular aspects of the standpoint of women that correlate with events experienced before transition; but after transition those standpoints become available, because the experiences do. Perhaps not all, though, for there are aspects of embodied experience that transition, even medical transition, may not make available (cf. Young 2005). Social aspects do become available, though, assuming the legibility and acceptance of one's gender. This is the same for race: if one is treated as being part of a particular racial or ethnic group, one is positioned to take on, in those parts, the standpoint of that group.

From these observations, we conclude that there is a way out of the sincerity problem pointed out above. In order to occupy a standpoint associated with a particular social group, it's not enough just to sincerely take oneself to be able to project the relevant persona. Rather, one's interlocutors must also take one to be able to do so, for if they don't, one won't be able to learn how it is to be treated as a member of that group, and won't be able to modify one's priors in the needed way. All this is just to say that uptake is required on the part of the people around one. This makes sense: standpoints are after all in large part about social facts and visibility, and the epistemic advantages coming from standpoints require a particular social positioning and observation of how one is treated as a result of that positioning for their efficacy.

We are left with the conclusion that standpoints in our theory amount to having the capacity to sincerely project certain personas with hearer uptake, together with the kinds of probability distributions that satisfying the relevant predicates would result in. To our knowledge, this is a new take on the issue.

Before we move on to possible ways in which standpoints relate to linguistic interpretation, we want to briefly augment the discussion in the last section for the identity persona case, as the reader might wonder if identity personas behave differently with respect to the questions raised there. We think the answer is: not significantly. They don't seem to generate implicatures either and their domain doesn't seem to have more structure than the Voronoi tesselations observed for most predicates: if anything, one might argue that identities have less, to the degree that one views all instances of a particular identity as equally satisfying the predicate in question ('valid'). It feels odd to claim that there is a prototypical woman; doing so again starts to approach the worries about privilege and category centrality raised by Lugones and Spelman (1983) and others. We conclude that (not unexpectedly) identity personas don't have more structure than other kinds of personas.

However, they do differ in one way: if what we say above is right, there is something like a presuppositional structure in play with identity personas. If I want to self-predicate *dyke* or present with a *dyke*-type persona, I must be able to sincerely self-predicate *woman*; this can be understood as a presupposition. It is, however, a presupposition that operates outside the social meaning domain narrowly construed as the space of personas. If we are on the right track, this means that certain personas depend on the truth of certain propositions, indicating some dependence across domains of meaning. Perhaps this is unshocking given what we know about how the indexation of social categories works in language; still, here it has a formal realization which shows that truth-conditional meaning and social meaning are not fully independent, at least at the pragmatic level of sincere use of linguistic expressions.

Let us now conclude this section with some remarks about standpoints, dogwhistles and linguistic interpretation. Hesni (2019) makes the observation that people's backgrounds and identities are partly determinative of their intuitions about socially significant pragmatic phenomena, such as slurs and dogwhistles. This is already incorporated in our theory via the priors, of course, but it might be that pairing dispositions to present with a particular persona and priors allows us to find patterns in priors which correlate with presentational dispositions. If so, that would mean that there is a relationship between the available personas a speaker can sincerely present with and the personas they can recognize, here not just in terms of 'standard' social meanings but also with dogwhistles and even slurs: it could be that some 'dogwhistled' slurs can only be recognized as such by individuals coming from particular perspectives. If standpoints do indeed turn out to even partly determine what personas can be recognized, much less other aspects of linguistic content, that would be an extremely interesting result; we aim to explore this in future work in a more philosophical context.

8.5 Differential communication: The scope of the theory

This book has been about dogwhistles: terms which allow the recognition of social personas by some but not by others. We have given an account in terms of how probable agents find the association between message and persona to be. We have shown that this idea yields an empirically solid treatment of dogwhistles, and of various related questions. One might wonder though: are dogwhistles the end of the story?

To us it seems clear that they aren't. Pretty much every social meaning bearer, linguistic or not, is going to be intelligible to some agents and not to others. Dogwhistles piggyback on this fact, but lots of other things do too. Consider the 'hanky code' used in gay communities to covertly signal sexual interests, introduced in its modern form around the early 1970s. To the uninitiated, people on the street just have handkerchiefs of various colors in the back pockets of their jeans; to those in the know, the color and position of the hanky signify a lot more. But without identifying the hanky wearer as (potentially) gay, the code seems to be irrelevant; in other words, it depends on identification of a social persona. Would we want to call these dogwhistles? Obviously not, but they absolutely are coded communication, and we think there isn't any reason our theory wouldn't apply to them as well.

We think, in fact, that the theory we've proposed speaks quite generally to coded communications, especially to those which depend in some way for recognition of social identity to be extracted. One would be more likely to ascribe meaning to the color of a hanky in a back pocket on someone one knew from the gay club than to someone who looked to be visiting from out of town and part of a straight couple (though of course all this is probabilistic, just as one would expect). But this observation holds for lots of things, not just subcultural codes or dogwhistles. Even the most innocuous and vanilla language carries some social meaning, at least insofar as it relates to register and community. Consider the word *dog*, as boring and basic a word as one can get, as evidenced by long usage in linguistic and philosophical communities as the canonical example of a 'normal' bit of language. Even *dog*, when considered as alternative to *canine*, exhibits aspects of register selection and formality, and further tags its user as a member of an English-speaking community (with a high degree of probability). All these are social meanings.

Once the sheer scope of social coding in language is recognized, in fact, one might start to wonder if any expression lacks a social meaning element, or a 'secret code.' From this perspective, every term becomes a dogwhistle, because every term arguably carries some social meaning, and because any given term yields different information to different audiences depending on their backgrounds. In this sense, the theory we have developed here has a much more general application than the narrow analysis of dogwhistles for which we built it. We think there is a lot more to be done in the area of how differential probabilities lead to differential meanings, how those differences are filtered through social groups, and how speakers recognize each other as belonging to the same or different 'meaning communities.' This is basically sociolinguistics under the rubric of formal pragmatics. We hope that this book helps to make sense of the way these two fields interact, and to open up new possibilities for the future.

References

Aaker, Jennifer, Anne Brumbaugh, and Sonya Grier. 2000. Nontarget markets and viewer distinctiveness: The impact of target marketing on advertising attitudes. *Journal of Consumer Psychology* 9:127–140.

Acton, Eric K. 2022. Sociophonetics, semantics, and intention. *Journal of Linguistics* 1–30.

Albertson, Bethany L. 2015. Dog-whistle politics: Multivocal communication and religious appeals. *Political Behavior* 37:3–26.

Austin, John Langshaw. 1975. *How to do things with words*. Vol. 88. Oxford University Press.

Baltag, Alexandru, and Sonja Smets. 2008. A qualitative theory of dynamic belief revision. In *Logic and the foundations of game and decision theory*, ed. G. Bonanno, W. van der Hoek, and M. Wooldridge, number 3 in Texts in Logic and Games, 13–60. Amsterdam University Press.

Barrett, Liam. 2022. Labour promises to support the LGBT community, but they are currently taking our votes for granted. *i News*.

Benthem, Johan van, and Eric Pacuit. 2011. Logical dynamics of evidence. In *International Workshop on Logic, Rationality and Interaction*, 1–27. Springer.

Bowles, Samuel, and Herbert Gintis. 2011. *A cooperative species: Human reciprocity and its evolution*. Princeton University Press.

Breitholtz, Ellen, and Robin Cooper. 2021. Dogwhistles as inferences in interaction. In *Proceedings of the Reasoning and Interaction Conference (ReInAct 2021)*, 40–46.

Bucholtz, Mary, and Kira Hall. 2005. Identity and interaction: A sociocultural linguistic approach. *Discourse Studies* 7:585–614.

Burnett, Heather. 2017. Sociolinguistic interaction and identity construction: The view from game-theoretic pragmatics. *Journal of Sociolinguistics* 21.2:238–271.

Burnett, Heather. 2019. Signalling games, sociolinguistic variation and the construction of style. *Linguistics and Philosophy* 42:419–450.

Burnett, Heather. 2020. A persona-based semantics for slurs. *Grazer Philosophische Studien* 97.1:31–62.

Calfano, Brian Robert, and Paul A Djupe. 2008. God talk: Religious cues and electoral support. *Political Research Quarterly* 62.2:329–339.

Camp, Elisabeth. 2013. Slurring perspectives. *Analytic Philosophy* 54:330–349.

Camp, Elisabeth. 2018. Insinuation, common ground. *New work on speech acts* 40.

Campbell-Kibler, Kathryn. 2007a. Accent,(ing), and the social logic of listener perceptions. *American Speech* 82:32–64.

Campbell-Kibler, Kathryn. 2007b. What did you think she'd say?: Expectations and sociolinguistic perception. In *Annual Conference on New Ways of Analyzing Variation*. Philadelphia, Pennsylvania, October.

Cappelen, Herman. 2018. *Fixing language: An essay on conceptual engineering*. Oxford University Press.

Chierchia, Gennaro. 2004. Scalar implicatures, polarity phenomena, and the syntax/pragmatics interface. In *Structure and beyond*, ed. Adriana Belletti, 39–103. Oxford.

Chierchia, Gennaro, and Raymond Turner. 1988. Semantics and property theory. *Linguistics and Philosophy* 11:261–302.

Chun, Wendy Hui Kyong. 2021. *Discriminating data: Correlation, neighborhoods, and the new politics of recognition*. MIT Press.

Dénigot, Quentin. 2022. Formal approaches to the communication of conflicting identities in discourse. Doctoral Dissertation, Université Paris Cité.

DeRose, Keith. 1991. Epistemic possibilities. *The Philosophical Review* 100:581–605.

Devitt, Michael. 2012. Whither experimental semantics? *Theoria* 73:5–36.

Eckert, Penelope. 2008. Variation and the indexical field. *Journal of Sociolinguistics* 12:453–476.

Eckert, Penelope. 2012. Three waves of variation study: The emergence of meaning in the study of sociolinguistic variation. *Annual Review of Anthropology* 41:87–100.

Eckert, Penny. 1989. *Jocks and burnouts: Social identity in the high school*. Teachers College Press: New York.

Elga, Adam, and Agustín Rayo. 2016. Fragmentation and information access.

Farrell, Joseph. 1993. Meaning and credibility in cheap-talk games. *Games and Economic Behavior* 5:514–31.

Frank, Michael C., and Noah D. Goodman. 2012. Predicting pragmatic reasoning in language games. *Science* 336:998–998.

Franke, Michael. 2008. Meaning and inference in case of conflict. In *Proceedings of the 13th ESSLLI student session*, 65–74.

Franke, Michael. 2011. Quantity implicatures, exhaustive interpretation, and rational conversation. *Semantics and Pragmatics* 4:1–1.

Franke, Michael, and Judith Degen. 2016. Reasoning in reference games: Individual-vs. population-level probabilistic modeling. *PloS one* 11:e0154854.

Franke, Michael, and Gerhard Jäger. 2016. Probabilistic pragmatics, or why Bayes rule is probably important for pragmatics. *Zeitschrift für sprachwissenschaft* 35:3–44.

Fricker, Miranda. 2007. *Epistemic injustice*. Oxford University Press.

Gärdenfors, Peter. 2004. *Conceptual spaces*. MIT Press.

Gintis, Herbert. 2000. Strong reciprocity and human society. *Journal of Theoretical Biology* 206:169–179.

Goodman, Noah D., and Michael C. Frank. 2016. Pragmatic language interpretation as probabilistic inference. *Trends in Cognitive Sciences* 20:818–829.

Goodman, Noah D., and Andreas Stuhlmüller. 2013. Knowledge and implicature: Modeling language understanding as social cognition. *Topics in Cognitive Science* 5:173–184.

Grice, H. Paul. 1975. Logic and conversation. In *Syntax and semantics*, ed. P. Cole and J.L. Morgan, Volume 3, 41–58. Academic Press.

Groenendijk, Jeroen, and Martin Stokhof. 1991. Dynamic predicate logic. *Linguistics and Philosophy* 14:39–100.

Gutzmann, Daniel. 2011. Expressive modifiers & mixed expressives. In *Empirical issues in syntax and semantics 8*, ed. Olivier Bonami and Patricia Cabredo Hofherr, 143–165 http://www.cssp.cnrs.fr/eiss8/eiss8.pdf.

Haslanger, Sally. 2000. Gender and race: (what) are they? (what) do we want them to be? *Noûs* 34:31–55.

Heim, Irene. 1982. The semantics of definite and indefinite noun phrases. Doctoral Dissertation, University of Massachusetts.

Henderson, Robert, and Elin McCready. 2017. How dogwhistles work. In *Proceedings of LENLS 14*. JSAI.

Henderson, Robert, and Elin McCready. 2018. Dog-whistles and the at-issue/not-at-issue distinction. In *Secondary content*, ed. Daniel Gutzmann and Katherine Turgay, 191–210. Brill.

Henderson, Robert, and Elin McCready. 2019. Dogwhistles, trust and ideology. In *Proceedings of the 22nd Amsterdam Colloquium*, 152–160.

Hesni, Samia. 2019. Philosophical intuitions and socially significant language. Manuscript, MIT.

Hessick, Carissa Byrne. 2006. Motive's role in criminal punishment. *South California Law Review* 80:89.

Hitchler, Walter Harrison. 1931. Motive as an essential element of crime. *Dickinson Law Library* 35:105.

Horn, Laurence Robert. 1972. On the semantic properties of logical operators in English.

Hurwitz, Jon, and Mark Peffley. 2005. Playing the race card in the post-Willie Horton era: the impact of racialized code words on support for punitive crime policy. *Public Opinion Quarterly* 69:99–112.

Jäger, Gerhard. 2010. Natural color categories are convex sets. In *Logic, language and meaning*, 11–20. Springer.

Kanner, Bernice. 2000. Hide in plain sight. *Working Woman* 25:14.

Kaplan, David. 1989. Demonstratives. In *Themes from Kaplan*, ed. Joseph Almog, John Perry, and Howard Wettstein, 481–566. Oxford University Press. Manuscript version from 1977.

Kennedy, Chris. 2007. Vagueness and gradability: The semantics of relative and absolute gradable predicates. *Linguistics and Philosophy* 30:1–45.

Khoo, Justin. 2017. Code words in political discourse. *Philosophical Topics*.

Kukla, Quill, and Mark Lance. 2023. Telling gender: The pragmatics and ethics of gender ascriptions. *Ergo an Open Access Journal of Philosophy* 9 URL https://journals.publishing.umich.edu/ergo/article/id/2911/.

Labov, William. 1963. The social motivation of a sound change. *Word* 19:273–309.

Labov, William. 1966. The social stratification of English in New York City.

Labov, William. 2012. *Dialect diversity in America: The politics of language change*. University of Virginia Press.

Lackey, Jennifer. 2008. *Learning from words: Testimony as a source of knowledge*. Oxford University Press.

Lackey, Jennifer, and Ernest Sosa, ed. 2006. *The epistemology of testimony*. Oxford University Press.

Langton, Rae. 2012. Beyond belief: Pragmatics in hate speech and pornography. *Speech and harm: Controversies over free speech*, 72–93.

Lascarides, A., and A. Copestake. 1999. Default representation in constraint-based frameworks. *Computational Linguistics* 25:55–105.

Lazarsfeld, Paul F., and Robert King Merton. 1948. *Mass communication, popular taste and organized social action*. Bobbs-Merrill, College Division Indianapolis.

Lewis, D. 1969. *Convention: A philosophical study.* Harvard University Press.
Lewis, David. 1975. Languages and language.
Lo Guercio, Nicolás, and Ramiro Caso. 2022. An account of overt intentional dogwhistling. *Synthese* 200:1–32.
Lugones, Maria, and Elizabeth Spelman. 1983. Feminist theory, cultural imperialism, and the demand for "the woman's voice." *Women's Studies International Forum.* Vol. 6.
Mallon, Ron. 2016. *The construction of human kinds.* Oxford University Press.
McCready, Elin. 2010. Varieties of conventional implicature. *Semantics and Pragmatics* 3:1–57.
McCready, Elin. 2012. Emotive equilibria. *Linguistics and Philosophy* 35:243–283.
McCready, Elin. 2014. Expressives and expressivity. *Open Linguistics* 1:53–70.
McCready, Elin. 2015. *Reliability in pragmatics.* Oxford University Press.
McCready, Elin. 2019. *The semantics and pragmatics of honorification: Register and social meaning.* Oxford University Press.
McCready, Elin, and Robert Henderson. 2020. Social meaning in repeated interactions. In *Proceedings of the Probability and Meaning Conference (PaM 2020)*, 69–72.
McCready, Elin, and Grégoire Winterstein. 2017. Negotiating epistemic authority. In *New Frontiers in Artificial Intelligence (JSAI-isAI 2016 work-shops, LENLS, HAT-MASH, AI-Biz, JURISIN and SKL revised selected papers)*, ed. Setsuya Kurahashi, Yuiko Ohta, Sachiyo Arai, Ken Satoh, and Daisuke Bekki, volume LNAI 10247, 74–89. Berlin: Springer.
McCready, Elin, and Grégoire Winterstein. 2019. Testing epistemic injustice. *Investigationes Linguisticae* 41:86–104.
McGowan, Mary Kate. 2004. Conversational exercitives: Something else we do with our words. *Linguistics and Philosophy* 27:93–111.
McGowan, Mary Kate. 2012. On 'whites only' signs and racist hate speech: Verbal acts of racial discrimination. *Speech and harm: Controversies over free speech*, eds. Maitra, Ishani, and Mary Kate McGowan, 121–147. Oxford University Press.
Mendelberg, Tali. 2001. *The race card: Campaign strategy, implicit messages, and the norm of equality.* Princeton University Press.
Nyhan, Brendan, and Jason Reifler. 2010. When corrections fail: The persistence of political misperceptions. *Political Behavior* 32:303–330.
Ochs, Elinor. 1992. Indexing gender. In *Rethinking context: Language as an interactive phenomenon*, ed. A. Duranti and C. Goodwin, 335–358. Cambridge University Press.
Pal, Joyojeet, Dinsha Mistree, and Tanya Madhani. 2018. A friendly neighborhood Hindu. In *CeDEM Asia 2018: Proceedings of the International Conference for E-Democracy and Open Government*, 97. Edition Donau-Universität Krems.
Palmer, Kimberly. 2000. Gay consumers in the driver's seat: Subaru's new ad campaign is among those signaling to homosexual buyers. *The Washington Post.*
Podesva, Robert. 2004. On constructing social meaning with stop release bursts. In *Sociolinguistics Symposium*, volume 15, 1–5.
Podesva, Robert J. 2007. Phonation type as a stylistic variable: The use of falsetto in constructing a persona 1. *Journal of Sociolinguistics* 11:478–504.
Popa-Wyatt, Mihaela. 2016. Not all slurs are equal. *Phenomenology and Mind* 150–156.
Potts, Christopher. 2005. *The logic of conventional implicatures.* Oxford University Press.
Potts, Christopher. 2007. The expressive dimension. *Theoretical Linguistics* 33:165–198.
Quaranto, Anne. 2022. Dog whistles, covertly coded speech, and the practices that enable them. *Synthese* 200:1–34.
Quine, W.V.O. 1951. Two dogmas of empiricism. *Philosophical Review* 60:20–43.
Recanati, Francois. 2003. *Literal meaning.* Cambridge University Press.
Reiter, Ray. 1980. A logic for default reasoning. *Artificial Intelligence* 13:91–132.
Saint-Croix, Catharine. 2020. Privilege and position. *Res Philosophica* 97:489–524.
Sauerland, Uli. 2004. Scalar implicatures in complex sentences. *Linguistics and Philosophy* 27:367–391.
Saul, Jennifer. 2018. Dogwhistles, political manipulation, and philosophy of language. *New Works on Speech Acts* 360–383.
Saul, Jennifer M. 2017. Racial figleaves, the shifting boundaries of the permissible, and the rise of Donald Trump. *Philosophical Topics* 45:97–116.
Schlenker, Philippe. 2012. Maximize presupposition and Gricean reasoning. *Natural Language Semantics* 20:391–429.
Scontras, Gregory, Michael Henry Tessler, and Michael Franke. 2021. A practical introduction to the rational speech act modeling framework. *arXiv preprint arXiv:2105.09867.*

Simon, Mallory, and Sara Sidner. 2019. Trump says he's not a racist. that's not how white nationalists see it. *CNN Politics*.
Spencer, Hayley. 2020. A brief history of the Fred Perry polo shirt and its complicated connections to hate groups. *Independent*.
Sperber, Dan, and Deirdre Wilson. 1986. *Relevance: Communication and cognition*, volume 142. Cambridge, MA: Harvard University Press.
Stalnaker, Robert. 1974. Pragmatic presuppositions. In *Semantics and philosophy*, ed. M.K. Munitz and P. Unger, 197–213. New York: New York University Press.
Stalnaker, Robert. 1978. Assertion. In *Pragmatics*, ed. P. Cole, volume 9, 315–332. New York: New York Academic Press.
Stanley, Jason. 2015. *How propaganda works*. Princeton University Press.
Starmer, Keir. 2021. The road ahead. *Fabian Ideas* 657:1–34.
Thurston, Alexander. 2017. Coded language among Muslim activists: Salafīs and the prophet's sermon of necessity. *Die Welt des Islams* 57:192–222.
Tirrell, Lynne. 2012. Genocidal language games. *Speech and harm: Controversies over free speech*, eds. Maitra, Ishani, and Mary Kate McGowan, 174–221. Oxford University Press.
van Rooij, Robert. 2008. Game theory and quantity implicatures. *Journal of Economic Methodology*: 261–274.
Väyrynen, Pekka. 2013. *The lewd, the rude and the nasty: A study of thick concepts in ethics*. Oxford.
Welsh, Kaite. 2016. Xena lesbian warrior princess is back—and she's gayer than ever. *The Telegraph*.
White, Ismail. 2007. When race matters and when it doesn't: Racial group differences in response to racial cues. *American Political Science Review* 101:339–354.
Yoon, Erica J., Michael Henry Tessler, Noah D. Goodman, and Michael C. Frank. 2016. Talking with tact: Polite language as a balance between kindness and informativity. In *Proceedings of the 38th Annual Conference of the Cognitive Science Society*. Cognitive Science Society.
Young, Iris Marion. 2005. *Throwing like a girl and other essays in feminist philosophy and social theory*. Oxford University Press.
Zhang, Qing. 2008. Rhotacization and the "Beijing smooth operator": The social meaning of a linguistic variable 1. *Journal of Sociolinguistics* 12:201–222.

Index

advertising 4–5
affective value 49, 51, 60, 66–67, 80–81

backfire 135
belief revision 82–83, 108
bias 87–89
big pharma 59–65
bricolage 73–74, 145

cheap talk 13, 106, 108–110
community of practice 83–84
conventionalization 7, 11, 16–18, 27, 37, 70–73
covert 3–4, 6, 9–10, 23, 29–30, 31, 32

deniability 6, 17, 27, 68–69
differential communication 147–148
discourse breakdown 111–113
Dred Scott 21, 24–25, 86–87
dyke 79–80

enriching dogwhistle 75–89
    analysis 85–89
epistemic injustice 117

fake news 123–125
fig leaves 125–127

Grice 16, 20–23, 35–36
Gritty 71

hedging 125–127
homophily 120
honorific 7, 16–18, 81
hypervigilance 106–113

ideological basis 81–82
ideology 12, 25
    formal treatment 76–85
implicature 12, 20–23, 35–36
    conventional 7, 16–18
    manner 20–23
    in Rational Speech Act models 93–94
    relevance 21
    scalar 41–44
    social meaning and vigilance 94–99
indexical field 44–46, 46–48, 51, 59
inferentialist 18–20, 27
inner-city 1–3, 7, 9, 12, 18, 20–22, 30–31, 68, 85–86
intentionality 9–10, 29, 36, 99–104

Jeremy Corbyn 107, 110–111

Keir Starmer 106–111
kind-mapping function 78

lesbian 79–80
literal listener 37–39, 48–49, 56

MAGA 78
mask-off moments 133
Maximize Presupposition 142
meme 71–72
motive 99–104
multivocal appeal 6, 8, 30–31

Obama gerund 76–77
overt 3–4, 6, 9–10, 29–30, 31, 32

polarization 13
political science 2–3, 65–66
pragmatic enrichment 85–86
pragmatic listener 37, 40–41
pragmatic speaker 37, 39–40, 49–50, 58
prior 52, 60
pronouns 145

QAnon 81, 138

reliability 116–119

slurs 5, 7, 16–18
social meaning 11, 15, 26–28, 44–46
    and presupposition 146–147
    structure of 138–139
social meaning games 35, 44–54, 56–58
Social Sincerity 82–85
speech act, 8–9, 23–24
standpoint epistemology 142

temperature 40, 50
testimony 13
trans rights activist (TRA) 76
trust 13

utility 39, 49, 53, 57–58, 62–65, 67–68

vigilance 12, 92–105

wonder-working power 3–4, 23, 26–27, 29–30, 30–31, 55, 70–71
world knowledge 'axioms' 77

Xena 72

OXFORD STUDIES IN SEMANTICS AND PRAGMATICS

General Editors
Chris Barker, *New York University*, and Chris Kennedy, *University of Chicago*

PUBLISHED

1
Definite Descriptions
Paul Elbourne

2
Logic in Grammar
Polarity, Free Choice, and Intervention
Gennaro Chierchia

3
Weak Island Semantics
Márta Abrusán

4
Reliability in Pragmatics
Elin McCready

5
Numerically Qualified Expressions
Chris Cummins

6
Use-Conditional Meaning
Studies in Multidimensional Semantics
Daniel Gutzmann

7
Gradability in Natural Language
Logical and Grammatical Foundations
Heather Burnett

8
Subjectivity and Perspective in Truth-Theoretic Semantics
Peter Lasersohn

9
The Semantics of Evidentials
Sarah E. Murray

10
Graded Modality
Qualitative and Quantitative Perspectives
Daniel Lassiter

11
The Semantics and Pragmatics of Honorification
Register and Social Meaning
Elin McCready

12
The Meaning of *More*
Alexis Wellwood

13
Enriched Meanings
Natural Language Semantics with Category Theory
Ash Asudeh and Gianluca Giorgolo

14
Parenthetical Meaning
Todor Koev

15
Actuality Inferences
Causality, Aspect, and Modality
Prerna Nadathur

16
From Perception to Communication
A Theory of Types for Action and Meaning
Robin Cooper

17
Signaling without Saying
The Semantics and Pragmatics of Dogwhistles
Robert Henderson and Elin McCready

IN PREPARATION

Comparing Comparison Constructions
M. Ryan Bochnak

Meaning over Time
The Foundations of Systematic Semantic Change
Ashwini Deo

Plural Reference
Friederike Moltmann

A History of Formal Semantics
Barbara Partee

On *De Se*
Hazel Pearson

Objects and the Grammar of Countability
Peter R. Sutton and Hana Filip

Bayesian Argumentation in Language
Grégoire Winterstein